Practice Teaching – Changing Social Work

of related interest

Handbook of Theory for Practice Teachers in Social Work
Edited by Joyce Lishman
ISBN 185302 098 2

Learning and Teaching in Social Work
Towards Reflective Practice
Edited by Margaret Yelloly and Mary Henkel
ISBN 185302 237 3

Competence in Social Work Practice
Edited by Kieran O'Hagan
ISBN 185302 332 9

Creative Training
Sociodrama and Team Building
Ron Wiener
ISBN 185302 422 8

Good Practice in Risk Assessment and Risk Management
Edited by Hazel Kemshall and Jacki Pritchard
Two volume set
ISBN 185302 552 6

Negotiation for Health and Social Service Professionals
Keith Fletcher
ISBN 185302 549 6

Practice Teaching – Changing Social Work

Edited by Hilary Lawson

Jessica Kingsley Publishers
London and Philadelphia

Acknowledgements

I would like to thank all the practice teachers and social work tutors who contributed to this book. Many readily agreed to the task on top of busy work schedules little realising how time consuming it would be!

I have appreciated the 'how's it going's from family, and friends and colleagues in the Social Policy and Social Work Group at Sussex University. I would particularly like to thank John Jacobs for his initial kick-start to the project. Thanks, too, to Jenny Clifton, Deborah Clow, Carole Ballardie and Teresa Madden who read various drafts of chapters and gave invaluable comments and encouragement.

For Terry, Beth and Anna. It's...a book, 300 grammes.

First published in the United Kingdom in 1998 by
Jessica Kingsley Publishers Ltd
116 Pentonville Road, London N1 9JB, England
and
325 Chestnut Street, Philadelphia, PA 19106, USA.

Copyright © 1998 Jessica Kingsley Publishers

Library of Congress Cataloging in Publication Data
A CIP catalogue record for this book is available from the Library of Congress

British Library Cataloguing in Publication Data
Practice teaching: changing social work
1.Social service 2.Social work education
I.Lawson, Hilary
361.3'2

ISBN 1 85302 478 3

Printed and Bound in Great Britain by
Athenaeum Press, Gateshead, Tyne and Wear

Contents

Introduction

Practice teachers – the highly skilled, specially trained educators of social work practice – rose from the ashes of the old student supervisors at the beginning of the 1990s. Their emergence stemmed from the publication of two documents, the *Requirements and Regulations for the Diploma in Social Work* (CCETSW 1989a) and *Improving Standards in Practice Learning* (CCETSW 1989b). Together, these documents had a significant impact on social work education, by sharpening the focus on the practice placement as a crucial element in the social work curriculum, and thrusting the practice teacher into centre stage.

To equip both the agencies and the practice teachers for this demanding new role, agencies had to be approved by the Central Council for Education and Training in Social Work (CCETSW) for the task, and practice teachers were encouraged to enrol on programmes leading to the CCETSW-accredited Practice Teaching Award. Many social workers interested in student supervision joined those first programmes with little awareness that the role of practice teacher was not just the old supervisor wearing different clothing, but was in fact an entirely different animal. Undoubtedly skills of supervision – skills in which many social workers are highly proficient – are crucial to the role. But the role demands more. It demands an understanding of adult learning theories (in fact not an entirely different body of knowledge from that with which social workers are familiar (for example Rogers 1969; Egan 1994) but the connections need to be made and added to), methods of teaching and assessment, and the explicit integration of theory and practice. In that 'the practice teacher is the manager of an educational experience' (Thompson 1990), practice teachers need also to be equipped with elements of management theory. In addition, practice teachers had to learn the language of competence frameworks. Rooted in the new approaches to training policy specified in a series of government white papers in the 1980s, CCETSW devised statements of competence for the qualifying social worker and these formed the new *Requirements and Regulations for the Diploma in Social Work*. Social work had been dissected into knowledge, values and skills and the social work student needed to demonstrate competence in a wide range of indicators to pass the placement.

Subsequent CCETSW documents (1995; 1996) have modified the framework to reflect changes in the perceived role of the social worker and more general changes in education and training (*see* Vass 1996), but units and elements of competence, evidence indicators and practice requirements have become the language of assessment. Competence frameworks do introduce a greater clarity and accountability into the assessment process, but they can also impart a reductionist superficiality. A good practice teacher knows that the sum of the parts do not necessarily make the whole and the skill lies in teasing out and evaluating those essential qualities of social work that resist the more tangible tick-box mentality of the competence schedule. As social workers are only too well aware about client assessment, frameworks are only as useful as the skill of the practitioner using them. Here is another area of learning for the new practice teacher, and one which much of the recent practice teaching and learning literature has not adequately addressed.

Since the inception of the first practice teaching programmes, practice teaching has developed into what Boswell has termed 'a near-precise professional art' (1997, p.348). A burgeoning literature has both informed and reflected the practice teachers' growing acquisition of a range of theoretical material drawn from social work, management and education. The purpose of this book is twofold. First, it addresses what seems to be a gap in the literature; the question practice teachers are now asking themselves is no longer *what* skills and knowledge base are needed to equip them for the task of practice teaching. It has shifted to *how* that learning can be applied in the various social work contexts in which they find themselves working. This book focuses on the *practice* of practice teaching. Second, it explicitly draws on the experience and expertise of the practice teachers themselves.

Social work agencies have been slow to acknowledge and value the pool of skilled practice teachers in the same way that they might validate and reward other specialisms. Most practice teachers manage to negotiate some workload relief to undertake their practice teaching duties, but this has always been dependent on other pressures in the team, and hardly ever reflects the onerous, time-consuming – and crucial – nature of the practice teaching task. The fact that practice teachers have not felt intrinsically valued is evidenced by the steady stream of accredited practice teachers moving into other areas of work, predominantly management, soon after gaining their Practice Teachers Award. The pool of practice teachers has never become the reservoir anticipated by CCETSW because of some strange mis-match between the values placed on the skills and knowledge the practice teachers gain through their training and work with the student, and the value of the practice teaching role itself. As soon as they become good practice teachers, they are seen by the organisation as becoming 'too good for practice teaching' – and 'springboard' into management.

CCETSW's recent development of the post-qualifying framework of awards has, however, recognised practice teaching as a means by which social workers can gain the PQSW (Post Qualifying Award in Social Work), and specialism in Education and Training can lead to the Advanced Award. Practice teaching will be an element of this, but agencies will need to recognise the broader role practice teachers could develop in research, education and training within the agency if their professional development in this area is to be sustained.

Practice teachers are crucial to the social work organisation because they represent the point at which social work culture is transmitted. They are in a pivotal position between the academic debates about what constitutes good social work practice, and organisational demands generated by the wider social and political changes. They must mediate and define social work for their students. 'Their position is a measure of the worth of practice in social work and their reflections a unique channel for social work to describe and understand its practice' (see Hugh England, Chapter 16).

Much has been written about the concept of the 'reflective practitioner' and its importance in social work. Pietroni highlights its particular relevance in times of change: 'Schön's work is intellectually located in a world in which critical change is not only recognised but was responsible for the generation of his theory' (1995, p.48). The reflection-in-action and reflection-on-action that Schön discusses requires a self-consciousness and the time and space that eludes most practitioners working under conditions of high pressure and enormous demands. However practice teachers *must* reflect on their work in order to articulate its elements and 'make sense' of it for the student. In times of change, it is particularly important that practice teachers help students make sense of changes in the organisation and in the role of social work. Many contributors to this book have discussed incorporating 'new learning' into the practice curriculum, for example, new policies, legislation, multi-disciplinary working, change itself. But the practice teacher is also in a prime position not just to reflect, but to influence changes. Much of the writing in this book is concerned with the question of how social work can adapt to new demands while still holding on to its fundamental values and key qualities.

Practice Teaching – Changing Social Work is, then, about both the changing nature of social work and its contexts, and also the recognition of the skill and experience of practice teachers and potential of practice teaching to inform those changes. Pietroni describes the current climate where 'anxieties about job security and organisational survival', and where political dictates and policy and legislative guidelines supersede professional judgement as producing a context which is 'intrinsically antagonistic to thoughtful practice' (1995, p.38). She goes on to express surprise that so much excellent social work continues to take place 'against these odds' (p.38). I would argue that practice teachers, in their work with students, play a large part in the maintenance and perpetuation of thoughtful practice. Not only is it necessary for them to both have and teach the skills of reflective practice, they also have access, through their pivotal role between practice and the academic institution, to current thinking and debates in social work. Parton argues: 'The social-work academy has been marginalised. Yet, if social work is to think independently and reconstruct itself, academic debates, drawing on contemporary developments in social theory are important' (1996, p.5). The practice teacher and student are well placed to contribute to these debates.

The practice teacher is also one of the few practitioners who is frequently engaged in practitioner research. This may be by way of supervising their student's practitioner research – and these can be quite sophisticated and insightful pieces of work of which, although too often they are simply assigned to the tutor's filing cabinet, many have been used to develop services in the placement. Practice teachers also frequently undertake their own practitioner research, particularly if they are working on a Post Qualifying Award in Social Work or enrolled on a practice teaching programme. As a tutor on one of these programmes I have been impressed by the range and quality of these pieces of work. Many of the chapters in this book originally stemmed from practice teachers' research undertaken while on their qualifying programme and the book represents an attempt to ensure their work is valued, shared and taken forward.

This book is about the *experience* of practice teaching: practice teaching at the sharp end. All of the contributors have had extensive experience of working with social work students or practice teachers and are familiar with the different aspects of practice teaching that are most challenging. Contributors were invited to write about those aspects of their work, their struggles, their research and their resolutions. In the spirit of 'joint provision' (CCETSW 1996) of social work education and training, the writers of the different chapters come from both academic and a range of practice settings, and represent a diversity of experience, but the focus of each chapter is on practical solutions that are offered as a way of sharing experiences and contributing to the development of practice teaching. The chapters fall roughly into three sections which reflect three aspects of the role which seem to exercise practice teachers the most: how to ensure anti-discriminatory practice remains the corner-stone of good social work practice, the integration of theory and practice, and the need for practice teachers to understand and respond to the constantly changing nature of social work and its settings.

In the 1996 DipSW Rules and Requirements, CCETSW states that students should 'identify and question their own values and prejudices' and 'demonstrate clear, consistent and thoughtful integration of values in practice'. The values espoused by CCETSW seem to shift and get blown about by political wind changes. This is evidenced in, for example, the curtailing of references to anti-discriminatory and anti-racist practice in the recent document. However, the task for the practice teacher lies in helping the student make sense of what values do constitute effective social work whatever the prevailing political climate might be, and consideration of how best they may be taught. The contributors to this book believe that practice teachers must continue to ensure anti-discriminatory practice remains at the heart of the social work curriculum and that they should help students effectively challenge all forms of discrimination.

Focusing on the practice teaching relationship itself is one way in which differences in power in society more generally can be recognised and addressed. Michelle Lefevre's chapter (Chapter 1) discusses the effects of the dynamics of oppression on the student's ability to learn and the practice teacher's capacity to teach and assess effectively. Other contributors, for example, Jacqui Jenkins (Chapter 2) and Helen Cosis Brown (Chapter 3), have written about particular oppressed groups in society (people with disabilities, and gay and lesbians respectively) and argued the case for an understanding of the political, theoretical and legislative contexts which reinforce their oppression. Practice teachers have a role in identifying ways in which the student social worker can work effectively within constraining and essentially discriminatory policy and legislative contexts. Both authors give practical examples to help the practice teacher facilitate the student's development of anti-oppressive practice with particular client groups, and

Helen Cosis Brown also considers the practice teaching relationship itself with reference to gay and lesbian students and practice teachers.

Elaine Arnold's chapter focuses on the knowledge base of anti-racist practice in an attempt to speak to those practice teachers, often coming from a work setting or part of the country where there is a relatively small representation of people from black and ethnic minority groups, who feel ill-equipped to teach anti-racism. She argues the importance of having an understanding both of the law in relation to anti-discrimination and also social work education's response to society's acknowledgement of racism. Finally in this section, Phil Jones offers a personal reflection of how being male affects the practice teaching role, particularly where the student is female, and how good use can be made of learning agreements to ensure gender dynamics are effectively explored.

Several studies (for example Walker *et al.* 1995) have reported the fact that facilitating the integration of theory and practice continues to be a part of the practice teacher role which causes the practice teacher some anxiety. Application of learning theory to the practice teacher's own development may give some clue as to why this might be. The practice teacher, being a skilled practitioner with at least two years' post-qualifying experience, will be at a high level of learning, 'unconsciously competent'. All those theories, methods and models that were once consciously applied to practice have now become an integral part of the practice teacher's implicit knowledge base and 'intuitively' used 'practice wisdom'. Thompson writes: 'If "theory" or new knowledge succeeds in changing our thinking, we tend to take it on board and no longer regard it explicitly as theory because it has become part of our "commonsense"' (Thompson 1990, p.39). Helping the practice teacher make explicit the implicit in their own work gives them confidence to do the same with their student. While several contributors have made explicit theories of practice teaching in their chapters (for example adult learning theories in Hoad's chapter and management theories in Cox's chapter), practice teachers have also illustrated how theoretical concepts and methods of intervention drawn from social work may be used within practice teaching. Two contributors, Fiona Mainstone (Chapter 6) and Di Metson (Chapter 7), have directly applied theories of intervention, Solution Focused Therapy and Transactional Analysis respectively, to the practice teaching task itself and give excellent examples of theory-in-use. Hilary Lawson (Chapter 15) draws on concepts more usually associated with family work to describe processes at play within the long-arm model of practice teaching. Charlotte Clow (Chapter 8) has used psychodynamic theory and theories of loss and change to shed light on the importance of the ending phase of the social work relationship, and to explore the benefits of a carefully managed ending. Corinne Pearce's chapter (Chapter 9) is a discussion of how practice teachers could introduce the What Works theory base to probation students. She gives an overview of cognitive, behavioural and structural casework approaches in practice with offenders and examines how these methods may be taught, and their use by the student assessed.

The final section includes chapters that focus on the changing nature of social work and the response practice teachers must make to those changes. The task for the practice teacher is to create learning conditions that enable students to understand and feel able to influence the changes. Often this entails re-framing the 'this is no time to have a student' thinking to one which identifies the learning that can be achieved – for both student *and* team – by offering a placement at what may initially seem an inopportune time. Tina Cox (Chapter 10) describes the challenges and opportunities placements undergoing significant change afford. She draws on models of change and adult learning theories to discuss how the practice teacher can ensure students learn to embrace and feel empowered within change, rather than be demoralised and disorientated by it. Where changes of legislation dictate changes of role and task, practice teachers are involved in helping students adapt to the new role while at the same time using discretion and professional judgement to ensure good client-centred social work practice is maintained. Chapters by Andy Mantell (Chapter 11) and Carole Ballardie (Chapter 12) explore these dilemmas in different settings. Andy Mantell describes the role of the student social worker in multi-disciplinary medical settings and Carole Ballardie scrutinises the 1995 National Standards for their potential for both oppressive and anti-oppressive practice and discusses how good interviewing and report writing can be achieved within them. In recent years social workers' knowledge and use of the law has become a more prominent aspect of their role. In Chapter 13 Polly Hoad explores the challenges of using the law in social work and suggests ways in which practice teachers can develop student social workers' competence in this important area. Carol Kedward has drawn on research which demonstrates another development in the role of the social worker: the need to be equipped for preventing and managing violent and threatening behaviour. In her chapter (Chapter 14) she underlines the importance of seeing good practice in managing violence as an integral part of staff care and stress management. The practice teacher needs to ensure the whole team reinforces the learning about safe practice.

In Chapter 15 Hilary Lawson describes a model of practice teaching, the long-arm model, that is becoming more widely used as its potential for creating placements in new and changing settings is being recognised. She analyses both the advantages and disadvantages of the model for the practice teachers, on-site supervisors and students and suggests ways in which practice teacher programmes and academic institutions may do more to support the model and increase its effectiveness. Finally, in Chapter 16, Hugh England traces changes in social work education and assesses both positive developments and those that present challenges for the practice teacher. The chapter raises speculation about the future role of the practice teacher.

My hope is that the chapters in this book demonstrate the complexity of the role of the practice teacher, and the skill and expertise required to undertake effective practice teaching. Practice teachers, by virtue of their role in transmitting social work culture, their involvement in practitioner and student research, and their pivotal position between the academic institution and the practice setting, are in a prime position to raise standards of social work, and contribute to the current debates about its future. With the recent government announcement that CCETSW itself is soon to be replaced by another training organisation, practice teacher involvement in these debates is particularly crucial.

References

Boswell, G. (1997) 'The role of the practice teacher.' In M. Davies (ed) *The Blackwell Companion to Social Work*. Oxford: Blackwell.

CCETSW (1989a) Requirements and Regulations for the Diploma in Social Work. London: CCETSW.

CCETSW (1989b) *Improving Standards in Practice Learning*. London: CCETSW.

CCETSW (1996) *Assuring Quality in the Diploma in Social Work – 1. Rules and Requirements for the DipSW* (Revised Edition). London: CCETSW.

Egan, G. (1994) *The Skilled Helper, Fourth Edition*. California: Brooks/Cole.

Parton, N. (1996) *Social Theory, Social Change and Social Work*. London: Routledge.

Pietroni, M. (1995) 'The nature and aims of professional education for social workers: a post-modern perspective.' In M. Yelloly and M. Henkel *Learning and Teaching in Social Work*. London: Jessica Kingsley Publishers.

Rogers, C. (1969) *Freedom to Learn*. Ohio: Columbus.

Thompson, N. (1990) 'More than a supervisor – the developing role of the practice teacher.' *Journal of Training and Development 2*, 33–43.

Vass, A. (1996) *Social Work Competences: Core Knowledge, Values and Skills*. London: Sage.

Yelloly, M. (1995) 'Professional competence and higher education.' In M. Yelloly and M. Henkel *Learning and Teaching in Social Work*. London: Jessica Kingsley Publishers.

Walker, J., McCarthy, P., Morgan, W. and Timms, N. (1995) *In Pursuit of Equality: Improving Practice Teaching in Social Work*. Newcastle.

CHAPTER I

Recognising and Addressing Imbalances of Power in the Practice Teacher/Student Dialectic

An Anti-Discriminatory Approach

Michelle Lefevre

The ability to learn is often related to confidence and feelings of empowerment, so social work students may find that anxiety about their skills and
performance on placement is a major stumbling block to their learning
(Thompson, Osada and Anderson 1994). Conversely, some measure of security, enjoyment and positiveness in their experience of the placement is likely
to enhance their ability to learn (ILPS 1993). Trust and safety will be central
to the fostering of this type of environment for the student by the practice
teacher. A crucial area for development will be within the supervisory relationship, which lies at the heart of the practice placement. It should provide a
source of support to the student as well as the educative, managerial, mediation and assessment/evaluation functions (Richards and Payne 1990).

Inherent in the dynamics of trust and safety between practice teacher and
student is the role and influence of power. Hugman (1991) defines coercion,
influence and authority as the main forms of power wielded by practitioners
within social care settings. The role of influence is not only related to observable conflicts of interest, but can be covert and hidden. For example, a social
worker may attempt to achieve a desired aim, such as the client's compliance
with a written agreement, whilst maintaining the appearance of consensus.
There may be no legal mandate to this plan, but the client may feel powerless
and unable to challenge the worker. The social worker may intimidate the client through their personal style or conduct, ignoring what the client says, or

using non-verbal expression to devalue the client. The client may feel unclear about their rights to challenge the plan and have fears about the consequences of challenge, such as resources being withheld unfairly. Whereas some social workers may deliberately use their influence to manage or manipulate such a situation, others may be less aware of their power.

The power of authority can be defined as 'the exercise of legitimate command based on social status' (Hugman 1991, p.34). Social workers have a mandated role which requires particular tasks to be carried out even where this conflicts with the expressed wishes of the client, for example where Approved Social Workers may advise the detention of an adult where their mental health places themselves or the public at risk.

The roles of influence and authority are demonstrated within the dialectic between the practice teacher and the student. The practice teacher holds explicit authority to assess whether the student has reached an adequate level of competence and, ultimately, to recommend whether they should pass or fail the placement (Kaiser 1997). The student may experience anxiety in relation to whether their practice meets the required standards or whether they will receive a fair and objective assessment. This may affect their confidence and, consequently, their ability to learn. The assessment role is not, then, a neutral player: it may have a significantly detrimental impact on the very skills it is designed to assess.

Many social workers feel uncomfortable with this authority role due to concerns about disempowering and oppressing others. They may try to deny its reality or work to lessen its influence (Davies 1985). Morrison (1993) points out that some supervisors may abdicate their appropriate authority role with their staff because of concerns that they may be perceived as being discriminatory, particularly where the supervisee belongs to an oppressed group by virtue of their race or gender, for example, and the supervisor does not. I decided to explore this issue as part of a small-scale survey on power and discrimination in the practice teacher/student relationship which I carried out amongst practice teachers in my own area. Three-quarters of my respondents felt there was a danger they might avoid giving criticism to, or failing a student, so as not to exploit their power. Although the sample is too small (eleven respondents) to be statistically significant, this does reflect the relevance of the issue for some practitioners.

Further comparisons can be made about the use of authority within other areas of social work. Yelloly and Henkel (1995) describe how trainers who are aware of the extent of their authority are less likely to collude with course participants to avoid learning experiences or to 'wield it unthinkingly and impose rigid, unresponsive courses' (p.169). Practitioners in the child protection field will need to use the power conferred by their position to clarify concerns and expectations to parents and take protective action in respect of children experiencing significant harm. Many social workers wish to avoid further disempowering clients who are already experiencing oppression, perhaps due to violence, racism or financial difficulties, but this can be dangerous if it obscures the child's need for safety (Reder *et al.* 1993).

A practice teacher who accepts and works with the authority with which they are invested, can use this to be proactive in creating a safe and constructive learning environment for the student within the agency. They will also feel more comfortable in developing a partnership with the student in which they will be explicit with the student about the criteria they must meet in order to pass the placement. If the student is clear about areas where improvement is needed and given adequate support, the opportunity for them to develop these is maximised (Kaiser 1997).

Like Hugman, Kadushin (1992) differentiates between the formal types of power in supervision, which derive from the authority and role of the supervisor (reward, coercive and positional power), and that which the student confers upon the supervisor, which is dependent on a number of factors. The student may accord the practice teacher referent power for the personal qualities which they admire and respect. The practice teacher's influence will also depend on the student's perception of the knowledge and skill they bring to the job. This will not only be related to their task of supervisor, but also to their role as social worker, as they will model this to the student.

How much influence they will allow the practice teacher will be determined by the student's own needs, their stage of learning and their willingness to make themselves vulnerable in asking for input and assistance. The more unsure they are about their abilities, the more dependent they will become on guidance from the practice teacher and the more influenced they will be by their responses (Kaiser 1997). If the student thinks the practice teacher has less expert status, they may well question their authority in the evaluation role (Brown and Bourne 1996). If they feel intimidated by the disparity in experience and skills, they may lose confidence and this will have the negative effects previously described on their ability to learn. The practice teacher may notice this dilemma more readily in a student who is overtly self-critical. Other students, however, may attempt to hide their anxieties by a reluctance to open their work to scrutiny. Practice teachers should be alert to students withholding information about particular cases, avoiding reflection on their practice and deflecting opportunities for their practice to be observed.

In this situation, the practice teacher should question their own role in the process. It may be that they have themselves a need for admiration or positive feedback, which is being fed by their own insecurities or inadequacies in their own supervision. A secure supervisor, whose own needs are being met, is more likely to be able to enhance the student's confidence by demonstrating their faith in the student's ability to develop and to value their areas of skill.

An anti-discriminatory approach

In determining a way forward which will empower both student and practice teacher, so that the potential of each is maximised, an approach which is both anti-discriminatory and anti-oppressive should be adopted. These terms are often used with clearly differentiated definitions. Discrimination refers to the unequal treatment of a person, based on 'personal factors such as their race, sex, age, (dis)ability or sexual orientation' (Philipson 1992, p.30). An anti-discriminatory approach would then be one which challenges unfairness and can be applied legally. Oppression is used more to refer to structural differences in power. An anti-oppressive approach would 'recognise and try to understand the obstacles to growth that may have developed for that person in the face of their past oppression and discrimination and works actively to enable them to increase their personal confidence and professional competence' (Brown and Bourne 1996, p.37). Thompson (1993), however, does not draw clear distinctions between the two approaches as, although recognising the distinct characteristics of discrimination and oppression, he sees them both as 'aspects of the divisive nature of social structure' (p.11). He uses 'anti-discriminatory' as an over-arching term to cover both approaches and this is how it will also be used within this chapter.

Empowering the student

Kadushin (1992) asserts the importance of empowering the student within the context of both student and practice teacher recognising the latter's legitimate power deriving from their role. The student should be accorded equal worth as a human being in the relationship and the validity of their contribution recognised. A partnership approach which still recognises the power imbalance, but focuses on working together towards the common placement goals, may assist this process (Yelloly and Henkel 1995). Although the practice teacher is more powerful by virtue of their role, the student should be able to feel they have a valid contribution to the planning of the placement and the assessment process. Preston-Shoot (1989) suggests explicitly involving the student in their evaluation through the development of a placement contract. This would clearly define 'relevant, realistic ... and clearly understood objectives' which the student is required to demonstrate and 'clarify the criteria by which the work will be assessed' (pp.3–4).

It will not merely be the content of such a discussion, but also the process of it which will contribute to the student's feelings of empowerment. The practice teacher may use their power in a negative way; by failing to demonstrate to the student that their contribution is valid and welcomed, they may block their participation. A more 'nutrient' or caring approach will ensure the practice teacher is aware of the student's needs for encouragement and being valued. This should enhance the process of collaboration (Grimwood and Popplestone 1993 in Brown and Bourne 1996).

The student's fears around unfair assessment are likely to be alleviated by clear procedures if it seems at all likely that the practice teacher might fail the student. CCETSW's Paper 30 originally recommended that a second opinion practice teacher be appointed to reassess the student's competence as soon as such concerns are raised (CCETSW 1991). Part of their role would be to ensure that power imbalances between practice teacher and student are recognised and addressed. Although this suggestion was changed in more recent regulations (CCETSW 1996), it could be argued that such practice is preferable and it may be that such a process could be adopted locally. The student should be included in the process of planning the review and reassessment. They may feel empowered by being able to bring a supportive person or advocate to meetings. When the second opinion practice teacher is appointed, issues such as their race and gender should be considered in consultation with the student (Branicki and Horncastle 1993).

Adopting a model for gaining evidence in practice could also empower the student by involving them in the assessment and evaluation process. Shardlow and Doel's (1993) three-stage model can be used to provide a more objective basis for gathering evidence of the student's competence. The methods for measuring competence will be selected depending on the particular skill area to be assessed. Different pieces of evidence will be examined to see if there is correspondence between the student's level of competence in a number of different situations. The student's competence will also be sampled over time, throughout the course of the placement. The openness of this approach will facilitate a partnership which will allow the student to measure their own development and the fairness of the assessment.

Empowering the practice teacher

Whilst the assessment role is one area in which the practice teacher is more powerful than the student, the relationship between the two is dialectical, that is, the attitudes and actions of each will influence the feelings and behaviour of the other. Consequently, there may be other dynamics which impact on the power relationship and cause both student and practice teacher to feel more or less powerful at different times. In my own survey, just over half of experienced practice teachers had felt, at times, that their student was more powerful than they were. This might have been in areas where the student has greater knowledge, skills or experience.

It will be important for the practice teacher to examine their own attitudes, motives and potential feelings of disempowerment prior to a placement. For example, whilst preparing for my first student placement, at the same time as undertaking a practice teachers' course, I considered that there might be the potential for me to feel less powerful than my student due to issues such as my age and gender. When first in social work, as a childless woman in my late twenties, I had sometimes felt disempowered when clients had questioned my abilities and skills, based on what they perceived as my lack of life experience. For the same reason I had, on occasion, experienced similar feelings of being deskilled and disempowered by other workers older than me, and I was concerned that this could also occur if I had a student older than me. For me, this would seem even more potentially disempowering with an older student who was male as the interplay between the dynamics of oppression can be particularly significant (Davis and Proctor 1989).

Such feelings of potential disempowerment need to be reflected upon as they may reduce the practice teacher's ability and skills to provide a trusting and educative placement experience for the student. The objective quality of their assessment of the student's learning and skills may also be impaired as, if the practice teacher is feeling under-confident, this may reduce their reliance on their own judgement. Consequently, they might fail to recognise and challenge areas in which the student does not demonstrate competency. The result of this could be an inadequate or even dangerous practitioner.

The practice teacher may attempt to redress their feelings of disempowerment by engaging in game playing. Kadushin (1976) suggests that supervisors are as likely as their supervisees to play games as social work is an area in which not only the work of the practitioner is exposed but also the self. This can cause both student and supervisor to feel inadequate and vulnerable. Anxieties related to early experiences may also be awakened causing unhelpful patterns to be enacted in the relationship. The practice teacher may attempt to regain a one-up position by criticising and intimidating the student, which is likely to reduce the student's confidence and hinder their development. They may also assess the student too strictly, in an attempt to assert their own authority inappropriately. Such behaviour will reduce the effectiveness of the placement and could ultimately cause the student to fail.

For the practice teacher to work effectively on these issues, they will require good supervision. This may be from the line manager, a peer group of other experienced practice teachers or an external consultant (Morrison 1993). The essential elements will be for a situation in which the supervisee has trust that they will be able safely to explore their personal views, feelings and concerns without fear of being judged and that they will receive constructive challenge which will enable them to move on. Supervision will also be a place where the practice teacher can try out forms of words to use with the student which may feel unfamiliar and difficult to start to say. This may include experimenting with how it feels for white practice teachers to acknowledge their whiteness to a black student or for female practice teachers to raise the issue of gender with a male student.

Working with difference

An anti-discriminatory approach in practice teaching will be one which prioritises 'a consistent and thorough conversation about the differences between supervisor and supervisee and the implications of these differences for their relationship' (Kaiser 1997, p.57). Morrison (1993) notes that some supervisors are worried about putting difference on the agenda 'in a constructive and proactive way, fearing either that they will make things worse, or that they will themselves be the subject of discrimination' (p.15).

In my own survey of practice teachers, I was able to explore their views on the importance of difference within the supervisory relationship. There was a broad consensus amongst respondents that issues such as race, gender, age, disability, sexual orientation and class would have an impact on the dynamics within the supervisory relationship. It was suggested that this could potentially disempower not only the student, but also the practice teacher. A number of suggestions were made for addressing these issues so that they do not inhibit the student's learning, nor the practice teacher's teaching and assessment role. Open acknowledgement by the practice teacher of the power dynamics was felt to be helpful in itself in dealing with these issues. This could lead to a more honest and open discussion within supervision about the impact on both parties of the power imbalances. In order to do this effectively and sensitively, practice teachers found they needed to prepare sufficiently in advance by being clear about their own views and issues. A helpful way forward was for both practice teacher and student to restate their shared aims, acknowledging that they both held responsibilities for dealing with these issues (albeit the practice teacher having a greater ascribed responsibility due to their qualified status and teaching role). This could be done in the very early stages, even prior to the placement, whilst drawing up the placement contract.

Race/Ethnicity

The practice teachers in my survey believed that having a practice teacher and student of a different ethnic or racial background to themselves could alter the power dynamic. Black students might feel particularly disempowered by a white practice teacher because of the impact of racism (ILPS 1993). This may be expressed in subtle ways which are difficult for the student to name to the white observer. However, the 'inability to explicitly pinpoint the racism does not by any means negate its very real, although often nebulous, presence' (Kaiser 1997, p.42). For example, black students have felt that their competence is more closely questioned than that of white students (p.42).

If the working environment is one in which black social workers and students are under-represented, the student may lack the support of peers who have shared experience of discrimination and who have developed helpful coping strategies. This isolation is likely to give added significance to feelings of discrimination and disempowerment. The white practice teacher could prepare for this by discovering if there are formal support networks for their black student and building their own links with black workers and organisations (Ferns 1989). They should also support their student in developing their own support networks, for example by ensuring they have placement space to pursue this.

Some white practice teachers felt deskilled and, consequently, disempowered in attempting to raise issues of racism with their black student. This may be due to perceiving their student as an expert on racism, due to their experiences of discrimination. There may also be a fear of being discriminatory themselves, through their own lack of knowledge or experience (Brown and Bourne 1996).

It is difficult for any white person growing up in Britain to evade the influence of prejudicial attitudes and beliefs about people based on their race and ethnicity which have been inculcated from an early age (Davis and Proctor 1989). An anti-discriminatory approach requires these attitudes and values to be brought to the surface so that their influence can be discussed and worked through. This could be an important area to be explored within supervision. However, some white students might find it more difficult to examine their own attitudes and assumptions regarding racism from a black practice teacher. This may be because they are concerned about being perceived as being racist and discriminatory (Morrison 1993). It may also be due to their discomfort at recognising their role in a white-dominated and racist society.

I have experienced the latter in training staff on anti-racist practice in my local authority. When a black trainer worked alone, some white staff felt they could sideline the issue of racism as the concern solely of black people. They tried to deny the reality of racism by accusing the black trainer of raising issues because they had a 'chip on their shoulder'. By co-working as a white trainer alongside this black trainer I was able to model the responsibility white people should take in accepting the reality of racism and acknowledging their responsibility for working to mitigate its effects. Co-working also provided support to the black trainer in dealing with the personal stress of confronting and challenging racism. I would suggest, then, that black practice teachers with white students could consider carrying out some co-work with a white colleague if there are issues which provoke particular stresses, difficulties or concerns. Similarly, white practice teachers can consider co-working with black colleagues as one of a range of strategies in adopting an anti-discriminatory approach.

Respondents to my survey suggested strategies for white practice teachers in raising their own awareness of racism in order to minimise the power imbalance with their black student. They had found their own awareness level had been raised by experience of work in multi-cultural areas. This had encouraged them to work on issues of power and discrimination in relation to their black clients. They had found it important to widen their experience through reading appropriate literature (e.g. Thompson 1993; Ahmad 1990;

Ahmed *et al.* 1986; Dominelli 1988) and to explore their own views and attitudes. This would normally be done within their own supervision, but if their supervisor lacks the appropriate skills and experience in these issues, it might be helpful to seek out specialist consultation and training. Many local authorities have set up support and development groups for practice teachers, to share information, raise issues and further their practice. This could be an appropriate setting for provision of training or for setting up practice seminars where workers can share their experiences and learn from each other. As with many other suggestions in this chapter, this is, of course, a strategy which will be relevant to other areas of oppression and discrimination, such as gender and sexual orientation.

The white practice teacher should, then, prior to the placement, have identified what their own issues might be in relation to the black student and have reflected on what the student's concerns might be. The practice teacher should be aware of the personal and professional impact of racism on the student from clients, professionals and the wider community.

They should then take responsibility for raising whether the student has concerns and issues pertaining to racism and ethnicity – as opposed to them having 'problems' (Davis and Proctor 1989). It will be important to keep this issue firmly on the agenda so that the student does not feel that there has been a tokenistic reference to it. The student will need to feel that a safe environment has been created before they will feel comfortable in expressing their concerns and it will be important for the practice teacher to demonstrate through their words and behaviour that they have both awareness of, and commitment to, the issue.

If the white practice teacher is feeling deskilled about issues of anti-racist practice when working with a black student, it may be helpful to acknowledge this to the student. The practice teacher could openly validate the student's experience in this area and affirm their commitment to ensuring that the issues are helpfully explored and dealt with. This need not mean that the practice teacher's authority is undermined. Indeed, it can be a helpful live modelling experience for the student, that is, that experienced social workers need always to be aware of the areas in which they should be furthering their knowledge and skills.

Gender

Both female students and practice teachers are likely to have experienced discrimination and oppression throughout their lives. Its impact in relation to their education and career may be experienced at the personal, cultural and structural levels (Thompson 1993). Structural discrimination may have an impact through difficulties in access to education and employment. This may be particularly related to child care commitments and a lack of good quality, safe and inexpensive child care (Langan and Day 1992). Sexual harassment or derogatory prejudicial comments may be experienced from colleagues within the agency, clients, other professionals or at the college. Cultural attitudes about women's roles may feel confusing and undermining. For example, 'women in authority who present themselves as primarily nurturing are often labelled unclear thinkers, whereas those who present themselves as more in charge are seen as dangerous' (Kaiser 1997, p.54). They are likely to feel disempowered by male domination of 'the resolution of conflict, the definition of publicly disputed issues, the formation of the language through which actions and institutions are structured' (Hugman 1991, p.46). These factors contribute to women's struggle to break through the 'glass ceiling', that is, progression in career hierarchies beyond a certain level. This is observable in many social services departments where female workers dominate at the lower paid levels and males in the higher management posts (Langan and Day 1992).

Male students may also suffer from stereotyping as found that men in caring professions are still expected to have greater competence in theoretical and technical skills than in relational work, nurturing abilities or approachability (Kaiser 1997).

The practice teacher will need not only to have awareness of the impact of sexism on the student, but also to have sufficiently explored their attitudes so that they are able to discuss these issues openly and sensitively with the student. Male practice teachers will need to be particularly sensitive when raising the issues with female students as it may bring up painful past experience which can feel threatening to explore with a male. Sharing such vulnerabilities is made doubly difficult because of the assessment role. It could be arranged for the student to have external support with such issues where appropriate, perhaps with a female colleague. Male practice teachers who are concerned about being oppressive may also find adopting the authority role with a female student particularly difficult, fearing it may further the student's disempowerment. Their experience with working to empower female clients may be usefully drawn upon.

It should not be assumed that it is only male practice teachers who need to explore their attitudes and assumptions in relation to gender. Female practice teachers may also have internalised some of the notions of rigid gender roles and stereotypes which are pervasive and influential within British society (Davis and Proctor 1989). It will be helpful for practice teachers of either gender to broaden their knowledge of feminist perspectives in social relations, in particular that there exists 'a deep-rooted, often unconscious system of beliefs, attitudes, and institutions in which distinctions between people's intrinsic worth are made on the grounds of their sex and sexual roles' (Bullock and Stallybrass 1977, in Thompson 1993, p.38).

Respondents to my survey advised that they had found a non-confrontational approach most helpful with their students. This could be less threatening to students who had not yet adopted an anti-sexist approach. This matched my own experience with a female student who had not yet developed an understanding of the impact of gender. This student was already feeling deskilled and disempowered by her experience of returning to education after a break of many years and having little confidence in her academic abilities. I was aware that even constructive criticism was experienced as undermining by her. Consequently, I felt it would be important to explore the issue at a pace which felt comfortable to her, so that she felt it was an opportunity for her to explore her values and beliefs.

If this student had experienced it as being told she was wrong, it could have led her to become defensive. This could have had a number of negative consequences, such as her learning by rote the required response without any real understanding of, or commitment to, anti-sexism. It could also have caused her to project her resentment and feelings of powerlessness onto the issues of gender and sexism. Instead, I found it helpful to encourage her to consider what kind of messages she had received about growing up as a female which were different from those her brothers had received about growing up male. This was a powerful exercise as she was able to see how she had been influenced by these stereotypical messages in a way that had, at times, been negative or inhibitory.

Sexual orientation

The experience of gay men, lesbians and bisexuals in their day-to-day working lives is often of abuse, harassment and ostracism (GLC 1985). Therefore, it is likely that non-heterosexual students will experience homophobia and heterosexism during the course of their placement and the practice teacher will need to support them with this, where appropriate. However, these students are likely to feel wary of discussing their sexuality with a heterosexual practice teacher. This may be due to fear of (or actual experience of) homo-phobia by the practice teacher. This could be experienced in overt ways, with derogatory or stereotypical comments, such as 'lesbians are anti-men' or 'bisexuals spread AIDS' (George 1993). The student is also likely to experi-ence the heterosexist world view of the practice teacher, with the lifestyles or experiences of gay men, bisexuals or lesbians being treated as invisible (Brown and Bourne 1996).

The concerns about the impact of homophobia by the practice teacher is likely to make the student feel particularly vulnerable regarding the assess-ment. Their fears about 'prejudice and partiality can be minimised by the use of competency-based assessment and by careful monitoring by the pro-gramme organisers' (Trotter and Gilchrist 1996, p.80).

For students whose sexuality is not already known, there will also be the dilemma of whether to disclose their sexuality. Within the agency, there could be an environment which not only excludes the home-life of non-heterosexuals, but actively harasses and discriminates against them. There may be unfair employment practices (such as paternity or compassionate leave which applies solely to heterosexual partners). Non-heterosexuals may be discouraged from working with vulnerable clients because of the equation of homosexuality with paedophilia and the perception that older lesbians, gays and bisexuals can 'corrupt' young people (GLC 1985). Yet, if the stu-dent cannot be open about their sexuality, it will mean they cannot gain support from their practice teacher when homophobia is experienced. It can also be stressful in itself to hide away such an integral part of the self as one's sexual orientation, particularly when an important feature of social work training is to develop a coherent use of self within practice.

Heterosexual practice teachers will need to challenge their own homo-phobia and heterosexism in order to provide a safe and empowering environment for the student within the supervisory relationship. They will need to give the student positive indicators of an anti-heterosexist stance, which should be affirmed at the start of the placement, as an anti-racist stance would be. Such a stance should be adopted with all students as assumptions should not be made about the student's sexuality. This will also provide important modelling for heterosexual students in their practice with clients.

For all practice teachers to reveal their sexuality to their students can 'avoid stereotypical assumptions and ... challenge homophobia directly' (Trotter and Gilchrist 1996, p.78). However, some non-heterosexual practice teachers may not feel that the culture of their agency renders this safe for them. The issue of whether to disclose their sexuality may depend on the attitude of the student. The attitude of, and support offered by, other staff in the agency may contribute to this decision-making as an unsupportive working environment will serve to reinforce any heterosexist and homophobic attitudes of a student.

It is likely that the practice teacher will have already needed to consider their external support systems in order to deal with attitudes and responses of clients. These support networks can similarly be accessed if there are issues in relation to the student. It may be that there are specialist issues which will need to be considered in relation to the practice teaching role, however. A local practice teachers forum could potentially provide support and consultation with these issues. If not, it may be possible to build links with lesbian, gay and bisexual practice teachers from other authorities. Practice teachers' courses and practice placement co-ordinators from other authorities may be a helpful place to approach to begin this process.

Disability

Respondents to my survey suggested that the power dynamic could also be altered if either the practice teacher or the student were disabled. They felt that disabled students were likely to feel particularly disadvantaged in their learning if the practice teacher was unaware of the disabilism they faced and was unable or unwilling to be supportive at either a practical or emotional level. This is an under-researched area as structural discrimination has meant that work environments have failed to cater for the needs of students with physical impairments, reducing the number of placements available. Practice teachers may be unnecessarily pessimistic about whether their placement may be suitable for students with particular needs. There needs to be a detailed and thorough assessment of the student's needs to see whether the agency can provide appropriate support services and technical expertise (James and Thomas 1996). Non-disabled practice teachers might be influenced by the danger of 'identity spread' with some physically disabled students. This could mean that, for them, the student 'stops being a person … and becomes a disabled person, identified solely by his or her medical problem and the limitations it imposes' (Locker 1983, p.139). It may also be that the 'assumption of general incompetence' comes into operation, so that they generalise the difficulties the student has with some day-to-day activities, to the rest of their life and abilities, whether physical or cognitive (p.139). Certainly, James and Thomas found in their research of visually disabled students undertaking DipSW courses that 'students had to prove themselves competent in a manner which would not have been expected of non-disabled students in similar circumstances' (1996, p.42). Such attitudes are likely to disempower the student by lowering their levels of confidence and instilling feelings of anger and resentment. These are likely to be unhelpful in their relationship with the practice teacher if the student does not feel able to raise the issues with the practice teacher, or if they do not feel heard or respected, or feel that there is no subsequent change.

Again, it will be important for practice teachers to scrutinise their attitudes and assumptions. What will be important in terms of the student's placement experience is whether the student feels discriminated against. The practice teacher must create an environment in which the student feels safe to raise issues they are unhappy about. They will need to be proactive to achieve this, making it clear to the student that they are ready to hear if there are any difficulties.

Conclusion

Students on placement have less power than the practice teacher because of the authority of the latter's assessment role. They may also award influence to the practice teacher because of their skills and qualities. They may feel disempowered if the differential is too great and this may inhibit their feelings of confidence, trust and safety. This is likely to reduce the effectiveness of the placement. This does not mean the practice teacher should abdicate their authority role, which is essential to give credence to their teaching, the evaluation and the clarity of the assessment criteria. Issues of difference, discrimination and oppression, relating to issues such as race, gender, sexual orientation and disability will need to be addressed by the practice teacher, particularly as students from oppressed groups will have experienced discrimination in relation to education (ILPS 1993).

Practice teachers may also feel disempowered by their student due to dynamics of race, gender etc. within the dialectic with the student. They will need to scrutinise their own behaviour, values and assumptions, both prior to and during the placement, to test out how these dynamics will affect them personally in relation to different students (as, indeed, they should do in relation to work with clients). Similarly, they should consider how these dynamics might impact on the thoughts, feelings and behaviour of the student. Rather than assuming what the impact might be, this should then mean that the practice teacher is ready to begin the process of consulting with the student on these issues.

The placement contract can be used to define the assessment criteria and the student will be empowered by partnership in this process. A base-line of language and behaviour should be set by the practice teacher in the placement contract, which would form part of the assessment regarding the value-base which the student is expected to develop throughout their training. Issues such as race and gender would then be discussed explicitly, not only in relation to clients, but in how they affect the interactions between the practice teacher and student. This would not only assist in creating an environment in which the student felt safe and supported in raising their own issues regarding discrimination, but would also mean that the practice teacher would be less likely to experience overt personal discriminatory behaviour from the student.

The practice teacher will also need to consider challenging the culture of the workplace to empower both themselves and the student in relation to discrimination. At a reactive level, overtly discriminatory comments and behaviour by clients and colleagues will need to be challenged. At a more proactive level, training sessions could be organised within the team which encourage other workers to examine their own values and assumptions. Practice teachers who are, themselves, from oppressed groups may need to seek the support of particular colleagues, managers or the union or other professional organisation if they are, or feel, unable to do this without harassment or further discrimination.

References

Ahmad, B. (1990) *Black Perspectives in Social Work*. BASW. Birmingham: Venture Press.

Ahmed, S., Cheetham, J. and Small, J. (eds) (1986) *Social Work With Black Children and their Families*. London: Batsford, in association with British Agencies for Adoption and Fostering.

Branicki, M. and Horncastle, J. (1993) 'Second opinion.' *Community Care,* 14 October, 22–23.

Brown, A. and Bourne, I. (1996) *The Social Work Supervisor: Supervision in Community, Day Care and Residential Settings*. Buckingham: Open University Press.

CCETSW (1991) *Rules and Requirements for the Diploma in Social Work* (Paper 30). London: CCETSW.

CCETSW (1996) *Assuring Quality in the Diploma in Social Work: Rules and Requirements for the DipSW*. London: CCETSW.

Davies, M. (1985) *The Essential Social Worker: A Guide to Positive Practice*. Community Care Practice Handbooks. Aldershot: Wildwood House.

Davis, L.E. and Proctor, E.K. (1989) *Race, Gender and Class*. New Jersey: Prentice Hall.

Dominelli, L. (1988) *Anti-Racist Social Work*. Practical Social Work Series. Basingstoke: Macmillan.

Ferns, P. (1989) 'Getting the most out of placements.' *Community Care,* 31 August, 16–17.

George, S. (1993) *Women and Bisexuality.* London: Scarlet Press.

GLC (1985) *Danger! Heterosexism at Work: A Handbook of Equal Opportunities in the Workplace for Lesbians and Gay Men.* London: Greater London Council.

Hugman, R. (1991) *Power in Caring Professions.* Hampshire: Macmillan Press Ltd.

Inner London Probation Service (ILPS) (1993) *Working with Difference: A Positive and Practical Guide to Anti-Discriminatory Practice Teaching.* London: ILPS.

James, P. and Thomas, M. (1996) 'Deconstructing a disabling environment in social work education.' *Social Work Education 15,* 1, 34–45.

Kadushin, A. (1976) *Supervision in Social Work.* New York: Columbia University Press.

Kadushin, A. (1992) *Supervision in Social Work.* Third Edition. New York: Columbia University Press.

Kaiser, T.L. (1997) *Supervisory Relationships: Exploring the Human Element.* California: Brooks/Core Publishing.

Langan, M. and Day, L. (1992) *Women, Oppression and Social Work: Issues in Anti-Discriminatory Practice.* London: Routledge.

Locker, D. (1983) *Disability and Disadvantage: the Consequences of Chronic Illness.* London: Tavistock.

Morrison, T. (1993) *Staff Supervision in Social Care.* London: Pitman Publishing, Longman Group UK Ltd.

Philipson, J. (1992) *Practising Equality: Men, Women and Social Work.* London: CCETSW.

Preston-Shoot, M. (1989) 'A contractual approach to practice teaching.' *Social Work Education 8,* 3, 3–15.

Reder, P., Duncan, S. and Gray, M. (1993) *Beyond Blame: Child Abuse Tragedies Revisited.* London: Routledge.

Richards, M. and Payne, C. (1990) *Staff Supervision in Child Protection Work.* London: NISW.

Shardlow, S. and Doel, M. (1993) 'Examination by triangulation – a model for practice teaching.' *Social Work Education 12,* 3, 67–79.

Thompson, N. (1993) *Anti-Discriminatory Practice.* BASW. Hampshire: The Macmillan Press.

Thompson, N., Osada, M. and Anderson, B. (1994) *Practice Teaching in Social Work.* Second Edition. Birmingham: Pepar Publications.

Trotter, J. and Gilchrist, J. (1996) 'Assessing DipSW students: anti-discriminatory practice in relation to lesbian and gay issues.' *Social Work Education 15,* 1, 75–82.

Yelloly, M. and Henkel, M. (eds) (1995) *Learning and Teaching in Social Work: Towards Reflective Practice.* London: Jessica Kingsley Publishers.

CHAPTER 2

Community Care Assessments, Anti-Disablist Practice and the Social Work Student

An Exploration of the Issues and some Guidelines for Good Practice

Jacqui Jenkins

Introduction

This chapter has been written drawing on my experiences of being a practice teacher in a Physical Disability Assessment Team of a social services department. The team was set up in 1993 in response to the community care legislation requirement of a split between the purchase and provision of services. The team consists of two workers (one of whom is a qualified social worker) whose main role is to undertake social care assessments and case management of people aged under 65 with a physical disability.

The team has weathered an enormous amount of change since it was established. This includes several changes of line manager, the merge with the Assessment Team for Older People, a whole-scale change of all managers and management structure as well as two changes of office location. On top of this, budgets are increasingly stretched and caseloads very large. These changes have largely been due to rationalisation in an attempt by the local authority to cut costs combined with the move towards becoming a unitary authority.

The effect of such change on staff cannot be underestimated. Their general feelings are of confusion, chaos, anxiety, powerlessness and frustration.

In spite of this people remain highly motivated to provide a good service to clients and strive to work in an anti-oppressive way.

The incoming social work student is likely to feel quite bewildered. They may initially believe that their study and lectures have borne little resemblance to what they are actually faced with on placement and they are likely to be anxious about how they are going to meet the expectations of their course in this setting. The immediate task of the practice teacher is to give the student an understanding of the workplace politics, the continuous cycle of change, the ongoing uncertainty and its impact on staff and clients whilst at the same time ensuring that the student feels sufficiently positive and empowered to carry out the required role. On top of this there is the challenge of meeting the course requirements whilst carrying out agency practices and procedures.

The document *Assuring Quality in the Diploma in Social Work-1* (CCETSW 1996) sets out the requirements for qualification in social work. Much emphasis is given to the values of social work. Social work students are encouraged to 'recognise the interrelationships of structural and individual factors in the social context in which services operate, and the need to address their impact on the lives of children and adults' (p.18). Students must demonstrate an ability to 'identify, analyse and take action to counter discrimination, racism, disadvantage, inequality and injustice, using strategies appropriate to role and context' (*ibid.*). It is this last phrase which encapsulates the dilemma that this chapter addresses. In the first part of the chapter I shall look at disability and disablism and demonstrate how the assessment process, developed in response to the NHS and Community Care Act, 1990, embodies a view of disabled people that is oppressive and discriminatory. Social work students undertaking placements in assessment teams therefore face considerable confusion when attempting to resolve the seemingly contradictory tasks of empowering clients and countering discrimination and working within a legislative and policy framework that severely inhibits this. In the second part of the chapter I shall look at how the student can attempt to resolve these dilemmas in their practice, and work within agency policy and decision-making procedures in an anti-oppressive and non-discriminatory way. To this end, I have produced a list of 'do's and don'ts' to act as a guideline for students.

Disability and oppression

In order to identify the ways in which social policy and hence social work can contribute to the continued oppression of disabled people it is helpful to look at the different models and theories of disability.

Oliver and Finkelstein are the main theorists in this area and, although the terms that they use differ, their theories are, broadly speaking, very similar. The two fundamental theories of disability can be identified as the personal tragedy theory (often referred to as the individual model) and the social oppression theory (Oliver 1983). Finkelstein defines his theories as the social death model and the social barriers model (Finkelstein 1991). Although I have adopted Oliver's terminology, I have also drawn on Finkelstein's arguments.

Intrinsic to the *personal tragedy theory of disability* is the assumption that to be disabled means to be unable to function socially as an independent citizen having the same rights and expectations as 'normal' people. Disabled people are assumed to be dependent upon others either for 'cure' or for 'care' (Finkelstein 1991) and the problems that disabled people face are considered as being a direct consequence of their individual impairment. Assumptions are made about how the onset of disability requires difficult psychological adjustment and the role of the helping professional is often seen as helping the disabled person to adjust to their particular disabling condition.

This is demonstrated in the Catch 22 situation in which many disabled people find themselves. If you have a disability, you must have psychological problems· if you state that you have no psychological problems then this is denial and that is a psychological problem (Trieschmann 1980). Similarly, in the past, disabled people who were angry because they were denied their rights to full participation in society have been pathologised and dismissed as not having come to terms with their disability.

The personal tragedy view of disability also perpetuates patronising attitudes towards disabled people. Disabled people are seen as either superheroes or tragic victims, never ordinary people. As Shearer says:

> The 'norm' demands that people whose disabilities are obvious and severe must be at least sad and even tragic. And if that defence breaks down in the face of individual reality it is ready with its own flip-side. The reaction to people who break out of the mould becomes: Aren't they wonderful? (Shearer, quoted in Oliver 1983, p.20)

These attitudes to disability all conspire to deny the 'normality' of disability and reinforce able-bodied people's assumptions about disabled people's experiences.

Incorporated in the personal tragedy theory are what Finkelstein calls the medical and the welfare models of disability. The medical model consists of categorising people according to their diagnosis and interpreting their disability in medical terms, ignoring the disabled person's relationship with their social and physical environments. The welfare model equates disability with social death and dependence necessitating the intervention of able-bodied professionals to administer care solutions.

The acceptance of such views and assumptions about disability has meant that social policies and social services are designed to compensate for the disabled individual's loss and dependency. As Oliver says:

> As far as disability is concerned, if it is seen as a tragedy, then disabled people will be treated as if they are victims of some tragic happening or circumstance. This treatment will occur not just in everyday interactions but will also be translated into social policies which will attempt to compensate these victims for the tragedies that have befallen them. (Oliver 1990, p.2)

Rather than empowering disabled people and promoting their independence, social services provision has served to reinforce and further oppress disabled people. Oliver gives some examples:

> There are a number of ways in which dependency is created through the delivery of professionalised services. The kind of services that are available, notably residential and day care facilities, the transportation of users in specialised transport and the rigidity of the routine activities which take place therein, all serve to institutionalise disabled people and create dependency. (Oliver 1990, p.98)

To sum up, the personal tragedy theory accepts an individual pathology of disability. It assumes that disabled people are dependent and in need of professional help to assist them in accepting their limited function in society and to administer services to cope with their inevitable dependence.

The alternative to the personal tragedy theory of disability is the *social oppression theory* (Oliver), or the social barriers model (Finkelstein). This theory recognises that society has a role in disabling people. It focuses not on the physical limitations of a particular individual but on the way that physical and social environments impose limitations on certain groups or categories of people.

> Disability is not an individual problem. Rather it is a social problem concerned with the effects of hostile physical and social environments upon impaired individuals or even a societal one concerned with the way society treats this particular minority group. (Oliver 1983, p.2)

Rather than seeing them as tragic victims who are needy and dependent, this theory of disability views disabled people as a minority group whose rights are being denied. It is helpful here to draw the distinction between impairment and disability, as defined in the social oppression theory of disability. The Union of Physically Impaired Against Segregation state:

> In our view it is society which disables physically impaired people. Disability is something imposed on top of our impairments by the way we are unnecessarily isolated and excluded from full participation in society. Thus we define impairment as lacking part or all of a limb, or having a defective limb, organism or mechanism of the body; and disability as the disadvantage or restriction of activity caused by a contemporary social organisation which takes no or little account of people who have physical impairments and thus excludes them in the mainstream of social activities. Physical disability is therefore a particular form of social oppression. (UPIAS 1976, pp.3–4)

Impairment is therefore the functional limitation, disability the limitation of opportunity due to physical and social barriers.

Sapey and Hewitt accept the social oppression theory of disability when they argue that disablement arises from the following factors: lack of mobility, access and communication facilities, the viewing of disabled people as non-productive; the ways in which segregated amenities for disabled people are provided, and the placing of responsibility for disability issues in the charitable sector (Sapey and Hewitt 1991).

They go on to argue that social workers contribute to the continued oppression of disabled people by passively accepting the individual model of disability and by following procedures which are specifically developed to limit people's access to resources under their control. By this they mean that social workers act as gatekeepers for their agencies, thereby restricting resources to disabled people. This, they argue, constitutes a denial of disabled people's rights. That is, social workers reinforce the view that 'disabled people are ... people "in need" rather than ... people whose rights to resources are denied or rationed' (Sapey and Hewitt 1991). In this way, the concept of being in need can become disabling in itself.

It is important to point out that the social oppression theory of disability does not deny that some people will need help in adjusting to the onset of disability or in grieving or mourning their lost body. However, the requiring of such help is not universal amongst disabled people. The social oppression theory of disability seeks to point out that disability and dependence are not inevitable consequences of impairment and should not be regarded as such.

Sapey and Hewitt state that social work practice unwittingly espouses the personal tragedy view of disability by accepting the casework system. They state that casework relies largely upon medical and psychological social models of intervention with individuals and fails to question the way in which able-bodied people have defined the world of disabled people. Oliver concurs with this, stating that the personal tragedy model of disability dominates social work practice. People are processed through a system defined by able-bodied people, which ignores the disabling environment and concentrates on individual impairment and inadequacies as the causes of disability. The upshot of this, according to Oliver, is that resources have been mis-directed and mis-spent: resources that have been used to maintain registers and count numbers of disabled people should have been spent on breaking down the physical and social barriers in society. As a result, 'disabled people have not received what they need, and in many cases the services that they have received have created or reinforced dependency' (Oliver 1990, p.96).

Finkelstein and Oliver both believe that the challenge for social workers is to work to the social oppression theory of disability and to provide alternatives to current practice so that social workers and disabled people can concentrate on barrier identification and removal both at the personal level (for the individual setting of their own goals) and at the social level where public facilities need to be made truly public (i.e. not just for able-bodied citizens).

> In working with disabled people, the social work task is no longer one of adjusting individuals to personal disasters but rather helping them to locate the personal, social, economic and community resources to live life to the full. (Oliver 1983, p.31)

The challenge for the social work student (and the social worker) is therefore to work with disabled people from a social oppression perspective rather than, as has tended to happen historically, from a personal tragedy perspective.

Before one can identify how this might be put into practice, we need first to look at the work itself and the legislative framework.

NHS and Community Care Act and assessment

The NHS and Community Care Act with its emphasis on user and carer involvement in assessment and planning, plus its focus on needs-led rather than service-led assessment, could have signalled a positive move towards a recognition and acceptance of the social oppression theory of disability, away from an individual pathology of disability. However, with the transfer of budgetary responsibility to social services departments came the greater demand on social workers to act as gatekeepers of services: needs are assessed, eligibility determined and those in greatest need are provided with a service subject to available resources.

The whole tone of the Community Care Act stresses assessment of individual need. Thus there is the danger that the personal tragedy theory of disability is reinforced, as disabled people are inevitably seen as in need and dependent. There are no longer any rights as 'claimants' (as when the Department of Social Security held the budgets for Income Support and residential care) but instead there are assessed needs which may or may not be met.

Secondly, disabled people continue to be pushed into being clients of casework because they are reliant on social workers to assess their needs and to identify care packages. As discussed earlier, inherent in this is the risk of individualising the problem and of ignoring the significance of social barriers. In addition, social workers have to judge a person's eligibility for a service rather than accepting per se an individual's own perception and definition of their needs and providing services accordingly. In devising eligibility criteria, it is all too easy to make the assumption that there is a direct relationship between the level of impairment and the level of need. Given that it is the social and physical barriers which disable people, it is likely that many people do not get a service because they are not sufficiently impaired.

What follows on from this is the temptation for people to act as more disabled in order to gain access to certain benefits and services which should be theirs by right. This reinforces an individual pathology.

Finally, the NHS and Community Care Act places importance on the needs of carers and emphasises that they should be supported in carrying out their caring role. Parker makes the link between the personal tragedy theory of disability and the recognition of carers. 'All the factors which transform an impairment into a disability also tend to transform family members and friends into carers' (Parker, quoted in Twigg and Atkin 1994, p.6).

From a social oppression perspective policies should not endorse dependence through an emphasis on supporting carers but should underwrite the independence of the disabled people for whom they care.

Meeting carers' needs diverts attention from the oppression of disabled people and perpetuates the personal tragedy view of disability. Sapey and Hewitt make the point that emphasising the needs of carers disempowers disabled people and can result in the policing of disabled people.

> Generally it is a position of powerlessness that leads people to become clients and for disabled people it is a position that has been defined by able-bodied people. It is difficult to see how, in an age of consumerism dominated by monetary policies, relatively powerless people can hope to compete with those who are in power. The result will be that the social work task will not be concerned with assisting disabled people as the ones directly affected by disablement, but will primarily be a means of ensuring that they will not be an inconvenience to the able-bodied people. Sufficient help is offered to ensure that society feels free of any further responsibility but empowerment is discouraged as threatening to those in power. This policing of disability is a means of containing offenders and safeguarding victims. (Sapey and Hewitt 1991, p.31)

The growing awareness of young carers also disempowers disabled people. As care in the community has become synonymous with care by the community, the issue of young carers and their 'burden of care' has received much publicity and led to demands that young carers be protected. Keith and Morris are very suspicious of the focus on young carers and claim that the phenomenon of young carers is socially constructed and reinforces the oppression of disabled people.

As disabled mothers, they write:

> The social construction of 'young carers' and the media attention which has followed us affects us every time we go out with our children, every time we meet new people, especially health and social services professionals. The research and media presentation of 'children as carers' undermines our role as mothers and defines disabled parents as inadequate. (Keith and Morris 1995, p.43)

Thus, community care legislation encapsulates the personal tragedy view of disability. Policies and practices developed in response to the legislation reinforce the dependence of people with disabilities and deny disabled people their rights by rationing services to those in greatest perceived need.

So far this chapter has discussed the two major theories of disability and identified how the personal tragedy theory dominates social policy and social work with disabled people and underpins much of the thinking behind the NHS and Community Care Act and its implementation. The student, on gaining insight into this, is likely to feel very disillusioned. How they can achieve CCETSW's stated objectives of working within agency decision-making processes whilst attempting to work to a social oppression theory of disability (i.e. work to counteract the impact of discrimination and seek to promote practices which are anti-oppressive) will now be explored.

Implications for practice

The task seems very daunting. The student is expected to work in an anti-oppressive way in an institution which reinforces the oppression of disabled people. Passive acceptance of the institution is considered to constitute a reinforcement of the oppression (Finkelstein 1991). The challenge is to press for and effect change from within the organisation.

Smale and Tuson encapsulate the essence of the problem when they ask:

> How can we, the professionals in Social Services, conduct ourselves so that people are 'empowered' and not made more powerless by having to go through the process of 'professional help', of having their 'needs assessed' and their 'case managed'? (Smale and Tuson 1993, p.6)

Similarly, one could beg the question, how do we as workers counteract the discrimination that disabled people face and ensure that we do not merely erect more barriers which further disable?

The main tasks within the agency are assessment and care management. It is in the carrying out of these tasks that the student has most influence for change and scope for developing anti-oppressive practices. The framework for the social care assessment in the particular agency in which I work is a form with a number of headings such as: background information, health, personal care, domestic tasks, lifestyle, housing situation, helping networks, client's perception, carer's perception, client's wishes and needs, and eligibility. The expectation is that the worker completes the form during the initial interview with the client. It is this interview to which the guidelines outlined later in this chapter relate.

The social care assessment form and the whole assessment process as prescribed by agency procedures fit into what has been described as a procedural model of assessment (Smale and Tuson 1993). Yet, I would argue that an exchange model of assessment lends itself more easily to a social oppression model of disability as it encourages the client to identify their 'problems' and their likely solution themselves. In the exchange model the worker concentrates on an exchange of information between themselves and the client, their carers and significant others. The question and answer pattern of behaviour is avoided. Professionals give information and explain what service options are available and how agency procedures work, and the service users are given time to explain their situation, their perceptions of the problem and possible solutions (Smale and Tuson 1993).

I believe that the best the student can do is to try to combine the procedural model with the exchange model. To give the student an understanding of what this means in practice, I have identified the following 'do's and don'ts' for students to bear in mind when undertaking assessments. This list is by no means exhaustive and should therefore not be used as a checklist. Rather, it should be used as guidance for good, anti-discriminatory practice.

1. **DO:** Be honest

   It is essential that one is honest with one's client. This involves being clear about the fact that eligibility criteria are used, how they are used and what the criteria are. Honesty about the fact that services are provided on the basis of need and available resources which precludes rights to services is also vital. However, it is not helpful for the student to deny any allegiance with the agency. This is unlikely to be useful to the client nor is it helpful in earning their confidence and trust.

2. **DO:** Explain

   The student must explain about the assessment process, who makes the decisions, the client's right to challenge decisions via the Departmental Complaints Procedure, and how they gain access to information in their file. As Smale makes clear in his critique of the procedural model of assessment, much of the evidence gathered in the assessment is to determine eligibility (Smale and Tuson 1993). The student, when gathering information, must explain why the in-

formation is sought and make it clear that the information gathered
may or may not be helpful to the client. Failure to do this may
automatically reinforce the personal tragedy theory of disability.
For example, a client requests a home help service for assistance
with housework. If the assessor fails to explain the assessment procedure and eligibility factors, the client is likely to become confused, upset or angry (and rightly so) at being asked questions
about their support networks and their personal care.

3. **DO:** Inform

Before a client can be helped to identify possible solutions to their
problems, or to meet their needs, they have to know what their
choices are. Under the community care legislation, assessments are
supposed to be needs led rather than service led. I have argued
elsewhere that in reality assessments are needs and resource led.
However, I agree with Smale and Tuson in the assertion that people tend to want what they know rather than know what they
want.

Thus when making assessments with people with disabilities, one's
role is to facilitate the client's definition of the problem and likely
solutions. The client is unable to do this if they are unaware of the
range of options. In addition, when acknowledging the limitations
of the process with regards to rights and needs, it is vital to inform
people of campaigning organisations and advocacy groups so that
awareness is heightened. This also serves to reduce the individual
pathology regarding disability by emphasising the existence of the
structural and physical barriers and the fact that disability organisations are increasingly demanding civil rights.

It is also crucial to inform the client about the funding of care
packages and the fact that the client will have to pay a contribution
towards this. This gives some people greater choice. If someone is
aware from the outset that they are likely to have to pay the full
cost, they then have the option to bypass the whole assessment
procedure. This clearly gives them far more control and independence (provided that the student gives them sufficient information
about choices, care agencies etc. on which to base these decisions).

4. **DO:** Identify the social and physical barriers

Where necessary refer the client on to the appropriate agency, for example to the Housing Department, occupational therapy, or access officers. As I outlined earlier in the chapter, the importance of this cannot be underestimated.

5. **DO:** Be more aware of your own assumptions, feelings and attitudes

   It is essential that the student is aware of their own values with regards both to disability and more generally. Of particular importance is the student's assumptions about the 'perfect' and 'imperfect' body and how these might affect their work with clients. (Obviously, this is an area for discussion and exploration in supervision sessions. A good way of examining these issues is through discussion of euthanasia and abortion of disabled foetuses.)

   A student who is not able to recognise their own values is unlikely to be able to identify anti-oppressive practice with regard to disability.

6. **DO NOT:** Make assumptions about what disability might mean for any individual

   Ask the client what it means for them. I make this point for two reasons. First, the personal tragedy theory assumes that loss is a major factor in adjusting to disability and that the disabled person needs to grieve for their 'lost' body or limb. Therefore, do not assume that loss will be an issue, but do not ignore it if it is an issue.

   Second, the social oppression theory emphasises the way in which the physical and social barriers disable. Earlier, I discussed how disabled people are pathologised and oppressed. It is important to bear in mind that some disabled people have internalised this oppression and as a result devalue themselves and have taken on the passive and dependent role assigned to them in society. It is essential that such people are not further oppressed by a student social worker's lack of acceptance of them. It is helpful to identify how people view themselves and to give them the information, choices and support to move on if they wish.

7. **DO:** Pay attention to language

The personal tragedy model of disability is so entrenched that to ask someone 'what is wrong with you?' does not sound nearly as outrageous as it should. The phrasing of questions to emphasise the social and physical barriers rather than the impairment is covered well in Oliver's *The Politics of Disablement* (1990) and could be made the focus of a supervision session in which appropriate questions could be rehearsed.

It is also very important to clarify the terms that workers and clients use. An illustration of this is the term 'independence'. Professionals tend to define independence in terms of toileting, cooking and eating without assistance. Many disabled people, however, define independence differently, seeing it as the ability to be in control of, and make decisions about, their life rather than doing things alone or without help (Oliver 1990).

8. **DO:** Facilitate clients' definition of the problem

The student should not perceive themselves as expert at defining problems and their solutions. Each client is an expert in themselves. The student should be the expert in facilitating the client's identification of the 'problem' and what is needed as a solution. This involves using essential social work skills of facilitation and communication. Gerard Egan's helping model with its emphasis on skills such as attention giving, active listening, communicating empathy, probing and challenging is as relevant in social work education and training today as it has always been (Egan 1994). (Once more such skills can be practised in supervision sessions.)

To truly facilitate the client's definition of the problem one must avoid being ruled by paperwork. Following the format of the social care assessment form rigidly is not helpful as it results in the assessment being dictated by the form itself rather than the client's perception and definition of their 'problem' and 'needs'. For this reason, I suggest that the assessment form is only completed at the end of the assessment process.

9. **DO:** Recognise the importance of culture, race, gender and/or sexual orientation

The likely impact of these on the individual, especially in terms of 'double discrimination', and also on other people's attitudes, problem definition and on the appropriateness of service provision should not be minimised.

10. **DO:** Avoid the 'Helpful Worker' syndrome

This is when 'helpful workers' try to help the client to meet criteria that will enable them to get what they say they need and what the worker judges that they need when they do not meet the agency's eligibility criteria. The danger is that the client has a more patho-logical label attached as a result.

It is likely to be very tempting for a student to fall into this trap, ei-ther for political reasons – because they see that the client has a right to the service or for personal reasons – because that they find it hard to say 'no' in a helping relationship. (Hawkins and Shohet explore this topic in 'Why be a helper?' in *Supervision in the Helping Professions* (1994). This is interesting reading and could be used as a basis for discussion in supervision.)

10. **DO NOT:** Concentrate on routine service delivery only

By this, I mean avoid assuming that all packages of care should have a community care funding element. It may be labouring the point rather, but there is a real danger of becoming unnecessarily service dominated. One should be creative, imaginative and flexible when devising care packages with clients. These need not always have a resource element but may involve voluntary organisations, volunteer bureaux and informal carers. Social services departments have tended to become less flexible in the way community care monies are spent now that community care is well established. As workers, we have a responsibility to our clients to try to resist this by pressing our managers and requesting monies for services which are not routinely provided. For example, four years ago, my depart-ment agreed community care funding for a bus pass for one client. I doubt whether this would be agreed now. However, one should not pre-empt such a situation by ceasing to request community care monies for unusual ventures which may help to break down physi-cal or social barriers.

11. **DO NOT:** Focus on the carer and leave the disabled person out

As mentioned earlier, recognising carers' needs conforms to a personal tragedy theory of disability and may result in the policing of people with disabilities. Nevertheless, carers do have needs and social workers have a statutory responsibility to take this into account. My fear is that when assessing a carer's needs the disabled person becomes an adjunct of the carer. The student must ensure that this does not happen.

12. **DO:** Record unmet needs and gaps in service

It is essential that workers pass such information to their managers and to the community care planners. This is one of the ways in which workers can attempt to inform and change the institution from within.

13. **DO:** Network with local and national disability organisations

Keeping abreast of the debates and changes taking place means that we can give accurate information to clients and, if they wish to, encourage them to get involved in campaigning for rights.

As stated earlier, this checklist is neither exclusive nor exhaustive. It is designed to guide the student and to help them to get a picture of what constitutes anti-discriminatory practice when undertaking community care assessments with disabled people.

As I have argued throughout this paper, attempting to work in an anti-discriminatory way within an institution which oppresses disabled people by reinforcing dependency and rationing services is a considerable challenge. The student must be aware of the negative institutional and individual factors and attempt to combat these. Smale and Tuson (1993) sum this up neatly when they say:

> What is necessary is for the care manager to conceptualise, or theorise afresh in each situation: not by ignoring available knowledge, but by clearly making such knowledge of population and groups a guide to thinking about a particular situation, and not its leader. (1993, p.64)

Conclusions: the role of the practice teacher

The guidelines outlined above are intended as a tool in supervision sessions for both planning assessment interviews and evaluating them afterwards as well as being a starting point for debate about disability and disablism.

For many students it is likely that the placement is the first opportunity they have had to explore these issues. They may feel a mixture of anger, shock, guilt and possibly defensiveness on learning about the politics of disability. Having absorbed the theories of disability they are then likely to feel immense frustration at the ignorance within able-bodied society and the extent to which a personal tragedy view of disability is ingrained in our institutions and social policies. This may also give rise to a sense of inadequacy and powerlessness in the face of such systematic oppression and they may feel very uncomfortable about the prospect of working within an organisation which reinforces this oppression.

Discussions in supervision could draw comparisons between the student's feelings and how clients might feel. The student should be encouraged to reflect on the climate within the team and the wider social services department. This might include exploration of the way in which social workers in the field of physical disability tend to be ascribed low status reflecting the low priority given to people with disabilities both by society generally as well as within social services departments. How is the low status of the work experienced by the student and how does the focus on budgets, job insecurity and the level of uncertainty and change impact on the student, the other workers involved and the work itself?

The task for the practice teacher is to try to prevent the student from feeling defeated. An exploration of the student's motives for doing social work and the personal yardsticks that they use to measure their performance as a social worker could be helpful here. An understanding of the concept of empowerment is crucial if the student is to retain a positive attitude to the work. In supervision sessions the student can be guided to thinking about empowerment in general terms and then encouraged to apply it more specifically to the agency's different tasks, for example community care assessments. This makes the work seem more manageable and enables the student to identify the areas over which they can have an influence in combating the discrimination towards, and the oppression of, disabled people.

Thus the practice teacher facilitates the student's understanding of the theory of disability, how oppression is reinforced by current legislation, and how these might be addressed when working as a social worker in this field.

References

CCETSW (1996) *Assuring Quality in the Diploma in Social Work: Rules and Requirements for the DipSW.* London: CCETSW.

Davidson, R. and Hunter, S. (1994) *Community Care in Practice*. London: Batsford, in association with British Agencies for Adoption and Fostering.

Egan, G. (1994) *The Skilled Helper*. California: Brooks Publishing.

Finkelstein, V. (1991) 'Disability: an administrative challenge?' In M. Oliver (ed) *Social Work: Disabled People and Disabling Environments*. London: Jessica Kingsley Publishers.

Hawkins, P. and Shohet, R. (1994) *Supervision in the Helping Professions*. Oxford: Oxford University Press.

Keith, L. and Morris, J. (1995) 'Easy targets: a disability rights perspective on the "Children as Carers" debate.' *Critical Social Policy 44/45,* 36–57.

Oliver, M. (1983) *Social Work with Disabled People*. Basingstoke: MacMillan.

Oliver, M. (1990) *The Politics of Disablement*. Basingstoke: MacMillan.

Sapey, B. and Hewitt, N. (1991) 'The changing context of social work practice.' In M. Oliver (ed) *Social Work: Disabled People and Disabling Environments*. London: Jessica Kingsley Publishers.

Smale, G. and Tuson, G. (1993) *Empowerment, Assessment, Care Management and the Skilled Worker*. NISW. London: HMSO.

Trieschmann, R.B. (1980) *Spinal Cord Injuries*. Oxford: Pergamon.

Twigg, J. and Atkin, R. (1994) *Carers Perceived*. Oxford: Oxford University Press.

UPIAS (1976) *Fundamental Principles of Disability*. London: Union of Physically Impaired Against Segregation.

Further reading

HMSO (1991) *Care Management and Assessment: A Practitioners' Guide*. London: HMSO.

Morris, J. (1991) *Pride Against Prejudice*. London: Womens Press.

CHAPTER 3

Working with Lesbians and Gay Men

Sexuality and Practice Teaching

Helen Cosis Brown

Introduction

This chapter is concerned with the role of practice teaching in preparing students to become competent and reflective social work practitioners. Competent means that they base their practice on relevant knowledge, are aware of the value base of their practice, and are able to utilise relevant skills to enable them to be effective, in the interests of all service users. The chapter looks at the interface of practice teaching and sexuality. 'Sexuality' is a term carrying many different meanings. Here it is in the main referring to sexual preference, lesbian and gay sexual identity.

Social work practice placements have always been the fundamental core of social work education: 'the role of the practice teacher in qualifying social work training has enduringly been the provider of necessary and appropriate learning experiences which furnish students with the opportunity to demonstrate their ability in the practice of social work' (Boswell 1997, p.348). The practice teacher, in addition to being a key player in the provision of learning opportunities, is also central to the process of the transmission of social work culture. It is within the placement setting that students learn the realities of social work values. But social work culture has not had an exemplary past when considering the profession's practice record with lesbians and gay men. Very little has been written relating practice teaching and sexual identity, although there have been two important and useful contributions: Forrister (1992) and Logan *et al.* (1996). This chapter is one more contribution to the debate, aiming to facilitate good quality practice teaching in relation to social work practice with lesbians and gay men.

Two main sections follow; first, *knowledge* relevant to practice teaching in this area. In this section I consider the significance of sexuality to social work practice; the historical, social and political context and theoretical considerations when integrating theory and practice. The second section explores the actual *practice* of practice teaching and includes the practice teacher and student relationship; placement agency organisational issues; practice teaching and the integration of theory and practice. The chapter ends with concluding thoughts about competent practice teaching and learning relating to service delivery to lesbian and gay individuals and communities.

Relevant knowledge

The significance of sexuality to social work practice

Within the focus on homosexuality, same sex sexual practice and identity, many aspects of 'sexuality' are involved: sex itself, feelings about self, others, community and the wider society. Heterosexuality is also relevant to practice teaching, but is not the focus of this chapter. Sexuality in all its various manifestations is central to human relations and as human relations are central to social work practice, sexuality has to be integral to our reflection on both our practice and our social care provision. Yet despite the importance of sexuality to human experience, social work has often shied away from addressing it explicitly, too embarrassed and anxious to engage. This has had devastating consequences for service users, as it can lead to the ignoring of sexual abuse, inappropriate interventions, and a contribution to the oppression of lesbians and gay men. It is this last consequence that is the concern of this chapter.

Discussions and debates about bettering social work with lesbians and gay men have been primarily located within the discourses of anti-oppressive social work practice. They have also appeared within literature about social work and sexuality more generally (Davis 1993). Social work's historical contribution to the oppression of lesbians and gay men and its more general anxiety about sex and sexuality makes the business of practice teaching in relation to lesbian and gay experience particularly difficult. But from this location the question arises as to whether lesbians and gay men really are oppressed and whether or not this oppression is of any concern to social work. In the recent past the oppression of lesbians and gay men within Britain has changed, with some improvement in the conditions of many. That is not to say that oppression no longer exists, but rather that it has changed in some aspects, and that some changes have led to improved experiences and life chances for many lesbians and gay men.

Amnesty International's recent worldwide review of human rights violations (both inside and outside the law) based on sexual orientation acts as a sobering reminder that the progress experienced in Britain since 1967 (when the Sexual Offences Act 1967 decriminalised male homosexual acts between consenting adults in private) has not been the case for the vast majority of lesbians and gay men across the world. Out of the countries surveyed by Amnesty International, there were 65 where homosexuality was illegal; some of these only explicitly mentioning male homosexuality. The sentences for the 'crime' of homosexuality in these countries ranged from fines to imprisonment and execution (Amnesty International 1997). Oppression of lesbians and gay men at the extreme end of the continuum includes persecution and murder. In some countries such actions are explicitly sanctioned by governments and in others oppression occurs at an individual and community level taking the form of such activities as 'queer-bashing'.

However disturbing these facts may be, why are they the concern of the practice teacher? They are relevant because they are the reality that impacts on all lesbians and gay men, however peripherally, and affects their sense of themselves, their experience of others and their relationship to society, at a conscious and unconscious level. Lesbians and gay men are both social workers and service users. To work effectively social workers need to be conscious of how oppression may relate to the individual they are working with and the services that are available to them, and how it may impact on themselves, and on their interventions. To enable there to be this necessary consciousness it is helpful to start by locating today's social work practice within a wider historical, social and political context.

The historical, social and political context

Social work qualifying education and practice teaching is regulated by the Central Council for Education and Training in Social Work (CCETSW) (CCETSW 1995; 1996). CCETSW's position on lesbian and gay rights is somewhat confusing. In their equal opportunities statement they say: 'CCETSW recognises that equal opportunity is something each individual wants for themselves and to which they have a legal right' (CCETSW 1995, p.9). Lesbians and gay men in Britain have no such right, as there is no protective legislation, only laws that limit their activity and criminalise some aspects of same sex male sexual practices; unlike New South Wales whose

Anti-Discrimination Act 1977 covers lesbians and gay men explicitly. The question arises as to whether or not CCETSW was deliberately excluding lesbians and gay men. However, later in the same CCETSW document defining the requirements of the qualifying social worker, it reads: 'knowledge and understanding of the diversity of individual lifestyles and communities in the UK; of the significance of poverty, racism, ill health and disability, and of gender, social class and sexuality' (CCETSW 1995, p.9). In other sections of both documents sexual orientation is subsumed under either 'disadvantage', 'discrimination' (CCETSW 1996, p.13) or 'difference' (CCETSW 1995, p.21). Although CCETSW's concern to emphasise good practice with lesbians and gay men for qualifying social workers could be interpreted as a little weak, it is important that it is there at all, and certainly 30 years ago would not have been.

CCETSW's inclusion of sexuality as a legitimate area of concern for social work education is the result of a number of different interrelated influences over the last 30 or more years. The birth of the lesbian and gay movement in Britain can be traced to the early part of this century but is commonly recognised in its modern form from the 1960s. Legislative changes have often acted as a focal point for the strengthening of the movement. Ironically the increased visibility and vociferousness of lesbian and gay communities in Britain coincided with the Conservative government's concerted efforts between 1979 and 1997 to locate lesbians and gay men as 'baddies' in the public imagination, with their repeated efforts to criminalise and restrict lesbians' and gay men's lives. Legislation affecting lesbians and gay men can be divided into two aspects: first, that relating to male same sex sexual practices and second, lesbians and gay men's right to parent. 'Under English and Scottish Law it has never been a crime simply to be homosexual – only to indulge in homosexual activity' (Jeffrey-Poulter 1991, p.3), and this, 'homosexual activity', has only related to male homosexuality. The first time lesbian and gay identity appears in law is in Section 28 of The Local Government Act 1988.

The criminalisation of male same sex sexual activity has been a powerful aspect of the oppression of gay men since the Labouchere Amendment to the 1885 Criminal Law Amendment Act, which criminalised sexual activity between men whether in private or public. Since that time the law covering male same sex practices has become a complex and confusing affair. It is helpfully and accessibly covered elsewhere (Jeffrey-Poulter 1991; Gooding 1992; Wilson 1995). Familiarity with this area is crucial for probation officers who are sometimes working with men prosecuted for these victimless crimes. The Criminal Justice and Public Order Act 1994 reduced the age of consent for male homosexual sexual activity to 18 from 21, leaving it still two years older than for heterosexual sex. The Act left those responsible for young people being accommodated by a local authority in a compromising position. For example, a social worker may be working with a young man who is 17 who is in a happy consensual relationship with a 19-year-old who is technically committing an offence.

The Conservative administration from 1979 engaged itself on a number of occasions with the question of whether or not lesbians and gay men should be allowed to act as carers for children. The Conservative government was given four opportunities to address this explicitly: the Local Government Act 1988, Section 28; the Foster-Placement Guidance and Regulations of the Children Act 1989; the Human Fertilisation and Embryology Act 1990 and the white paper, *Adoption: The Future* (Department of Health 1993). The first, Section 28, as it is commonly known, was the first piece of British law to acknowledge homosexuality as an identity as opposed to homosexual male sexual acts. The Act prevented local authorities funding activities that would 'intentionally promote' homosexuality or for maintained schools to promote 'homosexuality as a pretended family relationship'. The other three legislative debates all focused on the appropriateness of lesbians and gay men to care for children. The consultation process in all three cases resulted in the government having to retract its original position, having taken cognisance of the arguments put forward from the child care lobbies. These lobbies argued that lesbians and gay men should be able to parent and to act as substitute carers if they had the necessary qualities and attributes (Campion 1995; Brown 1997). The government of the period was in part responding to a growing awareness of the increasing visibility of lesbian mothers (Romans 1992) and the fact that lesbians and gay men were, with increasing confidence, coming forward to child care agencies as prospective carers. The child care lobbies were also aware of the increasing research base in Britain and America that was concluding that the sexual orientation of the parent did not affect the emotional, educational, social, psychological or sexual development of children (Patterson 1992; 1994; Tasker and Golombok 1991; 1995).

Simultaneously with the Conservative government's efforts to restrict lesbians' and gay men's lives, there was a complex evolution of Labour-controlled local authorities engaging in a process of opening up the possibilities for equal opportunity. This process has been well documented (Cooper 1994) and linked to social work practice and provision (Brown 1997). The resulting liberalisation of attitudes towards lesbians and gay men in various quarters led to the eventual inclusion of sexual orientation in the equal opportunities agendas of many local authorities, of the relevant trade unions (NAPO and UNISON) and of the Labour Party. CCETSW was at the tail end of these developments but did include sexuality within its new Diploma in Social Work in 1989 (CCETSW 1989), having previously included it in key policy documents. Social work thus found itself in a complex position within the 1980s and 1990s, aware of a Conservative government that was intent on limiting lesbians' and gay men's full participation in society, at the same time as some local authorities, probation services and both NAPO and UNISON were trying to further it.

Theoretical considerations when integrating theory and practice

Competence is the hoped for outcome for students undertaking practice placements. O'Hagan offers a helpful discussion of the meaning of competence in social work and some of the controversies surrounding its use (1996). CCETSW has broken competence down into three areas; knowledge, values, and skills, which for the purposes of this chapter is helpful. Social work students need the appropriate knowledge to inform their practice, a sound value base and relevant skills.

The integration of theory and practice is a requirement for qualifying social workers; it is also one of the aspects of social work that is the hardest to fully achieve. The practice teacher acts as a facilitator, enabling the student to make sense of 'theory' learnt in college, and to reflect on its practical application. Elsewhere I have described the knowledge base of social work as falling under three headings:

> Knowledge that informs the practitioner about the client's experience and context; knowledge that helps the practitioner plan appropriate intervention; and knowledge that clarifies the practitioner's understanding of the legal, policy, procedural and organisational context in which their practice takes place. (Brown 1996, p.10)

The first heading covers knowledge drawn from such disciplines as psychology, sociology and the growing anti-discriminatory practice literature; the second from what has traditionally been referred to as 'social work theory and skills', theories, and models of social work intervention; and the last from law relating to social work, social policy and organisational theory. All three headings are relevant to practice teaching and sexuality. The disciplines of psychology, sociology, social policy and social work theory, like all academic disciplines, are subject to the social, cultural, geographical, political and economic influences of the moment, and are therefore never neutral. These disciplines have been subject to homophobia (the fear and hatred of homosexuality) and have sometimes been influenced by it.

An example would be Erikson's work on the human life cycle (Erikson 1965), a developmental framework that many have found useful and applicable to social work practice. Gibson points out the inherent heterosexism in Erikson's sixth developmental stage, 'intimacy versus isolation'. He describes 'the ideal of genitality as: mutuality of orgasm, with a loved partner of the opposite sex, with whom one is able and willing to share a mutual trust and with whom one is able and willing to regulate the cycles of work, procreation and recreation, so as to secure to the offspring, too, all the stages of a satisfactory development' (1991, p.44). According to Erikson it would seem that the sixth developmental crisis can only be satisfactorily resolved if the person is heterosexual. The practice teacher needs to help the student critically reflect on the social, cultural, geographical, political and economic specificity of the 'knowledge' from which they draw. This 'reflection' needs to become an integral and automatic part of the student's practice. 'Reflection' will hopefully prevent the knee-jerk rejection of ideas because of their lack of 'political correctness', developing instead the ability to appropriately contextualise 'knowledge' and enable its critical use.

Debates about anti-oppressive practice have been primarily located within the arena of social work values. Such debates about how values are influenced by the cultural context take up much of a student's thinking. Values inevitably influence the selective use of knowledge, the relationship between knowledge and values being an extremely intimate one. For the purposes of helping students find their way through the quagmire of social work values, I have found it useful to consider them at four different levels:

> First, the values of the service user/client in relation to a particular piece of work; second, the values of the social worker in relation to the same work; third, the values of the agency in relation to the work; and last, the values enshrined in the policies and legislative context in which the piece of work is being undertaken. (Brown 1997, p.20)

For each piece of work the student is undertaking, the practice teacher can helpfully guide them to consider each level. These different levels may be in harmony, but are often in conflict. Consideration of them does not resolve the conflict, but makes the student conscious of it, and as a result there can be some anticipatory preparation. An example would be where a student is placed in a family placement team, and is responding to a gay male couple's application to become foster parents. The reaction to this application may well be affected by all four levels of values described above. The practice teacher would need to engage with the student in consideration of these different levels before the student responded to the applicants.

Social work skills have often been seen as neutral, outside the concerns of anti-discriminatory practice. However, interpersonal interactions with others are often where the experience of discrimination is located most acutely. The social worker avoiding eye contact, or the receptionist dismissively telling a person to wait can be experienced as directly relating to the service user's feelings of exclusion and marginalisation. There has been a growing literature raising sensitivity about the application of skills (d'Ardenne and Mahtani 1989; Munro et al. 1989; Dutton and Kohli 1996). Lesbians and gay men approaching a social work agency may come feeling a sense of potential marginalisation and exclusion. They may be hesitant about revealing the full details about their lives, fearing a homophobic response, which has often historically been the case (Hart and Richardson 1981). The skills involved in the CCETSW core competence of 'communicate and engage' (CCETSW 1995) are particularly crucial. If, for example, an assessment is to be undertaken to identify the care needs of a chronically sick lesbian then a trusting engagement has to be established for the woman to feel confident in sharing the full details of her domestic life. Unless this is done a comprehensive assessment will not have taken place and a potential inappropriate deployment of resources may result.

It is not the task of practice teachers to teach students all the knowledge, values and skills they need for competent and reflective practice; however it is their role to facilitate the student's proactive reflection.

Practice Teaching
The practice teacher and student relationship
The degree to which the practice teacher can act as an effective facilitator in this reflection process is dependent on the quality of the practice teaching relationship that is developed. This relationship is the central vehicle of the

learning process, the arena of constructed learning and role modelling and is where social work culture is transferred. That is not to say that these aspects of learning do not happen in other areas of the placement, but it is within this relationship that they take place in a concentrated way, both conscious and unconscious. The transmission of an agency's culture and attitudes towards lesbians and gay men is rarely conscious or explicit but imbued through asides, jokes and innuendo.

The practice teacher and student relationship is often intense, as by the nature of its content it is close, and it is not unusual for feelings of 'in loveness' to raise their head for both parties. This is an aspect of practice teaching and sexuality (heterosexual or homosexual) that often remains unvoiced. Much emphasis has been placed on the acknowledgement of 'difference' in the relationship between practice teacher and student (Shardlow and Doel 1996; Doel *et al.* 1996), but no mention of attraction. If sexual attraction does arise it is the role of the practice teacher to contain it within the placement period and seek out appropriate supervision within the agency to enable this containment. The practice teacher, as the assessor of the student's competence in practice, cannot (to put it bluntly) have sex with the student while the practice teacher is in any way connected with the student's assessment.

Historically, lesbian and gay students have experienced some direct homophobia on placements and within the practice teacher and student relationship. This history, as well as current experiences, makes many students reticent about being 'out' about their sexuality. The current preoccupation with 'difference' within social work education, sometimes discussed as if this awareness will delete difficult feelings relating to power, may carry with it an edge of superficiality and rhetoric. Articulating 'difference' in relation to perceived power relationships is not in itself anti-oppressive practice. Shifting the balance of power between individuals is a highly complex process and power itself is often a shifting and circumstantial phenomenon. Shardlow and Doel argue that: 'At the beginning of the placement, the practice teacher has a responsibility to introduce discussions about socially constructed difference' (1996, p.18). The intention is good, however this is a complex area in relation to lesbians and gay men. It is also worth noting that the quality of the welcome, respect, warmth, trust and integrity that the student has experienced from the practice teacher and the agency will convey a much stronger message to the student about 'valuing diversity' than an esoteric discussion about socially constructed differences.

'Coming out', the process by which an individual acknowledges to themselves and others their lesbian and gay identity, and the complex nature of this process for social workers, has been written about for the last 20 years but gets no simpler (Hart 1980; Brown 1997). The interface between racism and sexual orientation is particularly pertinent for social work as the belief that lesbians and gay men *should* be 'out', both for their own psychological health and for reasons of political solidarity, has been particularly inappropriate for some black lesbians and gay men. Mason-John and Khmbatta (1993) write about the need for individual black lesbians and gay men to decide for themselves when, where, and under what circumstances they are 'out', as they may choose to take refuge from racism in some arenas where they do not wish to be 'out'. The practice teacher needs to be sensitive to the individuality of the decision to be 'out' or 'in' for the student. The least oppressive approach to diversity in this arena is never to assume anyone's sexual orientation until told by the person themselves; this is the climate in which both lesbian and gay practice teachers and students are likely to feel their diversity truly recognised and the one where they will feel safe and comfortable enough to be most productive.

Practice placement agency organisational issues

The creation of a safe and comfortable learning environment is the responsibility of the individual practice teacher and the practice learning agency. The practice teacher can directly control the quality of their contribution to the practice teacher/student relationship in terms of boundaries, clarity, rigour, consistency, reliability, warmth, trust and integrity, but has to be in negotiation with others in relation to the agency's contribution to a safe and comfortable enough learning environment for lesbian and gay (or bisexual) students.

The practice teacher/student relationship is one sub-section of the larger practice placement system. All parties to this three-way relationship, whose concern is the development of practice competence for the student, are subject to other systems. For example the tutor is part of the college structure and subject to its regulations and procedures, the same is the case for the practice teacher in relation to the practice agency. All three parties are working to a learning agreement created to ensure that at the end of the placement the student's report will be able to evidence practice competence by the student, as set out in the Diploma in Social Work (DipSW) programme practice placement assessment criteria. This has itself to meet the requirements for

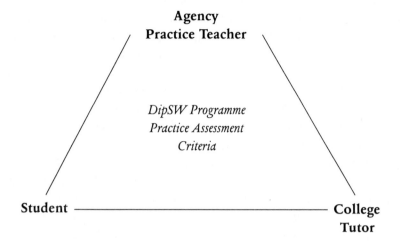

Figure 3.1

qualifying social work set down by CCETSW. For lesbians and gay students this practice placement system should act as a safeguard in relation to homophobia. CCETSW's equal opportunity policy includes sexual orientation and it is likely that the equal opportunity policies of the practice agency and the college will also include sexual orientation, although this is not always the case. Students are no longer quite so vulnerable to being subject to the prejudices of the individual practice teacher, as all three parties are now more accountable and have to work explicitly to the criteria for practice assessment set out by the student's DipSW programme. This increase in accountability should act as a safeguard against homophobia in the assessment of lesbian and gay students.

Preparing the placement agency about sexuality and practice teaching needs to happen before the arrival of a student. Homophobia is an area of oppression that is still not always recognised and often operates at a 'subtle' level, for example joking about sexuality and assuming everyone is heterosexual is common within social work agencies. This assumption of universal heterosexuality can act as a powerful negative controlling force for lesbian and gay students. It is the responsibility of the practice teacher to familiarise the agency (or the key people relating to the placement within the agency) with the placement assessment criteria, particularly relating to the values component and anti-oppressive practice aspects. This process in relation to sexuality can raise the awareness of agencies of the quality of their practice and provision to lesbian and gay individuals and communities, as well as to students. Such areas as the use of language (partner, for example is gender neutral and does not assume a sexuality), the diversity of images that are prevalent in the agency, and the quality and degree of welcome the agency conveys to the public all carry powerful messages for individuals who may feel marginalised and devalued (Brown 1997, p.77). For an agency to convey a culture that has respect for individuals and values diversity, it has to work at it in a conscious fashion, making it permeate all aspects and levels of its operations from the receptionist and telephonist to the director. The practice teacher engaging with the agency in preparation for the placement is not just of benefit to lesbian and gay students but to all students. The sexuality of a student often remains unknown to the practice agency, and it is equally important that questions of sexuality are considered in relation to heterosexual students as part of their competence to practice.

This process of agency preparation by the practice teacher usually runs concurrently with the preparation of the student induction period and the putting together of the placement induction pack. What goes into that pack is important (for example equal opportunity policies and harassment procedures) in conveying to students who are lesbian and gay (and all other students) how 'safe' the practice placement really is. Where there are clear omissions, for example the non-inclusion of sexual orientation within the equal opportunity policy it should be addressed directly and contextualised, so that the student can have a full understanding of the reasons for its omission and be reassured that its absence will not be injurious to the quality of their learning opportunities or their assessment. Once the practice teacher has done the work of the agency preparation, has taken responsibility for the induction process, and has confirmed the learning agreement based around the practice placement assessment criteria relevant to the student's DipSW programme, the practice teaching proper can begin in an environment that is conducive to practice learning.

Practice teaching: the integration of theory and practice
Earlier in the chapter there was some discussion of knowledge, values and skills. In helping students critically reflect on their use of knowledge when working with lesbian and gay service users it is important to be aware of the different areas of relevant 'knowledge'. Knowledge drawn from the mainstream social work sources to inform the practitioner: psychology, social

policy, sociology, social work theory and methods, anti-discriminatory practice literature, all need to be critically evaluated as to their relevance to
lesbians and gay men. Within these academic areas there is a growing discourse specific to homosexuality; within psychology Greene and Herek's
book on lesbian and gay psychology would be an example (1994). There is a
growing literature specific to social work and probation practice with lesbians and gay men (Brown 1992; 1997; Buckley 1992; Kus 1990; Logan *et al.*
1996; McCaughey and Buckley 1993; Woodman 1992) and a wealth of
writing from within the lesbian and gay communities that is of direct relevance to social work practice. The practice teacher cannot be expected to be
familiar with all the current literature relevant to social work practice with
lesbians and gay men. As with any other area of research and publication, the
expectation would be that they act as a facilitator for the student to integrate
the knowledge gained at college with their practice experience.

I have used a hypothetical supervisory session as the vehicle to illustrate
the integration of theory and practice in preparation for a piece of work. The
work that the student is to undertake is with a 16-year-old young man who
has recently 'come out' to his foster parents. The foster parents are finding
this impossible to accept. The placement agency is a children and families
team within a large city. Joe (the young man) is staying with a friend's family
at present, who have agreed to this for a week, while something else is
arranged. The student has had one telephone conversation with the foster
parents with whom Joe has lived since he was ten, when his mother died; his
father died when Joe was eight. The foster parents were angry and rejecting.
The conversation was full of 'homophobic' statements: 'he's turned out a
bloody poof after all we've done'; 'it's the school's fault employing queer
teachers'; 'he'll catch AIDS and be dead in a year'. The student was distressed
by the conversation and felt angry at these parents who had up to now, seemingly, had a good, solid and loving relationship with their foster child. Joe in
the meantime was feeling upset and frightened. The student has visited Joe,
but not the foster parents. The practice teacher and student meet for supervision to plan the work.

The student arrives very angry; Joe and his friend's parents are the heroes
and the foster parents are the homophobic baddies in her mind. She feels that
the foster parents should be 'struck off'. The practice teacher helps the student prepare for this work by focusing on skills, values and knowledge in the
following way. By using the three areas of knowledge set out earlier in the
chapter, the student is helped to focus on what she needs to reflect upon.

Within the first, 'knowledge that informs the practitioner about the client's experience and context', there are a number of areas that would need to be considered. The literature about 'coming out' and adolescence (Trenchard and Warren 1984; Kent-Baguley 1990; Brown 1997); crisis theory; and social work with lesbians and gay men (Kus 1990; Woodman 1992; Brown 1997) would all be relevant. The second area, 'knowledge that helps the practitioner plan appropriate intervention', would include crisis intervention and family work, to name only two examples. Lovell (1995) and Strommen (1990) are helpful in focusing the mind on the realities for families when a child 'comes out':

> By providing facilitating, non-pejorative assistance to the family, we can lessen the confusion and uncertainty these families experience as they wrestle with the reconstruction of long-held but never-examined beliefs and assumptions, and help them to keep the intimate circle of the family intact and healthy. (Strommen 1990, p.29)

Joe's 'coming out' has constituted a crisis for this family, therefore crisis intervention is relevant in enabling Joe to resume a dialogue with his foster family, whose 'homophobia' may be more related to the crisis than their feelings about Joe. The last aspect of knowledge, 'that clarifies the practitioner's understanding of the legal, policy, procedural and organisational context in which their practice takes place', must include the Children Act 1989 Guidance and Regulations, where the needs of young lesbians and gay men became the responsibility of placing agencies. 'The needs and concerns of young gay men and women must also be recognised and approached sympathetically' (Section 9.50, Vol. 3, Department of Health 1991) and 'Gay men and women may require very sympathetic carers to enable them to accept and develop their own self-esteem' (Section 9.53, Vol. 3, Department of Health 1991), are directions of which the student needs to be aware.

Earlier in the chapter values were considered. In preparing for the work with Joe and his family the four levels of values would need to be considered carefully. The student's values are at present conflicting with Joe's foster parents in this crisis period. The values of the agency are sympathetic to Joe's position. The legislative context gives conflicting messages. These conflicting and harmonious value systems need to be thought about carefully in supervision as they might impact on the skills deployed by the student. All parties are anxious and some are angry, and it is the role of the student social worker to focus on the interpersonal skills inherent within the CCETSW core competence of 'communicate and engage' so that all parties can be properly heard and enabled to communicate. Whatever the outcome, Joe will need lines of communication left open in the long term with the foster parents who love him and whom he loves. The approach the student takes could radically affect this. To 'challenge' their 'homophobia' in an angry way will not allow the possibility of the pain, confusion and anxiety lying underneath to be explored sufficiently for them to reconnect with the love they feel for their foster son. This does not mean collusion with homophobia, but enables all parties to engage in real communication and dialogue.

This case example is purely a construction to facilitate thinking about the preparation necessary in supervision, using the foci of knowledge, values and skills. Each piece of work will draw on different areas of knowledge and throw up different dilemmas. The generic theme running throughout is the need for there to be critical reflection within the practice teaching context in preparation for practice.

Conclusion

Lesbians and gay men are practice teachers, students and service users. Sexuality is a central part of all human experience, and when the sexual orientation of a person is a minority identity, this is thrown into sharp relief. Sexuality is an area that raises anxiety in social work and needs to be tackled during the social work education process to prepare practitioners to offer a competent service. It has been suggested, in this chapter, that a manageable focus for practice teachers is competence: knowledge, values and skills. Practice teaching is a fundamentally important role in the education of qualifying social workers and one which has to take on the area of sexuality and social work to be competent.

References

Amnesty International (1997) *Breaking the Silence: Human Rights Violations Based on Sexual Orientation.* London: Amnesty International.

Boswell, G. (1997) 'The role of the practice teacher.' In M. Davies (ed) *The Blackwell Companion to Social Work.* Oxford: Blackwell.

Brown, H.C. (1992) 'Lesbians, the State and social work practice.' In M. Langan and L. Day (eds) *Women, Oppression and Social Work.* London: Routledge.

Brown, H.C. (1996) 'The knowledge base of social work.' In A.A. Vass (ed) *Social Work Competences: Core Knowledge, Values and Skills.* London: Sage.

Brown, H.C. (1998) *Social Work and Sexuality: Working with Lesbians and Gay Men.* Basingstoke: Macmillan.

Buckley, K. (1992) 'Heterosexism, Power and Social Policy,' in P. Senior and D. Woodhill (eds) *Gender, Crime and Probation Practice.* Sheffield: PAVIC Publications.

Campion, M.J. (1995) *Who's Fit to Be a Parent?* London: Routledge.

CCETSW (1989) *Requirements and Regulations for the Diploma in Social Work.* London: CCETSW.

CCETSW (1995) *DipSW: Rules and Requirements for the Diploma in Social Work* (Paper 30). Revised Edition. London: CCETSW.

CCETSW (1996) *Assuring Quality for Practice Teaching: Rules and Requirements for the Practice Teaching Award. Approval, Review and Inspection of Practice Teaching Programmes.* London: CCETSW.

Cooper, D. (1994) *Sexing the City: Lesbian and Gay Politics Within the Activist State.* London: Rivers Oram.

Davis, L. (1993) *Sex and the Social Worker.* New Edition. London: Janus Publishing Company.

Department of Health (1991) *The Children Act 1989: Guidance and Regulations, Vol. 3: Family Placements.* London: HMSO.

Department of Health (1993) *Adoption: The Future.* London: HMSO.

d'Ardenne, P. and Mahtani, A. (1989) *Transcultural Counselling in Action.* London: Sage.

Doel, M., Shardlow, S., Sawdon, C. and Sawdon, D. (1996) *Teaching Social Work Practice.* Aldershot: Arena.

Dutton, J. and Kohli, R. (1996) 'The core skills of social work.' In A.A. Vass (ed) *Social Work Competences: Core Knowledge, Values and Skills.* London: Sage.

Erikson, E. (1965) *Childhood and Society.* Harmondsworth: Penguin.

Forrister, D.K. (1992) 'The integration of lesbian and gay content in direct practice courses.' In N.J. Woodman (ed) *Lesbian and Gay Lifestyles: A Guide for Counseling and Education.* New York: Irvington Publishers.

Gibson, A. (1991) 'Erikson's life cycle approach to development.' In J. Lishman (ed) *Handbook of Theory for Practice Teachers in Social Work.* London: Jessica Kingsley Publishers.

Gooding, C. (1992) *Trouble with the Law: A Legal Handbook for Lesbians and Gay Men.* London: GMP Publishers.

Greene, B. and Herek, G.M. (eds) (1994) *Lesbian and Gay Psychology: Theory, Research, and Clinical Applications.* London: Sage.

Hart, J. (1980) 'It's just a stage we're going through: the sexual politics of casework.' In M. Brake and R. Bailey (eds) *Radical Social Work and Practice.* London: Edward Arnold.

Hart, J. and Richardson, D. (eds) (1981) *The Theory and Practice of Homosexuality.* London: Routledge and Kegan Paul.

Jeffrey-Poulter, S. (1991) *Peers, Queers and Commons: The Struggle for Gay Law Reform from 1950 to the Present.* London: Routledge.

Kent-Baguley, P. (1990) 'Sexuality and youth work practice.' In T. Jeffs and M. Smith (eds) *Young People, Inequality and Youth Work.* Basingstoke: Macmillan.

Kus, R.J. (ed) (1990) *Keys to Caring: Assisting Your Gay and Lesbian Clients.* Boston: Alyson.

Logan, J., Kershaw, S., Karban, K., Mitts, S., Trotter, J. and Sinclair, M. (1996) *Confronting Prejudice: Lesbian and Gay Issues in Social Work Education.* Aldershot: Arena.

Lovell, A. (1995) *When Your Child Comes Out.* London: Sheldon Press.

Mason-John, V. and Khmbatta, A. (1993) *Lesbians Talk; Making Black Waves.* London: Scarlet Press.

McCaughey, C. and Buckley, K. (1993) *Sexuality, Youth Work and Probation Practice.* Sheffield: Pavic Publications.

Munro, A., Manthei, B. and Small, J. (1989) *Counselling: Skills of Problem Solving.* London: Routledge.

O'Hagan, K. (ed) (1996) *Competence in Social Work Practice: A Practical Guide for Professionals.* London: Jessica Kingsley Publishers.

Patterson, C.J. (1992) 'Children of lesbian and gay parents.' *Child Development 63*, 1025–1042.

Patterson, C.J. (1994) 'Children of the lesbian baby boom: behavioural adjustment, self-concepts, and sex role identity.' In B. Greene and G.M. Herek (eds) *Lesbians and Gay Psychology: Theory, Research, and Clinical Applications.* London: Sage.

Romans, P. (1992) 'Daring to pretend? Motherhood and lesbianism.' In K. Plummer *Modern Homosexualities.* London: Routledge.

Shardlow, S. and Doel, M. (1996) *Practice Learning and Teaching.* Basingstoke: Macmillan.

Strommen, E. (1990) 'Hidden branches and growing pains: homosexuality and the family tree.' In F.W. Bozett and M.B. Sussman (eds) *Homosexuality and Family Relations.* New York: Harrington Park Press.

Tasker, F. and Golombok, S. (1991) 'Children raised by lesbian mothers – the empirical evidence.' *Family Law 21*, 184–187.

Tasker, F. and Golombok, S. (1995) 'Adults raised as children in lesbian families.' *American Journal of Orthopsychiatry 65*, 2, 203–15.

Trenchard, L. and Warren, H. (1984) *Something to Tell You.* London: London Gay Teenage Group.

Wilson, A.R. (ed) (1995) *A Simple Matter of Justice?* London: Cassell.

Woodman, N.J. (ed) (1992) *Lesbian and Gay Lifestyles: A Guide for Counseling and Education.* New York: Irvington Publishers.

CHAPTER 4

Anti-Racist Practice Teaching

Equipping the Practice Teacher
for the Task

Elaine Arnold

Introduction

A Social Work Programme should 'aim to help students develop practice which combats the effects of prejudice and structural disadvantage in all its forms and to enable those who suffer from its effects, whether for reasons of age, disability, ethnic grouping, poverty, race, sexual orientation or social class to develop and take their place as citizens' (Master in Social Work/Sussex PostGraduate Diploma in Social Work Programme Handbook 1996–1998)

The above statement sets out a laudable aim which it is hoped that all practice teachers involved in the training of social work students would attempt to achieve. However even though anti-discriminatory practice has been a significant and integral part of the social work curriculum for nearly a decade, it is still recognised that a number of practice teachers feel ill at ease when asked to teach this crucial area of practice. In this chapter I shall be arguing that social work has a responsibility to recognise the diversity within society and to meet the needs of all groups. Where the population is changing, social work must adapt to ensure its relevance to new groups of users. The chapter will explore some of the essential knowledge and skills required by the practice teacher to ensure that students are effectively prepared to undertake anti-racist social work practice.

At the end of the 1980s the Central Council for Education and Training in Social Work (CCETSW) outlined its requirements for the new Diploma in Social Work programme and also those for the accreditation of practice teachers (CCETSW Paper 30 and 26.3 1989). The new model claimed that 'a practice teacher is indeed a teacher of practice', and stood in contrast to the old model student supervisor (Doel 1990). In the revised Paper 30 (CCETSW 1991) it was stated that:

> Social Workers need to be able to work in a society which is multiracial and multicultural. CCETSW will therefore seek to ensure that students are prepared not only for ethnically sensitive practice but also to challenge and confront institutional and other forms of racism. It will require that both the content of learning, and the context of learning promote and develop this approach. (p.21)

Although, as I argue below, CCETSW has since curtailed references to anti-racist practice, and substituted the more muted phrase 'counter discrimination' for 'challenge and confront', Thompson's statements that 'good practice is anti-discriminatory practice' and that 'social work practice which does not take account of oppression and discrimination cannot be seen as good practice, no matter how high its standards may be in other respects' (1993, p.10) should, I believe, remain at the heart of the practice teacher's value base.

Training for practice teachers

In the early 1990s Balen, Brown and Taylor conducted some research among practice teachers to ascertain how the prescribed changes in their role were being experienced. Apprehensions expressed largely centred on two areas: the new competence frameworks and anti-discriminatory practice. Of the latter, Balen et al. comment that a number of factors contributed to the anxiety. These were: working within agencies where there was little commitment to anti-discriminatory policies; a paucity of training among practice teachers themselves in this area which severely limited their ability to teach or assess; and finally, a growing awareness that their students were potentially far more competent in relation to anti-discriminatory practice than their practice teachers, given the college-based work they had undertaken (1993, p.22).

This echoes my own experience of teaching on a practice teacher programme and working with practice teachers in an area where the population was predominantly white. Some practice teachers had not experienced anti-racist training in depth, and some claimed to have been exposed to racism awareness training which had left them 'emotionally scarred' and reluctant to discuss issues of race. They also feared that in some instances they might express views and use language which would brand them as racists by

colleagues who were further advanced in their knowledge of racial discrimination, or by members of the groups discriminated against. However, most
trainee practice teachers were committed to anti-racist practice teaching and
were willing to engage with the teaching on race in spite of its emotive
nature. It was always necessary to establish clear ground rules. One which
was extremely important was that individuals be respectful of each other and
be given space to express their views so as to permit a free and frank discussion but that if something was said that someone else found offensive the
statement would be challenged and explored. When a 'safe' learning environment was established the practice teachers participated in exercises which
involved the use of case studies, trigger statements, questionnaires, role plays,
and much useful learning was achieved. However it is an area which requires
careful planning and the consideration of several strategies to ensure a successful outcome.

For example, if there are no black teaching staff should a black consultant
be brought in or does this take the teaching of anti-racism out of 'mainstream
teaching'? In some instances where there is an all-white teaching team an
outside black consultant co-teaches with a staff member. This arrangement
often works well but it can be costly and sufficient time may not be given for
in-depth teaching on the subject. Thought needs to be given to whether
black trainee practice teachers, who may be very few, should be allowed to
absent themselves on the grounds that because they suffer racism they do not
need to be taught about it with white colleagues, or that they may be singled
out to answer questions about black people or that white colleagues may be
inhibited in expressing their true feelings. Black practice teachers also need
training, both to help them survive and confront racism, and also to reflect on
their feelings about people who are different from themselves. They should
be consulted as to their wishes to remain with white colleagues or to be
taught in a separate group with a black consultant. Whatever arrangements
are made, the aim should be to engage the participants and ensure that they
receive sound training on the issues with the express purpose of being effective practice teachers. I share the view of England (1986, p.134) 'that good
social work requires an intellectual, imaginative and emotional engagement
which is intimate and precise, and is highly taxing of the person'. There were
some participants who never felt 'safe' enough to participate fully and it was
therefore difficult to know if they would ever be imaginative in finding ways
of helping their students to consider the issues, or if they themselves would
practice anti-racist social work.

Changing society: the social work response

Gould claims that 'arguably the major transformation in British social work education during the last decade has been the emergence of anti-racism and anti-discrimination as dominant perspectives' (1995, p.3). There are several reasons for this transformation. By the 1970s it was recognised that there were very definite demographic changes, especially in the inner cities, as a result of immigration. Between 1955 and the early 1960s, black workers had been encouraged to migrate from the New Commonwealth and Pakistan. At the beginning of the 1960s the Commonwealth Immigrants Act (1962) limited black immigrants entering the country. By then migrants realised that their plans for a temporary stay were unrealistic since their economic situation had hardly changed; neither had that of their homelands, so return was well nigh impossible. They became settlers.

Some of the countries in the Caribbean, such as Jamaica and Barbados, from which the settlers came had become independent, and this had caused a change in the settlers' status. They were now no longer children of the mother country but seemed to be poor relations or unwanted guests. Settlement was usually in the inner-city areas and jobs were only available in urban areas where there was poor housing. Apart from doctors and nurses whose services in hospitals were valued, migrants were employed in manual occupations. They experienced the antagonism of white workers and discrimination from employers at the first stage of recruitment, or having been recruited remained unpromoted. A comprehensive review of the living conditions of Asian and West Indian immigrants showed that their jobs were inferior ones, they were less well paid and lived in poorer housing than the general population (Smith 1977). It is fair to assume that feelings of security and safety for themselves and their children were very fragile.

The consequences of the disadvantages which the immigrant population suffered were very often disrupted family lives. In some areas about 80 per cent of mothers from the Caribbean worked, as did about 50 per cent of Asian women. Some of the children were not eligible for day care provided by the local authority, because they did not meet the criteria for admission as they were not children of single mothers. Many had limited knowledge of the social services and some for whom English was not their first language suffered difficulty in being understood. Cheetham (1982) noted that some people from the ethnic minorities may have found social services so inappropriate that they avoided contact save in the most desperate circumstances.

Cheetham also deplored the slow and grudging moves that social work had taken towards the recognition that the usual approaches were not equal to meet the needs of their new clientele. Four years later she commented that:

> Black families in Britain face many problems, the consequences of racial discrimination and migration; the latter, while it gave opportunities, also imposed strains extending well beyond the generations of people who were newcomers to Britain (1986, p.11).

There are still concerns today about the slow pace of recognising the need for non-discriminatory services for users from black and minority groups. Another challenge for the social services is trying to meet the needs of refugees who are extremely needy and vulnerable. Many of them arriving in the country seeking asylum have fled from their homes leaving family behind or having lost them altogether in very tragic circumstances. On arriving in this country they may find their problems exacerbated by institutions reluctant to change, or social workers frozen by their anxieties about how to meet the needs of such a diverse group of people.

CCETSW's response to training for anti-discriminatory, anti-racist practice

It is important to understand the historical context of CCETSW's response to training for work with black and other minority groups.

During the 1970s some practitioners began to express their dissatisfaction with the services to clients. As black and other clients from ethnic minority groups became more confident in their status as settlers they began to complain that their needs were not being adequately met by social workers, especially in the field of child care.

The need for training became apparent. CCETSW in 1979 declared the importance it attached to the teaching of areas related to ethnic minorities on its programmes. Subsequently CCETSW emphasised to all relevant bodies providing social work courses that, in view of the growing diverse student population, it was important to encourage students to question cultural assumptions about family patterns and the social lives of families. This was relevant not only in college-based teaching but also in practice in agencies (CCETSW 1985, p.31).

This was a tentative step and though it assisted in the explanation of different customs, value systems and beliefs of some of the minority groups, there was the tendency for workers to generalise and treat people from those groups as a homogenous mass, rather than relating to individuals and trying to meet their particular needs. The concepts of individual, cultural and institutional racism were not considered until later when black clients and workers began to be vocal about the oppression and discrimination meted out to them by the decisions and actions of social workers directly or indirectly. Examples of this were particularly noted in the assessment of black people's capacity to care for their children and the resulting disproportionate numbers of black children taken into the care of the Local Authority. This led to research by several concerned individuals (such as Lambert and Rowe 1973) and organisations, for example the Soul Kids Campaign (1977).

Students black and white, practitioners and tutors, demanded that attention was given to the inclusion of race issues in the training of social workers. At first this was piecemeal and was treated as an addition to a full curriculum. Black people and those from minority ethnic groups were invited in to 'give a talk on race issues', but this was often unsatisfactory as the time allocated was often too short and most of the time participants were left feeling confused, guilty, angry and paralysed. Nevertheless social workers, and other professionals, particularly probation officers, began to be more aware of the use of stereotypical and often derogatory language in reports on black and minority ethnic clients. There were also prolonged and heated debates over the issues of transracial placements, following the publication of a report (Owen and Jackson 1983) which claimed that black children were not being helped by their white adoptive parents to develop their racial identity. The Association of Black Social Workers and Allied Professions (1983) along with several writers, for example Cheetham (1982), Ahmed (1986) and Coombe and Little (1986) were insistent that attention should be paid to the training on racial issues in social work.

CCETSW's research findings during its formal visits to all of the then CQSW and CSS courses throughout the British Isles during 1988–89 were that some of the courses had begun to address issues of race, but others were finding it difficult to do so. The following areas of concern were highlighted:

- The availability of appropriate practice learning opportunities for students to address issues of anti-racism
- Agency and college anti-racist and equal opportunity policies
- The lack of clarity of terminology such as 'multiculturalism', 'ethnic-sensitive practice', 'black'

- Agency and teaching staff unreasonably expecting black and ethnic minority students to act as experts in this area, and yet appearing to be unable/unwilling to acknowledge that students can find
themselves confronting institutional racism in their college/univer-
sities and on placements with variable ability and preparation to
deal with it (Divine 1991).

When CCETSW introduced the Diploma in Social Work (1989), it drew on
this research to include in the requirements anti-racist and anti-
discriminatory components. In order to help college and agency staff, a
National Steering Group on the Teaching of Race and Anti-Racism in the
Personal Services was set up in 1990 and this provided ideas for the promotion of effective delivery of service to clients (The Teaching of Anti-Racism
in Diploma in Social Work Programmes, CCETSW 1991). It was advocated
that rather than relying on discrete blocks of teaching on race, the issues
should be integrated in the teaching of all subjects. There was also the
requirement that social work students showed competence in demonstrating
an awareness of both individual and institutional racism and ways to combat
both through anti-racist practice. This requirement was not easily met but in
some instances it encouraged creative ways of thinking and engaging students to examine their own attitudes to racial difference and to become aware
of incidences of racial discrimination within the workplace and in the wider
society.

The requirements of CCETSW that students practised in an anti-racist
manner generated an enormous amount of controversy, as did the statement
on anti-racism: 'CCETSW believes that racism is endemic in the values, attitudes and structures of British society including those of social services and
social work education' (CCETSW 1991, p.46).

The Council was accused of becoming politicised, and what I consider to
be a meaningless term 'political correctness' (Pinker 1993) was levelled
against it. I would argue that what was being suggested was the laudable aim
of 'professional correctness'. In 1993 the newly appointed chair to
CCETSW was reported as disagreeing with CCETSW's statement, in Annex
5 of Paper 30, about the endemic nature of racism within British society, but
he agreed that there was 'a lot of racism and discrimination which we have to
fight against' (Francis 1994, p.19). Some changes were instituted in the
structure of CCETSW and the Black Perspective Group which comprised
black academics, trainers and practitioners was abolished. Paper 30 was
revised and it is interesting to note that the word 'race' is not included when

explaining the diversity of the social settings in which social workers practice. 'The diversity is reflected through religion, ethnicity, culture, language, social status, family structure and life style' (CCETSW 1991, p.18).

Thompson warns that to focus exclusively on cultural or ethnic patterns without taking account of 'race' is indeed a naïve mistake (Thompson 1993, p.58).

Anti-discriminatory law for social workers

By the 1960s it was beginning to be recognised that racism was endemic in society at all levels. Legislation was enacted in an attempt to 'eliminate unlawful racial discrimination' and 'promote equality of opportunity, and good relations between persons of different racial groups' (these were based on 'grounds of race, colour, nationality and ethnic origins') (Race Relations Act 1976 Section 71). Particularly pertinent for those providing services such as social workers is Section 20 of the Act which states it is unlawful for anyone who is concerned with the provision (for payment or free of charge) of goods, facilities or services to the public to discriminate by refusing or deliberately omitting to provide them, or as regards their quality or the manner in which, or the terms on which, he provides them (Section 20.1). Further, the discrimination referred to may be direct (less favourable treatment) or indirect (applying a requirement or condition which has a disproportionately adverse effect on a particular racial group, and which cannot be justified) (Commission for Racial Equality 1989, p.11).

CCETSW (1995) has provided guidance for meeting the DipSw requirements with respect to the law for social work. It states that: 'Reference to the law on discrimination and equal opportunity should permeate all social work teaching within the academic and practice curricula'. Most students are now familiar with the Children Act (1989)'s recognition – for the first time in British law – of the importance of considering 'the child's religious persuasion, racial origin and cultural and linguistic background' in decisions regarding children being 'looked after' (Children Act 1989, Section 22(5)c, see also Sections 1(3) and Schedule 2(11) relating to race, culture, religion, and language). However, students may be less familiar with other legislation CCETSW lists as being designed to challenge discrimination: the Sex Discrimination Act 1975, the Race Relations Act 1976, the Welsh Language Act 1991 and the requirement in Section 95 of the Criminal Justice Act 1991 that those administering justice avoid discriminating against people on grounds of race, gender, or other grounds' (CCETSW 1995, pp.23–24). This

CCETSW document contains tasks and exercises which practice teachers may find useful in engaging students in thinking about the law and its relation to practice.

The role of practice teacher

The practice teacher needs to ensure that anti-racism becomes an integral part of the practice curriculum. As well as the knowledge base, practice teachers need sensitivity and understanding, and an ability to pace the learning to the students' level of understanding. Robinson (1995) highlights the fundamental and complex nature of such learning:

> Without a conscious awareness of one's own attitudes and anxieties that may be stimulated by the presence of a black client, the effectiveness of a social worker's interventions will be seriously diminished. It seems more common for social workers and mental health workers to assume that such feelings have been replaced either by a professional approach to all (patients) or by a conviction that somehow, they are different from other white people when dealing with the issue of race...the process of eliminating one's racial bias is much more difficult and involves an in-depth analysis of oneself and of a society that has fostered racism and oppression – it is a long term process. (p.160)

Practice teachers are in a prime position to enhance students' learning of anti-racist practice but only if they themselves have

- undergone training in anti-discriminatory practice
- understand the nature of racism
- accept that those socialised in a society that is racist internalise the beliefs, and frequently use terminology that may be derogatory to people different from themselves
- believe that it is necessary consciously to try to change words and behaviour which are offensive and hurtful to others
- believe that black people and other minority ethnic groups suffer from discrimination based on their racial difference. Practice teachers need to hold a balanced view about race relations legislation and realise that if they use it judiciously, social workers are enabled to challenge racism with confidence and authority.

For those practice teachers working in areas of the country where the population is predominantly white there are additional challenges. First, there is often the need to confront the 'race isn't an issue here' mentality of the agency which creates and perpetuates the 'invisibility' of any black and ethnic minority groups who *are* part of the local population. Second, in the absence of black users practice teachers need to be creative in how they effect learning; simulated practice by way of role play or rehearsal, or triggered discussions (often generated by a question such as 'and how would your understanding and practice be different if this family were black?) and case studies are all essential learning techniques. The point needs to be emphasised that Britain is a multi-cultural and multi-racial society and students must be equipped to work effectively with all groups in the population.

Students may themselves think of creative ways to facilitate practising in an anti-discriminatory and anti-racist way. For example, some students have made surveys of the catchment area of service users and tried to engage with people from diverse groups in order to discover the basis for their reluctance to use the service, and to encourage them to suggest ways in which their needs may be met. Students may discover that first attempts at using the service may have given the individual the feeling that there was no genuineness, warmth or empathy (Egan 1994). Analysing process recordings for language used, intonation of voice, issues of power, and values conveyed is a helpful exercise.

Terminology and definitions

Practice teachers and students need to have a clear definition of key words in discussing race issues. Often the term 'ethnic' is used to describe people who are different from the majority group without an understanding that all people are 'ethnic' (Thompson 1993, p.58). Over the years the terms 'ethnicity' and 'culture' seem to be used synonymously. Acharyya makes a helpful distinction between the terms ethnicity and culture as follows:

> The word ethnicity still refers us back to the putative racial origins of people, to their distinctive physical appearance as it is perceived by themselves and others. The word culture on the other hand refers to milieu, the process of living and the system of values, practices shared by particular groups of people. Ethnicity therefore (...) remains a relatively static concept for the individual. Culture by distinction is dynamic. It is ever changing and includes a whole gamut of experiences and learning

and includes all the distinctive practices of daily living, customs and attitudes. (Acharyya 1992, p.74)

Race is now widely defined as a social construct which attempts to group people by common ancestry, colour and other physical attributes. Roediger emphasises that:

> race is given meaning through the agency of human beings in historical and social contexts, and is not a biological or natural category. (Roediger 1994, p.2)

Racism, however, is:

> the belief that race is the primary determinant of human traits and capacities, and that racial differences produce an inherent superiority of a particular race. (Webster's New Collegiate Dictionary)

It has also been defined as:

> Belief in the inherent superiority of some races over others and discriminative treatment based on such belief. (Chambers Dictionary)

These definitions highlight superiority but do not state the element of power which is introduced by Judy Katz (1978) who believes it is the use of power added to the prejudice against other races which constitutes racism. Katz's definition has been criticised as its use of power puts too much emphasis on the individual at the expense of the structural. Thompson (1993) states that individual prejudice is not wholly accountable for the discrimination and oppression meted out to people from minority ethnic groups but that 'racism is built into the structure of society and in the dominant institutions' (p.61).

Dominelli (1997, p.16) explains that racism damages black and white people 'economically, socially and emotionally', and gives detailed exercises for use in training to examine personal, cultural and institutional racism. The practice teacher can engage the student in a discussion of these three forms of racism using the following definitions:

- Individual or personal racism comprises those personal attitudes and behaviours which individuals use to prejudge racial groups.

- Cultural racism consists of values, beliefs and ideas, usually embedded in history and 'common sense' which endorse the superiority of white culture over others.

- Institutional racism operates in institutions or organisations where racist beliefs and perceptions have become embedded in policy, procedures and practice and are used to exclude people (usually black) who do not 'fit in'.

This discussion, to be successful, will demand openness and trust and may be difficult for both practice teacher and student, but for practitioners to be competent in anti-racist practice it is essential that they are aware of their prejudices and values and have had an opportunity to examine their frame of reference. Using material from the student's caseload as well as the simulated exercises and projects already described will provide contexts in which such discussions can take place. Another way in which such learning can be addressed is by focusing on the practice teacher/student relationship itself.

Practice teacher/student relationship

The practice teacher needs to be mindful not only of the work done by the student and his or her client but also to keep a close eye on the interaction between practice teacher and student. Where students are black or from a minority ethnic group their previous encounters with the white establishment may affect their current experience. This needs to be acknowledged by the practice teachers, particularly if they, too, are white, and the students given time and space to discuss these matters. In working interculturally and cross-racially, it is well to bear in mind that:

> both social workers and clients bring to their interaction certain values acquired during socialisation within their own backgrounds. Frequently workers fail to recognize that clients from minority groups may have suffered previously unpleasant or belittling experiences at the hands of other professionals in health, housing, welfare or education agencies; experiences which may influence their more current meeting. (Arnold 1992, p.156)

All students need to be helped to recognise transference, which refers to the tendency to repeat a pattern of relating to an authority figure, be that positively or negatively, and similarly the counter transference which is the way the authority figure, in this case the practice teacher, responds to the student (Jacobs 1994). For example the student may have been used to being criticised by a parent or by a demanding teacher at school and he or she may be reluctant to produce reports for the practice teacher for fear of being criticised.

Similarly the practice teacher may be critical of his or her own child and realise that there is the tendency to be critical of the student. On the other hand the practice teacher may find criticism difficult. Both reactions create difficulty in forming an effective working relationship and the student's learning may be adversely affected.

Empowerment is a crucial aspect of social work practice and teaching about empowerment becomes live when the concept is applied to the practice teaching relationship itself. Rapoport (1995) cited in Warren (1997) urges us to be 'more critical and less casual about what we advocate as empowering'. Students, particularly if they are black or from another discriminated against group, will be able to inform the debate on empowerment from their own experience. Is the student included within the team's discussions, are the views of the student heard, and is the student allocated a cross-section of clients in order to gain experience with different categories of users? Are there opportunities created to discuss feelings of powerlessness in a predominantly white society? Or of how a black student relates to a white practice teacher who holds power not only as an authority figure in the agency but as a white person from a majority ethnic group?

If the practice teacher is black or from an ethnic minority group, and the student white, besides empowering the student as above the practice teacher needs to enable the white student to discuss the issues of racism without fear of offending the practice teacher.

The process of modelling facilitates learning behaviours and skills. The inexperienced social work student may enter the agency with many misgivings of 'getting it wrong' in his or her work with clients and more so if the clients are racially or culturally different from themselves. He or she looks to the practice teacher as a model in the early days before developing their own style. It may be useful for the student to be asked some questions before beginning work with a client who is racially or culturally different from themselves. These might be what assumptions were made about the individual, and what feelings are engendered by having to work with difference? Would the student make similar assumptions if the client were not different? All students, black and white, are in need of learning skills of interacting with people different from themselves.

There are times when black students may experience direct discrimination from clients who may refuse to accept a service from them because they are black. The practice teacher needs to be clear about the agency's policy and provide support for the student who may feel humiliated, angry and disempowered. It is important that the agency is unanimous in its agreement about how it deals with users who are disrespectful to members of its staff. Agencies should also be aware that black and ethnic minority students are not experts in the field of race relations and should not be used by them as such. This is not to say they are not to be heard when they make comments or suggestions for working with users of their racial or cultural group.

Conclusion

Within this chapter I have considered the context in which race issues have become important in the training of social work students, and the role of the practice teacher in effecting crucial learning about anti-racist social work practice. Practice teachers play an active role in imparting knowledge, assisting in the development of skills and encouraging the student to relate theory to practice in order to work effectively with all users of the service. Anti-discriminatory law is included in the legal mandate under which social workers perform their 'roles and tasks'. I have argued that practice teachers need to have knowledge of the law themselves, and to be able to help students see how judicious use of the law will be beneficial to themselves and users. Effective use of the law must, however, be underpinned by students' understanding of racism and commitment to challenging it.

Many of the families from black and minority ethnic groups experience poverty, discrimination, disadvantage, and to some extent have internalised feelings of inferiority within the powerful white society. When they come for help to the social services they may be feeling very powerless and inadequate. Student social workers need to understand and develop empowerment models of practice. Clients can be empowered when the social worker allows them time to tell their narrative, treats them with respect, takes an interest in their difference and acknowledges similarities and so builds a relationship that will facilitate working together. Invitation to participate in the decision-making processes which affect their lives will enhance their self-esteem. For some, social action may be a way of tackling their problems, for example, they may be involved in the setting up of a day-care centre for their young children, or for the elderly where they may speak the language of their homelands, prepare traditional meals and organise social activities of their own choice. The student could increase their knowledge base considerably by being involved in some of these activities with people from disadvantaged groups.

Whether working with individuals or groups, student social workers need awareness, sensitivity, understanding of the different cultures of groups in local communities and understanding, too, of the material and psychological effects of racial discrimination (Utting 1990).

I have also argued that the practice teaching relationship itself may raise issues of racial and cultural difference and these should be fully explored and exploited for their learning potential. This may be difficult work but it is essential if a good working relationship is to be built and if learning at a deep level is to occur. Because the power lies with the practice teacher, the responsibility of introducing the issues must be taken by them. This is explored further in other chapters in this book (*see*, for example, Chapter 1; and the use of the learning agreement as a strategy for focusing on issues of power imbalances in Chapter 5).

Finally, if anti-racist practice is to be effective it must be an objective of not just the student, the practice teacher and the social work programme. It must be embedded in the social work team and wider organisation. Managers of agencies which provide practice placements for students need to ensure that all practitioners are given time, space and support to ensure that effective social work practice is anti-racist practice.

Appendix

The following is an illustration of the pathway to anti-discriminatory/anti-racist practice. The role of the practice teacher is to help the student to arrive at Level 5.

Anti-racist practice (Level 5)

Acceptance that not only individuals discriminate but also institutions and their structures. Therefore there is a need for careful scrutiny of equal opportunity policies, and practices need to be in order to ensure that discrimination and obstacles which may prevent justice for all who use the services are eliminated.

Racism awareness (Level 4)

Examination of: individuals' values and their attitudes towards races different from themselves; how socialisation influences language used when referring to minority ethnic groups; the tendency to pathologise difference and to categorise individuals as superior or inferior. Recognition of how power is used to discriminate against minority ethnic groups in all areas of their lives.

Ethnically sensitive practice (Level 3)

Beginning to be sensitive to other groups whose ways of expressing themselves in language or actions are different from one's own ways, provided the behaviour does not put vulnerable members of the group at risk. Difference will not be used as an excuse for not exercising judgement and making a thorough assessment of the situation.

Multi-culturalism (Level 2)

Recognition that the dominant culture and values are not the only standard for measuring the values of other groups in society. Understanding that people's problems occur within diverse cultural backgrounds. Questioning cultural assumptions made by the dominant group, and refraining from attributing the reactions to injustice of those discriminated against as due to their differences of culture.

A colour-blind approach (Level 1)

Treating everyone the same. Denying that colour or belonging to a different ethnic group makes any significant difference to the individual's feelings. Paying little attention to the adverse circumstances which discrimination creates in the lives of black people and those from minority groups.

References

Acharyya, S. (1992) 'The doctor's dilemma: the practice of cultural psychiatry in multicultural Britain.' In J. Kareem and R. Littlewood (eds) *Intercultural Therapy: Themes, Interpretations and Practice.* Oxford: Blackwell.

Ahmed, S. (1986) 'Cultural racism in work with Asian women and girls.' In S. Ahmed, J. Cheetham and J. Small (eds) *Social Work with Black Children and their Families.* London: Batsford.

Arnold, E. (1992) 'Intercultural social work.' In J. Kareem and R. Littlewood (eds) *Intercultural Therapy: Themes, Interpretations and Practice.* Oxford: Blackwell.

Arnold, E. and James, M. (1989) 'Finding black families for black children in care: a case study.' *New Community 15*, 3, 417–425. Commission For Racial Equality, London.

Arnold, E. and Tulloch, J. (1996) 'Social work teaching not to blame for anti-discrimination setbacks.' *Professional Social Work, The Magazine of the British Association of Social Workers.* February. British Association of Social Workers, Birmingham.

Association of Black Social Workers and Allied Professions (1983) *Black Children in Care: Evidence to the House of Commons Social Service Select Committee.* London: ABSWAAP.

Balen, R., Brown, K. and Taylor, C. (1993) 'It seems so much is expected of us: practice teachers, the Diploma in Social Work and anti-discriminatory practice.' *Social Work Education 12*, 3, 17–35.

CCETSW (1989) *Improving Standards in Practice Learning,* Paper 26, 3. London: CCETSW.

CCETSW (1989) *Rules and Requirements for the DipSW,* Paper 30. London: CCETSW.

CCETSW (1991) *Rules and Requirements for the DipSW,* Revised Paper 30. London: CCETSW.

CCETSW (1995) *Assuring Quality in the Diploma in Social Work.* London: CCETSW.

CCETSW (1995) *Law for Social Workers.* London: CCETSW.

Chamber's Dictionary. (1993) London: Chambers Harrap.

Cheetham, J. (ed) (1982) *Social Work and Ethnicity.* London: Allen and Unwin.

Cheetham, J. (1986) 'Introduction.' In S. Ahmed, J. Cheetham and J. Small (eds) *Social Work with Black Children and their Families.* London: Batsford.

Commission for Racial Equality (1989) *Racial Equality in Social Services Department.* London: CRE.

Coombe, V. and Little, A. (eds) (1986) *Race and Social Work: A Guide To Training.* London: Tavistock Publications Ltd.

Divine, D. (1991) *Towards Real Communication.* London: CCETSW.

Doel, M. (1990) 'Putting the heart into the curriculum.' *Community Care, 797,* 20–22.

Dominelli, L. (1997) *Anti-Racist Social Work, Second Edition.* Basingstoke, London: Macmillan Press Limited.

Egan, G. (1994) *The Skilled Helper, Fifth Edition.* California: Brooks/Cole Publishing Co.

England, H. (1986) *Social Work as Art: Making Sense of Good Practice.* London: Allen and Unwin.

Francis, J. (1994) 'In the hot seat.' *Community Care, 999,* 19.

Gardiner, D. (1985) *Ethnic Minorities and Social Work Training,* Paper 21.1. London: CCETSW.

Gould, N. (1995) 'Anti-racist social work: a framework for teaching and action.' *Issues in Social Work Education 14,* 1, 3–17..

Jacobs, M. (1994) *Still Small Voice: a Practical Introduction to Counselling in Pastoral and Other Settings.* London: SPCK.

Katz, J.H. (1978) *White Awareness. A Handbook for Anti-Racism Training.* Oklahoma: University of Oklahoma Press.

Lambert, L. and Rowe, J. (1973) *Children Who Wait.* London: British Agencies For Adoption and Fostering.

Owen, G. and Jackson, B. (1983) *Adoption and Race: Black, Asian and Mixed Race Children in White Families.* London: Batsford.

Pinker, R. (1993) 'Commissars brainwash our social workers.' *The Daily Mail,* August 2.

Robinson, L. (1995) *Psychology for Social Workers. Black Perspectives.* London: Routledge.

Roediger, D. (1994) *Towards the Abolition of Whiteness. Essays on Race, Politics and Working Class History.* London: Verso.

Smith, D.J. (1977) *Racial Disadvantage in Britain.* Harmondsworth: Penguin.

Soul Kids Campaign (1977) *Report of the Soul Kids Campaign.* London: Association of British Adoption and Fostering Agencies.

Thompson, N. (1993) *Anti-Discriminatory Practice.* London: Macmillan.

Utting, W.B. (1990) *Issues of Race and Culture in the Family Placement of the Children.* London: Social Services Inspectorate, Department of Health.

Warren, C. (1997) 'Family support and the journey to empowerment.' In C. Cannan and C. Warren *Social Action with Children and Families.* London and New York: Routledge.

Webster, M.A. (1975) *Webster's New Collegiate Dictionary.* Massachussetts: Bell and Sons Ltd.

CHAPTER 5

Male Practice Teachers and Female Students

The Role of the Learning Agreement

Phil Jones

Introduction

My reasons for writing on this subject arise from my personal experience as a social worker. I am a white male practice teacher, the only male Child Protection Officer in a NSPCC Child Protection Team. I am a practitioner with little experience of managing or supervising staff. While preparing to become a practice teacher I realised that many of the students who would be placed with me at my agency would be women. In considering how I would be best able to ensure a high quality placement for a female student I was obliged to consider my experience of becoming a social worker, my training and my introduction to child protection. Highly relevant in this respect has been my developing understanding of men's role in gender oppression, child sexual abuse and domestic violence.

> Most men have been socialized to accept gender benefits and use them to their benefit. (Taylor and Daly 1995, p.63)

The unpicking of the issues surrounding the abuse of children and women fuelled by feminist and feminist-influenced writers was a heady process upon which I engaged during my qualifying training and beyond. This forced me to reflect upon my own gender and how I relate to others in my personal and professional life. During my training I was surprised by my women colleagues' distrust and suspicion of men, including, on occasions, myself. Dominelli and McLeod point out:

Women have recognised that they can share their experience more profoundly, more intimately and more sensitively with other women than
with men. (1989, p.88)

A student colleague at the time wrote in the conclusion of her research entitled 'How do women social workers feel about working with men as
colleagues and men as clients?':

What uniformly came across from this research are the powerful feelings of unease and suspicion these women (in this research) experience
when working with their male colleagues. (Chamberlayne 1990, p.68)

These observations, and others, caused me and my male colleagues to think
carefully about our role and relationships with women at work.

Some work has been done in examining the male practitioner's role in
child protection, most usefully by Simon Hacket (1997). It is my hope, in this
chapter, to add to the debate by focusing on the role of male practice teachers
in providing good learning opportunities for women students. How to go
about this has posed something of a dilemma! I wished to place the needs of
female students at the centre of the work but wouldn't presume to write from
a woman's perspective. On the other hand I have wanted to avoid the trap of
asking women what to do! I have opted, therefore, to attempt both by (i)
doing my 'own work' in trying to understand the issues from what has
already been written and from my own observations, and (ii) by undertaking
a small research project.

In order to ask women about their experiences of being on placement I
devised a brief questionnaire which focused on the learning contract as a
means of raising and addressing issues of gender. The questionnaire was distributed via a letter in *Community Care* magazine's 'Information Please' page
and to female colleagues who had expressed an interest in the research. The
respondent group was therefore composed of students and qualified practitioners. The research was not intended to provide 'hard' statistical
information but rather to help me understand some women's experience.
Many of the comments made by those who replied are included in this chapter.

Thirty-one questionnaires were distributed and eleven returned. This is,
of course, a very small sample which is not representative but nevertheless
has provided a useful contribution to my writing on the matter and my
approach to supervising women students.

I have begun this chapter by laying out my initial hypothesis. The following section considers the relevance of this subject within an anti-oppressive approach to practice teaching. The third part addresses the feminist critique, asking if it is possible for male practice teachers to ensure a 'good enough' placement experience for female students. The final section seeks to make some suggestions which male practice teachers (including myself) may wish to adopt in their practice with female students, drawing on the responses to the research project questionnaire.

Hypothesis: values made explicit and action planned

It is my belief that the learning agreement is an important opportunity to address crucial issues which may enhance or undermine the learning which it is hoped will take place during the placement. Although associated with the beginning of the placement the learning agreement should be a dynamic 'live' document which has real meaning for the practice teacher and student throughout the placement. The case for using learning agreements has been outlined by various authors, such as Preston-Shoot (1989), while others, Sawdon and Sawdon (1988), have pointed out the contribution made by learning agreements to partnership in supervision.

The hypothesis I shall be seeking to explore in this chapter is that practice teachers' values must be made explicit in the learning agreement and that 'action points' must be attached to the values expressed. These action points must directly address the needs of the student in question. It is my belief that practice teachers must clearly express their value base in social work and practice teaching in the learning contract.

> Educators need to be explicit about the value base on which their practice depends, and which informs any framework for learning offered to students. (Humphries 1988, p.11)

The values in question are, of course, those which underpin social work and are expressed in such documents as the British Association of Social Work Code of Ethics and in CCETSW's *Rules and Requirements for the DipSW* (1996). It is not sufficient that these values be tokenistic 'add-ons'; they must be fully understood and adopted by the practice teacher as integral to their own practice.

It is crucial that learning agreements should include plans to address the issues of oppression raised by the practice teacher/student relationship. A learning agreement which fully outlines the practice teacher's value position without a plan to address these issues in his relationship with the student is, at best, a lifeless document, and at worst one to be distrusted. Examples of such action points are ensuring access to a well-resourced black students consultation group or an arrangement with a female colleague to provide support to a female student. Further 'action points' will be explored in the concluding part of this chapter.

Anti-oppressive practice/anti-sexist practice

I use the terms 'issue(s) of oppression' or 'oppression issue(s)' in relation to those individuals or groups who have experienced oppression in western European society. This may include racism, sexism and/or oppression on the basis of (dis)ability, religion, class, age, sexual preference and/or health status. The complex, and often interlocking, nature of oppressive forces have been dealt with elsewhere (Dominelli 1988; Thompson 1993).

It is fair to say that the terms anti-oppressive and anti-discriminatory are often used as being interchangeable. Phillipson (1992) helpfully contrasts the terms. She describes 'anti-discriminatory practice' as being fundamentally reformist and concerned with equality of treatment and fairness. On the other hand she describes anti-oppressive practice as working

> with a model of empowerment and liberation and requir[ing] a fundamental re-thinking of values, institutions and relationships. (p.15)

I believe that the anti-oppressive approach has more relevance to the subject in question as it would not be adequate for a practice teacher merely to treat female and male students alike. Male practice teachers must critically review their own experience and consider the impact of gender oppression on all their women colleagues and how these dynamics may continue to be played out in these relationships.

In *Assuring Quality in the Diploma in Social Work* (1996) CCETSW requires that social work practitioners 'identify and question their own values and prejudices' and 'identify, analyse and take action to counter discrimination, racism, disadvantage, inequality and injustice, using strategies appropriate to role and context' (p.18). CCETSW's *Rules and Requirements for the Practice Teaching Award* (1996) again emphasises the importance of the practice teacher countering discrimination, racism and disadvantage in both the context of their own social work role and in their practice teaching. It can be argued, however, that the phraseology used in the 1996 Rules document exposes CCETSW's position in respect of these as somewhat diluted in com-

arison to previous Rules and Requirements. In 1989 CCETSW stated une-
quivocably that 'qualifying social workers must be able to recognise the need
for and seek to promote policies and practices which are non-discriminatory
and anti-oppressive' and, more specifically to the subject under discussion,
'develop an understanding of gender issues and demonstrate anti-sexism in
social work practice' (CCETSW 1989, p.16). But combating sexism, along
with other oppressions, must remain central to the tasks of social work and
practice teaching. However it is important in the context of anti-sexism that
the focus be on gender oppression rather than merely gender, that is, that the
experience of oppression rather than of difference should underline the
anti-sexist approach of the practice teacher. This distinction has not always
been made in the literature. Hawkins and Shohet write of the importance of
recognising worker and client background.

> This is especially relevant when there is a match between the age of the
> worker and the supervisor, but the client has a different age, gender and
> background, e.g. if the client is an old, working class, West Indian man,
> and the worker and the supervisor are both young, middle-class, white
> women. In such cases the supervisor has to work doubly hard to help the
> supervisee explore how her own background and attitudes are affecting
> how she sees and works with the client. (1989, p.48)

While this paragraph usefully advises supervisors to approach working with
difference in a sensitive manner it does little to address the possibility of
racism which may be present in the supervisee's knowledge base nor any
Eurocentric or 'colour blind' policies under which the organisation involved
operates, nor indeed the prejudice and abuse the client will have experienced.
It also seems to assume that difference is 'value free', that is, the supervisee is
encouraged to identify that the client is different but not to consider that
there may be a multi-dimensional set of power relationships 'present' in their
contact. This leaves the worker in danger of being part of the problem, not
part of the solution.

Phillipson (1992) describes the word 'gender' as 'an inadequate substitute' (p.56) as it fails to address structural inequality. The male practice
teacher will need to consider that the female student is not just of a different
gender but will almost certainly arrive at the placement having been subject
to gender oppression. The practice teacher will need to ensure that he does
not represent a further 'chapter' in the student's experience of sexism.

Male practice teachers and female students – an opportunity for learning?

Writers such as Chamberlayne, Dominelli and McLeod have clearly felt that women have a particular opportunity for supportive relationships through contact with other women which is not present in their interaction with men. Humphries (1988) quotes Mezirow (1983) in her assertion that in order to facilitate learning there needs to be created an 'ethos of support, encouragement, non-judgmental acceptance, mutual help and individual responsibility' (p.15).

Do we conclude from this that male practice teachers are therefore less likely to provide a safe learning environment for female students than their female colleagues? Further questions arise if the context in which this relationship takes place is explored. Hanmer and Statham (1988) write about the experiences of women entering social work, emphasising women's different employment patterns and lower pay than men and the under-representation of women in management positions. More recently Taylor and Daly (1995) have described the experience of Canadian women social workers:

> The multi-dimensional factors that define power in our society have had a devastating effect on women in society and women in social work in particular. Problems with professional status and social acceptability plague women in social work in an unique way. (p.1)

Brown and Bourne (1996) describe how sexism may be internalised by women during their earlier development:

> This experience will have included the relationship between her parents, and how she was treated by her father, and more generally what she observed at school, among her friends and in the community in which she lived. (p.33)

Women's experience of entering social work education may be in sharp contrast to many men's, particularly if the woman is black, has a disability or has children. Humphries (1988) quotes Robertson:

> The norms of our higher education system are the norms of the bachelor boy student...course design and planning has been implicitly related to a concept of a 'normal' student who is a cleanlimbed 18 year old white male. (p.7)

Higher education systems, including those which educate social workers, are significantly influenced by Knowles' (1978) work on adult learning. However, Knowles has constructed a model of adult learning which, in many ways, fails to address the experience of adults whose needs have gone unmet during their development. Humphries in her critique of Knowles' theories writes:

> Knowles assumes that all adults have similar opportunities for self direction…[he] also ignores contradictions and particular difficulties faced by, for example, women and black people from working class backgrounds who find a place in the higher education system. (1988, p.7)

I am not able to answer the question which began this chapter – is it 'OK' for male practice teachers to occupy this important role in respect of female students? An experienced child sexual abuse worker, in answer to a question about men's role in that field, said to me that none of us, men nor women, have a right to do such work but those of us who wish to must prove ourselves able through learning and reflection. I believe that this answer could similarly be applied to the issue under discussion. Male social workers do not have the 'right' to fulfil this role. However, many will wish to, particularly following CCETSW's introduction of the Post Qualifying Award in Social Work for which the Accredited Practice Teachers Award provides a convenient route to gaining the credits for 'enabling others'. The male practice teachers who wish to provide an anti-sexist service need to address the shortcomings of their position as described above and develop their own techniques to meet women students' needs.

Dominelli (1988) argues that white people cannot provide positive models for black people on how to survive in a racist society – the same could be said of men providing a model for women in a sexist one. Julia Phillipson (1992) believes that there is a role for men in this:

> Male tutors and supervisors can provide positive models to other men of anti-sexist practice and both women and men can model ways of challenging sexism and of building alternative ways of working. (p.42)

I am also sufficiently optimistic to be able to recognise that my male colleagues are working hard to address gender oppression in the workplace. This is not to be complacent, nor to fail to acknowledge how male-dominated and constructed management 'set-ups' act to seduce male workers into uncritically accepting them. In the fight against oppression would it not be unwise, or indeed dangerous, to exclude men?

Therefore the question is – what do male practice teachers need to do before agreeing to have a female student, meeting with them and beginning the learning agreement? I believe that the first task is to consider what Taylor and Daly refer to as 'the wisdom of women'. Women's work on patriarchy and sexual abuse has formed the biggest single contribution to child protection thinking in recent years. This debate is now being developed by black women who, while accepting their white sisters' analysis of the family as a place of oppression for women and children, emphasise that black families offer black people a life-saving haven from racism. This work has come from a wish for equality and safety for women and children and has a great deal to offer men. A radically enhanced focus on the 'wisdom of women' does not mean that men's views no longer count; however, there is a need for the value base of social work and child protection to be assiduously reviewed in the light of analysis of the impact of oppression.

The second task is for the male practice teacher to view his masculinity positively in his role as practice teacher. Having identified the insidious nature of sexism and committed himself to anti-sexist practice I believe that it is important to see the limits of his responsibility for sexism. This does not 'let him off the hook' in terms of his own behaviour at work, at home and/or in the community in which he lives. Neither should he become unwary of the 'benefits' to him of sexism. However, this does mean that on a day-to-day basis he can reject the accusations of sexism that belong elsewhere. He is only directly responsible for his own sexism. Although issues of gender oppression underlie all relationships between men and women, if a man and a woman have difficulty or disagree it is not necessarily because of sexism. It is crucial for male practice teachers to bear this in mind when negotiating difficulties in placements, including the possibility of failing a student. Practice teachers need to be clear about the basis upon which they hold power and authority in the relationship with the student. Male practice teachers need to critically reflect on this and ensure that their power is 'legitimate'. On the other hand it is important that the male practice teacher should not become so insecure in his gender identity that he may not be able to accept the legitimate authority due to him in his role.

The following suggestions are made assuming that the practice teacher has undertaken some preparation work of his own. To what extent has he addressed the traditional dictates of his masculinity? Indeed, why is he entering practice teaching? Is he interested in meeting the needs of students placed at his agency or is career advancement the principal motivation? The latter is an understandable aim, but one which, when viewed in isolation, tends to reflect stereotypical masculinity. Most critically he must be prepared to value survival in a sexist society when the traditional dictates of his masculinity require him to value only complete success.

Conclusions

1. Be explicit about values in the learning agreement

This has been mentioned on several occasions in this chapter but will not suffer from repetition. The values that social workers are required to hold are expressed in several documents already mentioned. The practice teacher will need to acknowledge his gender's responsibility for gender oppression and commit himself to an anti-sexist approach to practice. All eleven research respondents agreed that they wanted anti-sexist values expressed in learning contracts, seven said that they had been, but only five reported that this had been raised in a useful way. One reported that it had been 'agreed at beginning that it was OK to confront issues if one of us had disagreed – very useful to have this stated and encouraged'. Another wrote of the benefits of engaging in this process at the start of the placement: '...issues were on the table at the beginning so the personal feelings element can be unravelled from working issues (if possible)'.

2. Be action oriented

The purpose of being clear about values is to be enabled to act on them. As already stated, there is little worth in values without action. In addition it should be considered that one's actions may have as much or more benefit than one's thoughts. This is not to excuse a 'half-hearted approach' to anti-sexism but more a position which states that men should 'get on with it', address gender oppression and take some risks, not hide behind theoretical constructs and guilt. One respondent to my research described how the practice teacher's value statements had been supported in more practical ways: 'Issues of gender were discussed informally and two exercises undertaken from *Teaching Social Work Practice* (Mark Doel)'.

Additionally practice teachers need to be consistent in the behaviour that they agree to in the learning agreement in order effectively to model anti-sexist behaviour. I recall an economics lecturer telling me that what is 'mumbled into the blackboard is sometimes listened to more clearly than what is shouted from the lectern'!

3. Self-Awareness

Central to the ideas underpinning anti-oppressive practice are notions that workers should 'check out' their feelings about particular individuals/families/groups in order to try and address any blocks to learning and good practice. This is as true for practice teachers and I believe that it is important for male practice teachers to do the 'checking out' in relation to their sexuality. It is particularly crucial that male practice teachers conduct themselves with integrity in their work with female students and avoid all ambiguous comments and situations. They must ask themselves if there is any inappropriate sexual 'pay-off' in the manner in which they are working and take responsibility for this, ensuring that the practice teaching relationship is not distorted and that planned learning is not disrupted. I address these comments principally to heterosexual male practice teachers but believe that the interplay of gender and sexuality is a complex one and that a self-censorious approach is the safest, regardless of the practice teacher's sexual orientation.

4. Clarity about authority

There is a certain amount of 'legitimate' authority vested in the practice teaching role which arises from the tasks of teaching and assessing social workers in training. This should be distinguished from the oppressive forces arising from structural power differentials. Sawdon and Sawdon (1988) write:

> The effective supervisor does not deny his/her power and authority but uses it to ensure that, with the supervisee, s/he is clear about what is required and how they are meeting those requirements together. The effective supervisor does not lean over backwards, nor abrogate power and authority. (p.15)

The struggle to identify what is legitimate and what is not is a necessary process for the male practice teacher.

5. Address the shortcomings in the arrangement

It is useful to ask students what would have been their ideal practice teacher, therefore allowing for opportunities to be provided that will meet this need. Most obviously this might include the opportunity for women students to have access to a woman staff member with whom to discuss any difficulties or personal issues which are raised in the process of the work. One respondent reported, 'My practice teacher's line manager was female and she was identified as someone I could use should I want to talk to another woman. All parties agreed that this could happen.' However, it needs to be acknowledged that a student may not be able to let her practice teacher know that she is disappointed in the gender of her practice teacher or that it is an issue at all. One respondent in my research felt that she had been able to discuss this with her (male) Practice Learning Co-ordinator but worried 'that a less confident female might have problems addressing issues/feelings with a male practice teacher'. This level of trust and understanding may only develop as the placement develops and as the practice teacher models a mature and accepting approach to such matters. It would be useful to programme a review process into the learning agreement, enabling these issues to be raised alongside the developing relationship.

6. Organisational supports

In addition to (5) the practice teacher needs to recognise that certain services need to be offered in their organisation which should not be reliant on students asking or demanding them. The experience of students who are women, black, gay and/or have a disability is widely recognised and therefore organisations need to establish opportunities to allow these students' needs to be met. This may include support groups although I am nervous about organisations feeling that they have fulfilled their responsibilities by starting such groups without looking at what is needed back at the workplace. For example, is it enough to have a black students' support group if the establishment's policy is riddled with racist assumptions and there are no black workers at a senior management level? If such services are available the learning agreement should include reference to them and also address the implications their take-up will have on the student workload, or the costs involved either to the student or the agency, so that students are not disadvantaged by attending or effectively prevented from doing so.

7. Organisational policy

Most social work organisations have policies countering discrimination including a policy on sexual harassment and a complaints policy. The existence of such and how they are put into action must be made clear in the learning agreement. These documents serve as a useful adjunct to the values expressed by the practice teacher. In the early days of a female student's placement I was struggling with what I would include in the learning agreement about sexual harassment. In my eagerness to let her know where I stood on the matter I told her that I would not sexually harass her! On reflection this must have been quite unnerving for her and it would have been better to have clearly stated that I knew of this policy and that she would have access to it should she need it.

8. Supervision venue

It is important that the practice teacher and student meet for supervision at a venue which is suitable for this purpose. The practice teacher needs to arrange this in a way which maintains clear boundaries relating to physical safety and sexuality. One female student wrote in her reply that the location of supervision sessions became an issue during her placement: 'for example I had supervision in a flat alone with male practice teacher – could have/ *did* become an issue'.

9. Consider the 'whole' student

Thus far I have primarily thought about the gender of the student. However, it is important that other issues should be addressed in the learning agreement. This was referred to by one woman student as a 'holistic approach'. It is clear that a woman student's race and (dis)ability should be raised, but what of class? One respondent wrote 'I think this [class] is an important issue but often overlooked'. It may be useful to acknowledge that the relationship between classes has served to disadvantage working-class people and their communities and such disadvantage should not be replicated in the student/practice teacher relationship. The learning agreement may also address matters which may have arisen as a result of under-resourced educational experiences, for example difficulties in formal language and writing skills. Age was raised as an important issue in one reply to my questionnaire: 'Current practice teacher is 20 years younger than I am, this, likewise, discussed in supervision but not formalised in any context.' Other matters may become clearer as the placement progresses. One student for whom I have been practice teacher was a lone parent who had been experiencing difficulties with her children's 'absent' father. The student knew that I, too, was a father who did not live with his children. It was important to be clear that should such issues be raised in supervision it was my role to be attentive to her needs rather then identifying with her ex-partner. Responsibilities of caring, particularly when a child is sick, should be addressed in the learning agreement. This must, of course, also be the case where a student is a male parent if the current assumption that child care difficulties are the sole prerogative of female parents is to be challenged. Reference will need to be made to the college and agencies' expectations but every opportunity to be flexible will do much to support and reassure students who are also parents.

My literature search, observations and research project have convinced me that male practice teachers do have a role to play in female students' social work education. My research respondents indicated that many male practice teachers are grappling with the issue of gender oppression and how that can be addressed and challenged within the practice teaching relationship. A larger sample would have provided a greater range of valuable contributions from a wider base. It would have been useful if the respondents' age and race had been recorded. I would also have been interested to find out when those who replied had qualified/were hoping to qualify, as a number of colleagues questioned if practice teachers' practice had indeed changed over the years. There would have undoubtedly been great value in such research being undertaken by a woman researcher using face-to-face interviews. The subject deserves further exploration but I hope I have made a useful contribution to the continuing debate about the role of gender and gender oppression in social work education.

References

Bristish Association of Social Work (1986) 'Code of Ethics for Social Work.' BASW.

Brown, A. and Bourne, I. (1996) *The Social Work Supervisor: Supervision in Community, Day Care and Residential Settings.* Buckingham: Open University Press.

CCETSW (1989) *Requirements and Regulations for the Diploma in Social Work.* London: CCETSW.

CCETSW (1996) *Assuring Quality in the Diploma in Social Work-1. Rules and Requirements for the DipSW.* London: CCETSW.

CCETSW (1996) *Assuring Quality for Practice Teaching. Rules and Requirements for the Practice Teacher Award.* London: CCETSW.

Chamberlayne, S. (1990) 'How do women social workers feel about working with men as colleagues and men as clients?' Unpublished Thesis, University of Sussex.

Doel, M., Shardlow, S., Sawdon, C. and Sawdon, D. (1996) *Teaching Social Work Practice.* Aldershot: Arena.

Dominelli, L. (1988) *Anti-Racist Social Work.* Basingstoke: Macmillan Education Ltd.

Dominelli, L. and McLeod, E. (1989) *Feminist Social Work.* Basingstoke: Macmillan Education Ltd.

Hacket, S. (1997) 'Men protecting children? A study of male social workers' experiences of working with child sexual abuse.' Unpublished Thesis, University of Manchester.

Hanmer, J. and Statham, D. (1988) *Women and Social Work.* Basingstoke: Macmillan Education Ltd.

Hawkins, P. and Shohet, R. (1989) *Supervision in the Helping Professions.* Milton Keynes: Open University Press.

Humphries, B. (1988) 'Adult learning in social work education: toward liberation or domestication?' *Critical Social Policy 8,* 2, 4–21.

Knowles, M. (1978) *The Adult Learner: A Neglected Species.* New Jersey: Englewood, Prentice Hall.

Phillipson, J. (1992) *Practicing Equality: Women, Men and Social Work.* London: CCETSW.

Preston-Shoot, M. (1989) 'A contractual approach to practice teaching.' *Social Work Education 8,* 3, 3–15.

Sawdon, C. and Sawdon, D. (1988) 'The supervision partnership: a whole greater than the sum of its parts.' In J. Pritchard (ed) *Good Practice in Supervision.* London: Jessica Kingsley Publishers Ltd.

Taylor, P. and Daly, C. (eds) (1995) *Gender Dilemmas In Social Work: Issues Affecting Women in the Profession.* Toronto: Canadian Scholars Press Inc.

Thompson, N. (1993) *Anti-Oppressive Practice.* Basingstoke: Macmillan.

CHAPTER 6

Practice Teaching
A Solutions-Focused Approach

Fiona Mainstone

The first section of this chapter locates the solutions-focused approach in the wider traditions of social work, supervision and practice teaching and explores its contribution to anti-oppressive practice. The second section gives a brief account of the epistemological origins of solutions-focused therapy. In the third section I outline the principles which underpin the work of therapists in this model and examine how these principles might translate into practice teaching. In the final section I identify the key interventions employed in a solutions-focused interview and the nuances of their application in the relationship between social work student and practice teacher. I am indebted to Evan George, Chris Iveson and Harvey Ratner of the Brief Therapy Practice, who provided me with some notes prepared for their workshop on supervision and consultation. Their notes provided the inspiration and starting point for this chapter.

Practice teaching with a twist

Social work is a broad church. In most placements the practice teacher has the complex task of conveying a few key methods whilst facilitating the student's own grasp of a systematic eclecticism. The ideas and skills of the solutions-focused worker occupy somewhat scattered positions on the therapeutic continuum. I follow O'Hanlon in thinking of this as practice teaching 'with a twist' (O'Hanlon 1993).

At its most simple, the model is cognitive. The emphasis on specific behavioural goals creates a familiar territory for psychologists and educationalists. Practice teachers in social work could do well to shed their professional preoccupation with problem and pathology and adopt the teacher's focus on what the student might become. CCETSW's setting out of competencies and the growing expectation that practice teachers will evaluate student's practice against objective measures of achievement fits comfortably with this model's insistence on specified behavioural changes rather than insight as the indicator of progress.

Increasing prominence has been given in the field of practice teaching to contractual approaches. The range of solutions-focused techniques designed to elicit behaviourally stated objectives and to promote shared expectations of change are particularly helpful in the design of contracts which are specific to the student's needs and relevant to the nascent practice teaching relationship.

The social work profession has yet to provide a firm anchor for supervision. The dominant theme of government guidance has been that professional, old-fashioned casework supervision is essential. For example, the Cleveland Report said it is 'the skill and experience of social workers rather than a high level of commitment to child protection procedures which are in the best interests of the children' (p.85). Despite this advice, social workers in some settings receive no supervision and managerial supervision of form which merely checks that workers are fulfilling minimum tasks has prevailed over reflective and challenging supervision of content in most agencies.

The regular individual supervision meeting between practice teacher and student has remained a core ingredient of practice placements and serves the purposes of accountability, teaching and assessment. Having identified the qualities of the ideal supervisor as identical to those of the ideal therapist, albeit differently employed, Hawkins and Shohet (1989) provide a model for each practice teacher to develop a supervisory style determined by the developmental needs of the student and the necessary balance between the educative, supportive and managerial functions of supervision. They present the aspiring practice teacher with choices and issues to be considered in the process of establishing a personal style of supervising. The style chosen needs to fit the placement, the student and the personality of the practice teacher. These arguments legitimate my pursuit of a supervision style congruent with my politics and my pathological optimism! I am also reassured by Hawkins and Shohet's conclusion that good supervision is not so much objective truth as an act of faith hinging on relationship.

The solutions focus provides an especially helpful bridge between the supervision of form and of content. This model encourages conversations

which are collaborative and yet open the possibility of profoundly challenging and personal work. Psychoanalytical models of casework supervision are
potentially debilitating in the practice teaching relationship. The relationship between practice teacher and student is much shorter lived than the
conventional therapeutic relationship. The practice teacher's responsibility to
assess does not enable unconditional regard. The student feels and is inevitably vulnerable. Confidentiality cannot be guaranteed. The provision of safety
and respect is especially pertinent in the context of practice teaching where
the student has to be helped to relinquish the security of the known and take
the risk of failure.

I will refer in this text to some ways in which a solutions focus might
inform the practice teacher's contribution to fighting oppression. Thompson
(Thompston 1990, p.35) stresses that 'The development of antidiscrimina-
tory practice hinges on having the courage to tackle the complex and highly
sensitive value issues involved. A pragmatic...approach would miss this
dimension of social work education altogether'. His idea that learning takes
place primarily within the student's own personal life world echoes Erickson's (1954) concept of utilisation (Thompson 1990, p.38). Thompson
suggests that the perspective transformation required in anti-oppressive
social work education depends on working with the student's *weltanschauung*.
A solutions focus makes its contribution to this endeavour at several levels.

An approach which celebrates the achievements of the disempowered,
and takes account of adverse circumstances which have acted as constraints is
of especial value in working with a member of an oppressed group whether
student or client. This model allows for the need to clarify those aspects of
the problem which are within and outwith the control of the student or
client, and explore whether they have done all that they would like to do to
try to influence those in authority.

The practice of the Just Therapy group, which has structured its service to
enable all work with female clients to be accountable to the women in the
team and all work with any member of a minority ethnic group to be
accountable to a member of the same ethnic group, serves as a useful pointer
for the design of an anti-oppressive learning culture. In the practice teaching
context this might mean generating peer study groups, or ensuring that any
black student with a white practice teacher would have the oversight of a
black mentor.

Another dimension of the anti-oppressive thrust of this model is the way
in which the emphasis on strengths and resources has the potential to

depathologise experiences which are routinely given negative connotations. Solutions-focused conversations open up the possibility of re-authoring alternative versions of stories, drawing attention to strengths, resources, coping, survival and achievement in the face of adversity and injustice.

There is always an imbalance of power between client and worker and between student and practice teacher. Solutions-focused work, like other co-constructive approaches, minimises this power differential and makes it overt. There is a conscious debunking of professional mystique. The value placed on sapiential power over positional power helps undo the imbalance. The client or student is the expert on their own aspirations and has responsibility for choosing the action required to fulfil their wishes.

This move away from the traditional expert–novice model towards a more participative style of learning nurtures anti-oppressive practice teaching. It is also in tune with the principles of adult education identified by Freire as *critical consciousness* (Freire 1972) and by Rogers as *self-appropriated learning* (Rogers 1961).

Sources and inspirations

Solutions-focused therapy is oriented to searching for solutions and strengths in favour of examining problems and deficits. Although this work may be abhorred by some proponents of long-term psychotherapy, solutions-focused work has achieved a degree of respectability and credence. This method has found popularity in some areas of social services and health service provision because of the imperative to work with the largest possible numbers as quickly as possible because of spending constraints. I do not endorse the exclusive use of solutions-focused therapy to cut costs where other forms of help may be indicated. However, I do propose that these ideas are especially potent tools in encouraging purposeful and enduring change both in therapy and in adult learning.

The thinking which informs the current practice of solutions-focused therapy in Britain today is drawn from several diverse sources.

The published history of brief therapy can be traced from Milton Erickson's 1954 paper 'Special techniques of brief hypnotherapy'. In this paper he detailed, through seven case examples, an approach that focuses on 'intentionally utilizing neurotic symptomatology to meet the unique needs of the patient'. Haley, whose own work straddles the structural and strategic schools of family therapy, published an influential review of Erickson's work in 1973 which served to bring it to a wider readership.

In the late 1960s and early 1970s, a number of developments in working briefly occurred in the context of family therapy. Practitioners in the American strategic schools and in the Milan systemic school in Italy (Selvini-Palazzoli *et al.* 1974) developed an interest in dealing with problems, how they are maintained and how to solve them. Steve de Shazer began to use his model of Brief Therapy in Milwaukee, while the Brief Therapy Centre was established at the Mental Research Institute in Palo Alto, California.

The fundamental idea of a therapy which talks about solutions not problems has subsequently been developed by its protagonists across continents. America has generated an influential body of work from a cluster of therapeutic and teaching organisations all located in the mid-west. De Shazer's works to a deceptively simple formula which restricts the therapeutic intervention to examining exceptions to the problem, identifying goals and the concrete changes which achieve them. O'Hanlon emphasises respect and collaboration (O'Hanlon 1993). Dolan (1991) insistently unravels the unwanted symptoms of trauma victims by valuing survival stories and highlighting the sources of resilience. These American therapists share an optimistic approach and are highly accessible. In the Antipodes, the Dulwich Centre has published a range of material with a more political thrust. Jenkins adduces the 'grain of honour' (Jenkins 1990) to effect change in men who perpetrate physical and sexual violence. Tamasese and Waldegrave propose 'Just Therapy', to mean a therapy which is both fair and simple. Working from a black perspective this utilises the strengths and resources intrinsic to Aboriginal beliefs and ways of living to explicitly defy therapeutic traditions which support the white Anglo-Saxon hegemony in New Zealand. Within Europe, the Brief Therapy Practice in London has adopted a pragmatic and eclectic stance to both teaching and therapeutic practice.

Nowhere in this diverse and innovative literature is there any thorough exploration of how ideas about treatment for individuals and families might be applied to other levels of the helping system such as training, consultation, supervision, management and policy making. It is that exploration of application to the practice teacher relationship I now wish to consider.

First principles

As with all therapeutic practice, solutions-focused interventions rest on a set of values determined by both theory and ideology. My understanding is that these resolve into fundamental ideas which in turn hold the following four principles for supervision.

Respect

This style of work is non-normative in the sense that it is not based on any theory of human behaviour. In therapeutic practice this principle precludes both advice and interpretation.

Erickson's work contributes the concept of 'utilisation' (Erickson 1954). In the therapeutic context this principle means using whatever the client brings and lends itself to echoing the words and phrases used by the client, developing metaphors which resonate with the client's interests.

The focus on strengths and resources is not intended to minimise the client's distress or the severity of the problem they bring. These have to be given sufficient attention to ensure that the significance of the problem is understood and respected. The search for strengths and resources is a source of client empowerment whereas the more usual emphasis on problems maintains a clear contrast between the pathology of the client and the competence of the therapist.

In the context of practice teaching these three principles of being non-normative, utilisation, and respect for strengths translate into a commitment to respecting the individuality of the student. The intention behind applying these principles to practice teaching would be to maximise the possibility of the student reworking their personality, experience, skills and interests in such a way that they integrate these with the skills and professional identity required for qualification as a social worker.

The Brief Therapy Practice advise that

> it is better to develop the idiosyncratic ways in which the consultee will achieve their goals than for them to become a clone of the supervisor. In this way supervision and consultation can become contexts from which the consultee can take power. (Evans *et al.* unpublished)

Possibility

A second principle in solutions-focused work is that however difficult the problem, the situation will always contain exceptions which are signs of the solution happening.

In both therapy and teaching the search for exceptions may be closely linked to the search for strengths and resources. In directing the student's work and examining casework problems, any exception to the problem, indeed anything that may be instrumental in moving any part of the system towards a goal, is worth exploring in detail. Any exception to the prevailing problem, whether this is related to the client's dilemma or the student's interventions, contains valuable clues as to how best to proceed.

Simplicity

The very word 'solution' contains the principle that the model's orientation is to the future. It implies a vision of what the client can and shall be.

Some practitioners prefer the term Brief Therapy which reflects the principle of minimal intervention. I take this to mean both brevity and specificity as expressed in de Shazer's dictum (de Shazer *et al.* 1986) 'if it ain't broke don't fix it' (a phrase sometimes employed in less benign circles!).

The solutions-focused therapist makes a commitment to simplicity to the extent even of veritable parsimony.

For the purpose of practice teaching the three principles of future orientation, minimalism and simplicity come together to inform conversations which are resolutely goal centred. Whether the subject under discussion is a piece of direct work, case management, the student's personal journey, social work method, or the assessment of competence, it is fundamental to this model that the goals of the work are itemised in concrete, specific, behavioural detail.

Collaboration

Solutions-focused therapy is conceived of as a collaborative enterprise built on a relationship which has the principle of co-operation at its core. O'Hanlon's 'Therapy of Empowerment' (O'Hanlon 1993) adapts ideas from the paper 'Temptations of power and certainty' (Amundson *et al.* 1993) to develop a range of interviewing techniques which undo hierarchy, expertise, and unilateral control. Solutions-focused workers do not ascribe to the psychoanalytic idea of unconscious resistance, or to the systemic notion of homeostasis as a motivating force. Jenkins (1990) has elaborated ways of working with violent and abusive men which invite the client to identify and tackle those aspects of self which act as constraints on change and restrict personal growth.

In the practice teaching context, as in therapy, it should be acknowledged that any two parties in such relationships may choose to co-operate but are never equally powerful. It is therefore essential to name and act out the explicit intention to act collaboratively towards the achievement of named goals and to delineate the implicit and potentially paralysing effects of inevitable difference. This principle will be enshrined in a commitment to the student's personal learning goals. A collaborative approach should at best help enable the student to own their deficits and actively engage in change.

Action and change

Solutions-focused brief therapy emphasises clients' talents, resources, and existing problem-solving abilities. It is goal directed and generally more concerned with the present and future than with the past. These approaches are relevant to practice teaching and translate readily for use with a student on practice placement.

Problem-free talk

Some but not all practitioners make use of de Shazer's ideas about problem-free talk. De Shazer *et al.* (1986) recommend an introductory conversation which amounts to politely asking for everyday information about successful areas of the client's life. Before the placement starts the practice teacher could make respectful enquiries about the student's previous experience of life and work and acknowledge that the student role may not be congruent with the student's responsibilities and skills outwith social work. A section which accredits the student's skills and strengths can be included in the contract and practice learning agreement at the start of the placement.

Goals

In solutions-focused therapy the practitioner frames enquiries about the problem in such a way as to elicit the client's goals. Questions such as

- What do you hope for?
- How will you know when you no longer need this help?

are asked from the outset and are intended to identify goals which are specific and clear. In the context of practice teaching these questions could be helpful as the student begins to engage in the real work of the placement and might translate as

- How will you know that your work with this family has been successful?
- How will you know when your work has achieved your objectives?

In the therapeutic context clients can be characterised as customer, complainant or visitor. It is often helpful to ask circular and reflexive questions which ask the client to reflect on the problem from another person's point of view in order to frame active, properly owned goals which accurately reflect the client's status. In practice teaching it is similarly important to identify the student's goals from the perspective of the various absent participants, such as parent, child, Guardian *ad Litem*, practice teacher and university tutor, so that the student's work is helped to address client, agency and student need.

- What will the court need to see that will tell them this work is progressing in the right direction?
- What do you imagine is the client's miracle picture of life without this problem?

In the practice teaching context as in therapy the goals should be described in terms of behavioural change which can be observed and evaluated.

The 'Miracle Question' is a goal-setting and solution-finding technique which helps the client specify how things will be different once the problem is solved:

> Suppose there is a miracle tonight while you are sleeping and the problem that we have talked about today is solved. Since you are sleeping you do not know that a miracle has happened. What do you suppose you will notice that is different the next morning that will let you know that there has been a miracle overnight?

It could be especially helpful in tackling intractable problems experienced by the student, for example difficulty in internalising aspects of the professional role or trouble over producing process records on time.

Exceptions

In solutions-focused therapy, pre-session change and exceptions to the problem are perceived as important clues to motivate and inform progress. Once the goals of a particular piece of work have been clarified, the focus of discussions with the student would be to elicit and amplify the times when progress, however small, has already been made.

An emphasis on exceptions may be especially helpful when the student needs to transfer existing skills for use in an unfamiliar and perhaps more threatening arena. Exploring exceptions can be used to remobilise the student who finds themselves deskilled by the student role, or to encourage the student who is paralysed by a more general lack of confidence. The practice teacher would draw the student's attention to exceptions with questions such as:

- What has been happening at the times you have been progressing in this work?

- When are the times you have felt most hopeful? What was different about those times?

- When you have been successful in similar pieces of work how did you do it?

- What do you think the client has found most useful about the work?

In the process of having to explain to the practice teacher, it becomes clear to the student that they are already doing things to create exceptions to the problem and that these could be repeated. Having owned up to success it could become easier for the student to own up to some failures too!

Scales

Scaling questions are an especially versatile tool in the solutions-focused worker's repertoire. They provide a means to measure change and progress made towards the specific goals that have been set, and to identify what the next step might be. The therapist designs the scaling question according to the goals already named by the client so that 'ten' describes how they would like the situation to be while 'one' describes the worst it has ever been or could be.

Scales can be used to direct the student's interventions when picking up new work. They can also be used later in the placement to examine the progress of the student's casework with questions such as:

- With 'one' representing you believing that change is not possible in this piece of work and 'ten' representing your absolute confidence that progress can be made, what number best represents your position at the moment?

- What is it that you know about yourself and your client that puts you at 'x' and not at 'one'?

- How would you know that this case had reached one further point along the way?

- Where on the scale would your client say they had reached?

- What number would you/the client/the agency settle for on the scale?
- What number would represent sufficient change for people to feel real progress had been made, and there was no longer any need to worry?

Scaling questions can be especially useful in talking about issues which are painful to address, difficult to put into words and generally considered too abstract to concretise.

- If 'ten' represents you will 'give your all' to this placement, and 'one' means you no longer care what the hell happens to you, where would you put yourself in terms of your commitment to the course?
- If 'one' represented a firm decision never to work again with this client group and 'ten' represented your completion of a job application to this agency, where would you put yourself today in relation to this type of work?

Scaling questions can be used in this way to assess and bring under scrutiny the student's confidence, investment in personal change, willingness to work hard to bring about learning, prioritising of problems to be solved, perception of hopefulness, and evaluation of progress.

Coping questions

Just as some clients face desperate and intractable problems, some students have huge difficulties to overcome if they are to pass their placement and succeed as workers. These difficulties often seem insurmountable midway through the placement. In these circumstances glib reassurance is neither helpful nor just. Coping questions can be used to identify strengths and resources or to turn a hopeless and overwhelming situation into something workable. Questions such as

- What is it about the client, and what is it about you that stops you from giving up?
- How do you cope with this situation?
- If you were handing over this case now what would be your advice to the next worker?

- What have you learned in the course of this piece of work about what you would not want to do again?

are intended to support the student through difficult casework experiences while searching for ways to encourage optimism and access learning.

Coping questions could be useful too in helping the student address personal problems in relation to their development as a social worker:

- What have you learnt about your own work and indeed yourself during this journey?

- What have you learnt about the skills, the strengths and the resources that you are bringing to bear so that things are staying afloat at work despite all your worries about your family's health?

- Since you are the kind of person who takes criticism very seriously it must have been hard for you to keep going when your practice paper failed. How did you manage to get up and come in to work today?

Dolan (1991) provides a whole repertoire of ideas to help the survivors of trauma secure a degree of safety and containment which enables them to take the risk of changing and beginning to heal. For example, the client might identify and bring to therapy an object symbolising safety. Dolan encourages the client to build up an 'emergency tool kit' of items, letters, photos and souvenirs which represent the client's personal resources and capacity to survive. She sometimes sets the client the task of envisioning themselves in the future having successfully overcome their problem and asks this wise person/survivor-to-be to offer up words of advice and encouragement. These techniques could be adapted to facilitate the student's personal survival in instances where the student's potential for change has been immobilised or where placement failure is anticipated.

Solutions focused feedback

Therapeutic sessions routinely end with the therapist giving the client compliments to end on an upbeat note, leave a feeling of accomplishment and guide future development. The practice teacher would aim to end each discussion with a summary of the relevant qualities, resources and skills applied by the student and compliment them on any changes, however small, that have been achieved in the work.

I've been really impressed by your commitment to this case. You've persevered in trying to find a way of meeting with MsD. Her note to you shows me that this has paid off as it gives you an indication that she is now willing to 'talk about talks' with you when you meet her here.

Students often complain that they do not know or understand what is expected. Compliments give the student information throughout the placement about how their work is perceived by the practice teacher. Practice aspirations are endorsed and mistakes can be left behind.

The feedback should not be a general eulogy. It should identify that which has been useful in moving towards the student's goals.

In this chapter I have proposed that ideas and methods drawn from solutions-focused brief therapy are potent tools for the practice teacher. I have transcribed solutions-focused principles to the practice teaching context and demonstrated that this approach is useful both for analysing casework material and for addressing personal and developmental issues in the practice placement. I have explored the potential value to anti-oppressive practice teaching of a conscientious focus on strengths, achievement and receiver expertise.

References

Amundson, J., Stewart, K. and Valentine, L. (1993) 'Temptations of power and certainty.' *Journal of Marital and Family Therapy 19*, 2, 111–123.

Cleveland Inquiry, The (1988) *Report of the Inquiry into Child Abuse in Cleveland 1987.* London: HMSO.

Dolan, Y. (1991) *Resolving Sexual Abuse.* London: W.W.Norton.

Erickson, M.H. (1954) 'Special techniques of brief hypnotherapy.' *Journal of Clinical and Experimental Hypnosis 2*, 109–129.

Evans *et al.* Unpublished course material. London: Brief Therapy Centre.

Freire, P. (1972) *Pedagogy of the Oppressed.* Harmondsworth: Penguin.

Haley, J. (1973) *Uncommon Therapy.* London: W.W.Norton.

Hawkins, P. and Shohet, R. (1989) *Supervision in the Helping Professions: An Individual, Group and Organisational Approach.* Milton Keynes: Open University Press.

Jenkins, A. (1990) *Invitations to Responsibility.* N.Z.: Dulwich Centre.

O'Hanlon, W. (1993) Conference Notes. Unpublished, November.

Rogers, C. (1961) *On Becoming a Person.* Boston: Houghton Mifflin.

Selvini-Palazzoli *et al.* (1974) 'The treatment of children through brief therapy of their parents.' *Family Process 13.*

de Shazer *et al.* (1986) 'Brief therapy: focused solution developments.' *Family Process 25*, 207–222.

Thompson, N. 'More than a supervisor – the developing role of the practice teacher.' *Journal of Training and Development 1*, 2, July 1990.

Watzlawick *et al.* (1974) *Change: Principles of Problem Formation and Problem Resolution.* London: W.W.Norton.

Further reading

George, E., Iveson, C. and Ratner, H. *Supervision and Consultation: A Solution Focused Approach.* Unpublished workshop notes from Brief Therapy Practice, London.

Lethem, J. (1994) *Moved to Tears, Moved to Action.* Brief Therapy Press.

Lishman, J. (ed) (1991) *Handbook of Theory for Practice Teachers in Social Work.* London: Jessica Kingsley Publishers.

Waldegrave, C. (1986) 'Mono-cultural, mono-class, and so called non-political family therapy.' *Australia and New Zealand Journal of Family Therapy 6,* 4, 197–200.

Yelloly, M. and Henkel, M. (eds) (1995) *Learning and Teaching in Social Work.* London: Jessica Kingsley Publishers.

CHAPTER 7

The Practice Teacher and Student Dyad

Using Concepts from Transactional Analysis to Enable Effective Learning and Teaching

Di Metson

The International Transactional Analysis Association describes Transactional Analysis as 'a theory of personality and a systematic psychotherapy for personal growth and personal change' (*Transactional Analysis Journal. Official Journal of the International Transactional Analysis Association*).

Eric Berne (1910–1970), the founder of Transactional Analysis, was a psychiatrist who trained in psychoanalysis and who, during the war years, worked for the army in the USA. Whilst working on discharge assessments of soldiers, which needed to be undertaken speedily, Berne concentrated on the use of intuition as a basis for assessment and from this began to develop the concepts of Transactional Analysis. During this period, Berne found that he disagreed both with the established practice of discussing a patient's case in his or her absence and with what he felt to be the use of incomprehensible language. Berne created a language that could be taught to the patient, which could then be used as a tool to discuss with the patient his or her experiences and problems and which would facilitate the choices the patient could make.

The theory of Transactional Analysis offers an analysis of feelings, thoughts and behaviours and a method of communication to provide a forum for personal development. Transactional Analysis as a theory of communication has been developed to be used in other areas as well as the psychiatric setting. It is now seen as a valid tool to be used in organisational, educational and social settings (Barker 1980).

Kathy Ford and Alan Jones describe the function of the practice teacher[1] and student relationship as 'to help the student become aware of the nature of the job to be learned and to acquire the knowledge and skills involved in responding to people's needs in a helpful way' (Ford and Jones 1987). I want to use some of the concepts of Transactional Analysis, particularly the one of Games, to further an understanding of this relationship in order that each partner may develop their role, achieve their required aims and enjoy their experience. I will discuss the complexity of Game Analysis and then look at other ideas drawn from Transactional Analysis which ensure that the needs of each partner are addressed.

Some of the basic concepts in Transactional Analysis

The ego state model: Berne described three separate sets of ego states within the individual. These can be identified via the individual's feelings, thoughts and behaviours. So:

> I am in my Parent ego state when I think and behave in a way similar to my original carers or others whom I have introjected..

> I am in my Adult ego state when I am collecting and processing all available data as a basis for future action.

> I am in my Child ego state when I feel, think and behave in a way that I did in my childhood. (Berne 1961, p.75)

A **transaction** is a basic unit of social interaction between two or more people. The transaction involves a 'stimulus' from one person and a 'response' from the other. The stimulus can come from any of the individual's ego states and is addressed to any of the other person's three ego states. The stimulus can be at a conscious level (the social or overt level) or at an unconscious level (the psychological or non-verbal level) which is known as the 'ulterior' level. Likewise, the response from the other person will come from either the ego state the stimulus was directed at or from another ego state and again this can be at a conscious or at an unconscious level.

To illustrate this, here are some examples from the practice teacher and student relationship (Berne 1966, p.225).

---

[1]   I have referred to the practice teacher as 'she' and the student as 'he' throughout this chapter.

Example 1

The practice teacher welcomes the new student to the team by saying in a straightforward manner 'Welcome to the team' (labelled S). This is a stimulus from the practice teacher's Adult ego state to the student's Adult ego state. The student replies with a straightforward 'Thank you' (labelled R). This is an overt, parallel Adult-to-Adult transaction drawn as follows:

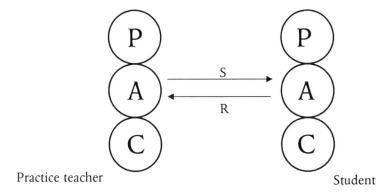

Practice teacher   Student

Figure 7.1

Example 2

The practice teacher continues by referring to the student assessment procedure. The practice teacher feels she wants to reassure the new student about the need for assessment so, speaking from her Parent ego state, says 'I expect you'll find the process of assessment quite daunting but, don't worry, I'm here to help you with it'. This is addressed to the student's Child ego state. It is the feelings behind the statement and the words which are used which indicate that the practice teacher is speaking from the Parent ego state. The student realises by the tone of voice and the verbal indicators that his Child ego state is being addressed. The student does not want to be intimidated by the assessment procedure nor does he want to be in a 'childlike' position with the practice teacher so replies from his Adult ego state saying 'Thank you. I have the assessment schedule and I would like to use it in supervision'.

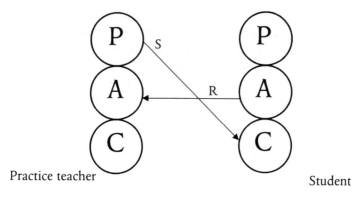

Practice teacher   Student

Figure 7.2

These are conscious social level transactions whereby the practice teacher appears to want to parent the student but the student, whilst acknowledging the practice teacher's concern, does not want to be made into a victim of the situation. The individual's feelings, thoughts and actions indicate the ego state from which the individual is speaking.

Example 3

This time, using the same example, the practice teacher wants to reassure the student and believes she is speaking from her Adult ego state to the student's Adult ego state. She says: 'The process of assessment is a difficult one and my role is to help you through it' (Ss on the diagram). However, on an unconscious psychological level (Sp) she speaks in a condescending tone with the implication that the student may not be able to cope and on the non-verbal or ulterior level she is addressing the student's Child ego state.

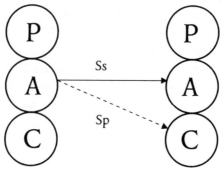

Practice teacher   Student

Figure 7.3

Example 4

Further on in the placement, the student has done his first process recording of an interview with a client. He says to his practice teacher, apparently on an Adult-to-Adult basis: 'I've found it difficult to evaluate my process recording' (Ss).

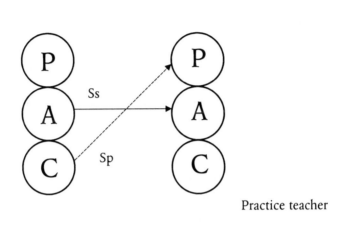

Student   Practice teacher

Figure 7.4

But he says this in a breathless, anxious manner which may indicate that his transaction is coming, on an unconscious level, from his Child ego state and is addressed to the practice teacher's Parent ego state (Sp).

Example 5

In reply to this the practice teacher might make a conscious decision to acknowledge the student's anxiety. She says 'I can see you have found this difficult; would you like to tell me more?' and her voice and manner are congruent with her desire to acknowledge the student's anxiety and there is no unconscious or psychological message.

A **complementary transaction** describes when the person's response comes from the ego state the original transaction was addressed to. Example 1 shows this.

A **crossed transaction** is one when the ego state addressed is not the one that responds, as in Example 2.

A **stroke** is a form of recognition of the person's existence. It can be verbal or non-verbal, positive or negative, conditional (based on what the person has done) or unconditional (based on what the person is). Any sort of stroke, Berne believed, is better than none, but for optimal learning in the practice teacher/student relationship I would argue that positive, conditional strokes are the most useful.

Games were defined by Eric Berne as 'an ongoing series of complementary ulterior transactions progressing to a well defined predictable outcome' (Berne 1964, p.44).

There are, according to Berne, a number of characteristics which define a psychological game:

- A Game occurs *between two or more people*, for example the practice teacher and the student. It can also occur with more people, for example the tutor on the social work course or the manager of the team.

- A Game requires an exchange at the *unconscious, psychological level* as well on the social level. In Example 2, the practice teacher might see herself as the student's 'knight in shining armour', leading the student through to a pass at the end of the placement without consciously checking with the student what learning and support the student thinks he needs.

- *Both participants* in the exchange are actively involved in Games. These may not be the same Games but may be linked in some way. The practice teacher in Example 2, with the expertise and knowledge she has, appears to want to organise or to rescue the student. The student may be an apparently confident, outgoing person but with little experience of social work who is feeling quite anxious about the placement and is loath to admit to these feelings. The student has found someone who will be willing to tell him what should be done and unconsciously the student is hooked into a Game.

- The people in the Game *do not realise* they are in a game until the closing stages unfold. So, to continue with Example 2, if the student had not replied from his Adult ego state thereby stopping the game it might have continued with the practice teacher happy to give lots of advice which the student might have followed for a while.

- Towards the end of the Game it appears *the roles of the participants have changed* and then one party may often be left feeling put down in some way. To expand Example 2 and the Game that could have started, as the placement continues the student may begin to feel that his voice is not being adequately heard, that there may be things that he requires from the practice teaching session which are not being provided. The student may begin to feel hard done by. The practice teacher meanwhile is concerned that, whilst the placement is already halfway through, the student does not seem to be taking much initiative. The practice teacher may begin to worry that perhaps she is not such an effective and helpful practice teacher after all. The student, from being a possible victim in the situation, may come unconsciously to persecute the practice teacher for not giving him what he wanted and the practice teacher moves from a position of rescuing the student to one of being a victim in the situation.

- A Game is *repetitive*, that is, the same person will play the same Game or Games and there will be a sense of *deja vu*. For the practice teacher and the student this will be a familiar situation for them even though neither consciously wanted to find themselves here and, unless they become aware of what is happening, similar scenes will be enacted in the future.

- A Game is *predictable*, going through a series of stages to the conclusion which will confirm each individual's world view. In the example, the practice teacher may be left believing that, no matter how hard she tries, she will never make a successful practice teacher. The student has confirmed his world view that his feelings or views are never taken into account. Also at this stage, there may be a moment's silence, a feeling of 'here we go again', a feeling of surprise or of confusion, all of which indicate that the person has been hooked into a Game. At this point the Game surfaces into awareness.

The **Drama Triangle** was devised by Stephen Karpman (1968) and is used as a method to analyse Games. The positions on the Triangle are known as Persecutor, Rescuer and Victim and these are the roles that are to be found in Games. As a Game unfolds, the individual starts in one position and moves around the Triangle until the end of the Game produces the final position. The origins of each position are to be found in childhood but the significance of them in adulthood and in the practice teacher/student relationship is how they affect current teaching and learning. This will be further developed later on.

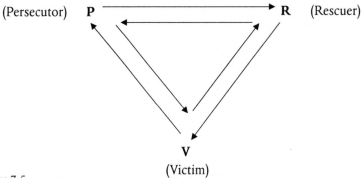

Figure 7.5

A Persecutor is someone who sees other people as inferior. A Rescuer believes that he/she is OK as long as he/she is helping others. A Rescuer sees him/herself as superior and the other person as inferior. A Victim sees him/herself as helpless and may seek a Persecutor to confirm this or a Rescuer to offer help.

Why engage in Games?

We have seen how both parties in the practice teacher/student relationship will engage in Games on an unconscious level and that the outcome is often undesirable in so far as at least one partner is left feeling put down or uncomfortable in some way. Games would not appear to facilitate helpful autonomous learning and teaching but there are reasons why individuals engage in Games.

Game structure is one of the ways in which Transactional Analysts describe people as organising their time. There are five other ways in which time is said to be organised and stimulation or strokes are to be found in each structure, although the level and predictability of the strokes change with each time structure. The Game structure provides an abundant source of strokes both negative and positive for the people involved (Berne 1966, p.229). (For more information on time organisation see the Further Reading section.)

As well as providing a structure on time and a source of strokes, a Game also provides one way of dealing with, or avoiding, discomfort. This happens at the unconscious level, when the individual uses a predictable sequence of events with a predictable consequence which the individual believes will be the least stressful or easiest way of dealing with an anxious situation. If the individual is aware that he or she is involved in a game then this is not a game, it is a social manoeuvre.

The practice teacher/student relationship is potentially full of discomfort, anxiety and tension which appear to occur on three levels:

- within the relationship itself
- between the practice teacher/student relationship and the wider social work team
- between the practice teacher/student relationship and the educational establishment.

Within the relationship, each partner brings their own personal and professional histories. This background affects how the individual feels and behaves which in turn may result in a tension in the relationship.

The relationship also provides a setting to re-enact each individual's personal experience of childhood and of parenting. To over-simplify, the practice teacher may represent the over-indulgent or disciplinarian parent or the student may rediscover the role of stroppy adolescent or of the charming 'apple of my eye'. There is also a parallel here with the educational history of each partner: past experiences of, and attitudes towards, authority may re-surface and affect current behaviour.

The practice teacher has considerable power and responsibility in the relationship. She has the responsibility to make the experience an interesting one for the student and she has the power to pass or fail the student. The student may be uncertain how much power and responsibility he has or may feel wary about exercising the potential which he might recognise he has.

Both practice teacher and student want to be seen as 'good enough', if not excellent, during the placement. This may develop into a tension between them, that neither is allowed to make mistakes.

The task of assessment itself provokes anxiety. No matter how well planned the placement is, how challenging it is, or how smoothly it runs the assessment has to be made. Both practice teacher and student have to deal with making it fair and accurate.

The main tensions between the practice teacher/student relationship and the wider social work team may also focus on these issues of power and responsibility particularly towards the student's role within the team. Colleagues may feel envy that such a supportive relationship has developed or critical at the way the practice teacher is handling her responsibilities. The practice teacher may feel resentful that she is not allowed sufficient time by the team or by the manager to do her job properly.

The practice teacher may feel she needs to prove to the team that she can do an excellent job or colleagues may feel irritated that they are expected to do too much or not enough for the student. This dynamic may result in the student not using colleagues sufficiently or asking for too much of their time.

The tensions between the practice teacher/student dyad and the educational establishment will include the above. The level of anxiety will also be affected by how integrated the placement is within the professional course and by whether the task and role of the placement setting is recognised and validated by the academic staff. The level of support from the educational establishment and the clarity of instruction will affect the amount of anxiety experienced by the practice teacher and student.

In fact the list of possible sources of anxiety for both the student and the practice teacher is considerable and the individual may unconsciously use a Game as a way of managing the feelings, particularly those of discomfort, that he or she is experiencing within the practice teaching relationship. The other person, in turn wanting to manage his or her own feelings, unconsciously connects with the first person in a Game. A Game enables a possibly difficult situation to be handled in a predictable way in which the individual's way of seeing the world will be confirmed.

Another useful concept drawn from Transactional Analysis, which also lends some insight into the relationship between practice teacher and student, is that of discounting. A discount is when the individual exaggerates, minimises or ignores a feeling, a thought, a belief, or an action to do with himself, or with another person or with the situation. The process of being hooked into a Game requires such a discount. To use an example from the practice teacher/student relationship, the student is halfway through the placement. He has considerable expertise and experience in undertaking initial assessments and has started an assessment but in a new area of work. The practice teacher has little experience or knowledge with this particular client group. The level of anxiety on both sides might be quite high when the student brings this piece of work to the practice teaching session.

The student knows that he should talk about the assessment in the practice teaching session but is unsure what he wants from supervision. The student believes that he should not be feeling so anxious as he has undertaken numerous assessments in the past. So the student says: 'This is how far I have got with the new assessment. I'm not sure what I'm doing and I don't know if it is OK'. The student is not directly asking for advice from the practice teacher but the unspoken message, indicated here particularly by the student's tone and demeanour, is to ask for help with the next stage. The student in this example appears to be discounting, that is ignoring, the reality that it is all right to feel some anxiety when undertaking a new piece of work. He is also ignoring the reality that what he has learnt from previous assessments is transferable to a new situation. He is also ignoring the possibility that he can ask the practice teacher directly for information. If he continues to carry on with these discounts the end of the Game may be that the student is left believing that he is never given the information that he needs or perhaps that the progress of his placement is not as good as it could be.

In this example, the practice teacher may also be feeling concerned in the supervision session because she has no recent expertise in this particular area. Rather than acknowledging, at least to herself, that she has no current experience, she chooses to ignore the significance of this feeling and discounts the fact that she or the student could consult someone more specialised in this area for advice. The practice teacher, in replying to the student, may at this stage offer the student various ineffectual suggestions as to the next stage of the assessment. Whilst the practice teacher may feel she is managing her own feelings of anxiety, she is minimising the teaching potential for the student. If this continues, the practice teacher may end up blaming the student for not being sufficiently competent or blaming herself for not being up to the job.

The process of discounting on both sides enables each person to believe that what is being felt is being contained. Each person then enters a game on an unconscious level in order to sustain this process.

What kind of Games are there?

Both partners in the practice teaching process will engage in Games at some time. Rather than deal directly with the issue that may be causing concern, the individual unconsciously makes use of a Game which then appears to achieve a desired outcome. The end result however is not usually as satisfactory as one would want.

Kadushin, in an article entitled 'Games people play in supervision' (1976), used the concept of games to describe interactions between supervisor and supervisee. Danbury (1994) has related these ideas to the practice teaching relationship. While Kadushin's article provides some helpful insight into the dynamics of the practice teacher/student relationship and certainly makes for thought-provoking (if somewhat dated) reading, the games he describes imply a conscious manipulation of the relationship. Berne, however, was clear in his writing that Games – in Transactional Analysis – take place outside of awareness. Once either party becomes alert to a Game being played, it ceases to be a Game but is a social manoeuvre. Both students and practice teachers often recognise the scenarios Kadushin describes and admit to engaging in the interactions to relieve anxiety or achieve some other outcome and both Kadushin and Danbury provide useful material for discussion in supervision. It is not my intention, however, to consider Games which are developed with the conscious awareness of the participants within this chapter.

Games and the Drama Triangle

The sort of psychological Games that might develop will be linked to the main areas of anxiety associated with the practice teacher/student relationship. The positions each person takes up at the beginning of the Game and finds themselves in at the end will always correspond to the positions on the Drama Triangle mentioned earlier.

For example, the insecure, inexperienced student might start the placement feeling helpless, believing the practice teacher to be a better social worker. The student ignores any experience he may have and the fact that he was accepted for the course and, in order to contain these feelings of inadequacy, moves into a Victim position. The student does not directly discuss how he is feeling and does not state clearly what he needs but rather gives out the psychological message to the practice teacher that he requires 'sorting out'. The practice teacher feels this invitation and may at the same time be experiencing her own feelings of insecurity with the mantle of practice teacher status. To deal with this, the practice teacher unconsciously feels that she is OK as a practice teacher as long as she takes the position of organising the student. The practice teacher moves to the Rescuer position by not checking out with the student what help the student feels he needs. With time, the student begins to feel that his needs are not really being met and might then move, unconsciously, to persecute the practice teacher for not being up to the job. The practice teacher might then move to a Victim position believing that, as has happened so often in the past, she does not get it right. The student is engaged in a Game of 'Look how hard I'm trying to be a good student…'; the practice teacher's Game might be 'I'm only trying to help'.

The following example may occur towards the end of the placement. The student, an older man with much work experience and confidence, came to the placement feeling slightly resentful that at this stage in his career he was having to study for a professional qualification. The practice teacher is also quite a bit younger. This fact has not been acknowledged and so has fuelled the student's resentment. The student unconsciously has been quite persecutory of the practice teacher who has been drawn into a Victim position believing she has not much to offer the student. By the end of the placement the practice teacher realises there is not enough written material on which to assess the student and may move into a position of persecuting the student for this omission. The practice teacher may argue that despite the student's experience the student is in fact not any good ('Now I've got you…'). The student goes into a Victim position thinking that, despite his experience, he will never make the grade.

The type of Game will reflect issues of experience each partner brings to the relationship. This obviously refers to professional experience but will also relate to personal experience. For example, the older student with no direct social work experience but who has raised his own family may have a practice teacher with no children and no real experience of parenting. In order to feel less like an inexperienced student, the student may move unconsciously to persecute the practice teacher who is seen as having little experience of the real world of parenting.

The practice teacher exercises power via the assessment procedure so Games may occur here and they will be connected with how each views and deals with this issue. For example, if the practice teacher feels uncomfortable with this role, perhaps with an obviously experienced student, the practice teacher may allow herself to be rescued or persecuted by the experienced student. If the practice teacher feels insecure in this role she may move to a position of persecuting the student who is seen as always getting it wrong.

Finally, there is the issue of how each views him or herself. If the practice teacher believes that she is only good enough when she is teaching the student all of the time, without leaving the student space to make a few, minor mistakes or without checking out with the student what teaching he wants, there will be many opportunities for Games to be enacted and the practice teacher may well find herself in a position of rescuing the student. Likewise, if the student believes he is only good enough if he is busy all the time with clients and does not need time to prepare and to reflect, the games may end with the student finding himself in a Victim position.

How to spot a Game

One indicator of a Game series is to monitor how one is feeling at the end of a sequence of transactions within the supervisory relationship. A feeling of superiority or of worthlessness, of anger or of glee, may indicate a Game as will a feeling of confusion or of surprise. It is worth noting that it is not just the feeling that indicates the Game but the process of silence, of confusion, or of surprise that is experienced just before the well-known feeling is acknowledged.

A way to help predict a possible Game, as well as spotting that one has occurred, is to consider the concept of discounting as I have discussed earlier. If the individual spends time considering whether anything is being exaggerated, ignored or minimised this will enable the individual to consider the situation in a different light. For example, the new practice teacher might be feeling quite anxious about this role for which she has no experience. She may then exaggerate her experience as a social worker believing this will help contain her anxiety at her lack of experience in this new role. Or, the practice teacher may ignore the feeling and approach the situation as a bull in a china shop. Both scenarios will lead to Games with the student.

Spotting the discount also enables both practice teacher and student to look at the position she or he may be most used to on the Drama Triangle – Persecutor, Rescuer or Victim. As the individual becomes more aware of the positions she or he favours on the Drama Triangle so it is possible to recognise that the next step is into a Game.

It is important here to emphasise that the practice teacher/student dyad is not a therapeutic or counselling relationship. One of its goals is to enable the student's learning and professional development. Hazel Danbury (1994) describes how the student will bring transferential feelings into the relationship with the practice teacher, as will the practice teacher. The feelings of transference and of counter transference are the beginning stages of the game, for example the student may 'transfer' onto the practice teacher feelings about his parents and teachers from the past. The practice teacher may bring feelings about how she was parented or taught from the past to the present situation. An awareness of these transference and counter transference feelings will also indicate that a Game might be about to begin.

Ideas for a Game-free relationship

Developing an awareness of an unhelpful dynamic within the practice teacher and student relationship is a useful start. However, its use is limited if we do not know what can be used instead.

If the student and practice teacher can develop an understanding of their own particular needs then the individual can think through whether these need to be addressed in the practice teaching relationship or whether they need to be addressed elsewhere. The individual can then develop the skill of asking for what is needed in a straight manner; that is, neither putting themselves down nor the other person; neither exaggerating nor ignoring their own needs. For example, if the student is aware that he is feeling anxious he can develop the skill to think through where this anxiety is coming from. Is he ascribing to the practice teacher feelings about learning that belong to the past or is this feeling the result of a genuine lack of experience, or perhaps a mixture of both? When the student is clearer as to the origins of the anxiety then he is in a position to think through what he requires from supervision.

Elizabeth Ash, in her statement 'Reflective supervision produces reflective practice' (Ash 1995), emphasises the need for reflection in the supervisory relationship. The ability to reflect and understand what one is feeling will then allow one to develop an awareness of whether one is in a position on the Drama Triangle; if this is so, which position it is and, finally, what should be done next.

The manner of asking is crucial as this could become the opening stage of another Game. The request for help needs to be stated in a clear, straightforward manner. Pre-placement planning seems to be an important place to start. Dave Barker (1980) describes a three-cornered contract between the trainer, the trainee and the sponsoring organisation. In social work practice there is also the social work team in which the practice teacher and student are based and this I believe is the beginning of the four-cornered contract based on:

- the student's history and current expectations
- the practice teacher's history and current expectations
- the educational establishment's expectations
- the social work team's experience and expectations of a student.

Once these issues have been aired, then the initial placement contract, or learning agreement, can be developed and used as a tool to be updated as necessary throughout the placement. The agreement, actively entered into by all parties, will minimise the need for positions to be taken on the Drama Triangle and therefore the need for Games.

Another useful tool is the agenda for the practice teaching session. Whilst the practice teacher has overall responsibility for its content, the student too has a responsibility in providing for the agenda and participating in it. Elizabeth Ash, in the above article, sets out a framework for the supervisory relationship. My belief is that time spent discussing how supervision is organised will enable the development of a vehicle which

- allows effective use of the time available
- encourages congruent strokes and effective feedback
- contains anxiety and other feelings.

If the individual becomes aware that they are not getting what is required or that the stages of a Game are being enacted, they can comment on the process or intervene in the exchanges in order to stop the unfolding of the Game. Likewise, when either individual realises they are in one of the Victim, Rescuer or Persecutor positions they can refuse to be there and move out of the Drama Triangle.

Connected with the above, and returning to the basic theory mentioned earlier on, if the individual concentrates on using their Adult ego state in supervision this decreases the likelihood of childlike or persecutory statements being made. This approach requires that the individual is as aware as is possible about what is happening within the session.

The concept of strokes is a useful tool to be used. We have already seen how Games ensure a steady supply of strokes. These may be negative, especially at the end of a Game when one partner may be feeling put upon, or may be seen as an acknowledgement of something that is not very helpful, for example if one person puts themselves in a superior position to the other. Strokes which are genuinely expressed by the practice teacher and which are congruent both verbally and non-verbally will mean there is less need for games and will help the student learn. An example of a positive, unconditional and congruent stroke is supervision that starts on time, using the focused and uninterrupted attention of the practice teacher. Likewise, the student who has prepared himself for supervision and is appropriately present and involved is giving both the practice teacher and himself a positive, unconditional and congruent stroke. Increasing stroke levels serves to acknowledge the other person, thereby containing or reducing anxiety and therefore minimising the need to enter a Game.

A way forward

Game analysis can be seen as a useful tool to highlight what may be happening in the practice teacher and student relationship particularly if something seems to be going awry. It also invites each partner to find other ways to provide an effective teaching and learning relationship. In particular, it offers the opportunity to:

1. recognise and acknowledge the importance of initial feelings in the practice teaching relationship as these may set the tone for the teaching and learning to be done in the future

2. understand that communication may be seen as a process involving separate stages

3. acknowledge that change is always possible

4. use the tools of contract and of agenda setting as useful aids for straight communication

5. understand that positive, unconditional strokes are an important way of developing an effective practice teacher and student relationship.

References

Ash, E. (1995) 'Supervision – taking account of feelings.' In J. Pritchard (ed) *Good Practice in Supervision.* London: Jessica Kingsley Publishers.

Barker, D. (1980) *TA and Training.* Farnborough: Gower Press.

Berne, E. (1961) *Transactional Analysis in Psychotherapy.* New York: Grove Press Inc.

Berne, E. (1964) *Games People Play.* New York: Penguin Books Ltd.

Berne, E. (1966) *Principles of Group Treatment.* Oxford: Oxford University Press.

Danbury, H. (1994) *Teaching Practical Social Work.* Aldershot: Arena.

Ford, K. and Jones, A. (1987) *Student Supervision.* Basingstoke: Macmillan.

Kadushin, A. (1979) 'Games people play in supervision.' In C.E. Hunson (ed) *Social Work Supervision: Classic Statements and Critical Issues.* New York: Free Press.

Karpman, S. (1968) 'Fairy tales and script drama analysis.' *TAB 7,* 26, 39.

Transactional Analysis Journal (1995) Statement by Susan Sevilla of ITAA printed in journal description.

Further reading

Lapworth, P., Sills, C. and Fish, S. (1993) *Transactional Analysis Counselling.* Oxford: Winslow Press.

Pitman, E. (1984) *Transactional Analysis for Social Workers and Counsellors.* London: Routledge and Kegan Paul.

Schiff, J.L., Schiff, A.W., Mellor, K., Schiff, E., Schiff, S., Richman, D., Fishman, J., Wolz, L., Fishman, C. and Momb, D. (1975) *Cathexis Reader.* New York: Harper and Row, Publishers, Inc.

CHAPTER 8

Managing Endings in Practice Teaching

Charlotte Clow

Introduction

I was astounded as a student social worker on placement, when in my last session with a client he expressed genuine shock and horror that I was leaving, denying vehemently that he had known in advance. How could this be? It had often been mentioned as part of my student status that I would be leaving in June and when I had raised it in previous weeks, he had hardly reacted. What was going on?

It was clear to me that my client was not dissembling. His shock and horror were genuine. He had 'forgotten' because the reality was too hard for him to accept – he had not wanted to hear that I was leaving. For my own part, I had been only too happy to believe that he did not mind because it made it easier for me. I wanted to believe that he would manage without me and I thought the easy-going nature of our last sessions indicated successful work. This sense of achievement was particularly important to me at the point of my assessment.

At this last session, however, I became aware of the gulf between what had appeared to be the case and the reality. It became clear to me that we had neglected to address a crucial aspect of our relationship, my leaving, and that this could threaten all the progress that we had so far established, as well as making it very difficult for the client to resume work with a new social worker.

This example, although specific to one case, gives a flavour of some of the issues that can be raised for both the social worker and client by the endings process. These are present for social workers generally, but particularly pertinent for student social workers who have to deal with ending dates that are outside their control and who have the added anxieties of the assessment process.

In this chapter I look at how the practice teacher can help the student manage the endings process effectively, using psychodynamic concepts and theories of loss and change as tools in understanding the complexity of issues raised. Since an ending only has significance in the context of a relationship that matters, I start by taking a brief look at the importance of the social work relationship and consider common responses to loss. I then examine the implications of endings for the service user, the student social worker and the practice teacher. Finally, I look at the benefits of a well-managed ending and suggest some guidelines for practice teachers for promoting good practice in this area.

The importance of the social work relationship

From birth, relationships provide the climate for the growth of the human personality. Despite a recent tendency to play down its therapeutic element, research still suggests that the quality of the relationship between the service user and social worker is the single most important factor in social work effectiveness, whatever the theoretical approach.

> The core of social work remains the relationship between worker and client...the attitudes shown by the social worker remain critical determinants of the service offered. (Bamford 1989, p.138)

Counselling skills form the medium through which we negotiate a safe and trusting relationship with our clients. Warmth, acceptance, unconditional regard and respect across any cultural divide are conveyed through good listening skills, open questions, and the use of accurate empathy, using a model such as the one advanced by Egan (1975). The aim is to achieve a good working alliance that empowers service users to make the changes they need.

One of the most helpful concepts in understanding why it is sometimes so difficult to achieve this working alliance is that of transference. Transference is the process that happens to some extent in all human relationships whereby feelings are transferred from significant relationships in the past to new relationships in the present, without consideration of whether they still apply. For example, a service user that has had early childhood experiences of abuse may well bring transferential feelings of mistrust, fear and anger to the social work relationship despite all the efforts of the social worker to reassure them. Or they may bring a desperate need for love and affection and idealise their social worker as the positive parent they never had.

Whether the relationship is considered supportive and validating or intrusive and difficult by the service user, it is likely to be a highly significant one precisely because it is about having to accept help from a professional at a time of stress and vulnerability. At these times the 'child within' is particularly reactivated, bringing attachment behaviour to the fore with powerful force. The likelihood of transference feelings is therefore already high and increased further by the position of authority held by the social worker.

For the service user allocated a student social worker, there can be additional dimensions that need addressing, such as worries about confidentiality, feelings about being a guinea pig or getting 'second best', or perhaps even a sense of not having been good enough (or bad enough!) to get a 'real' social worker. Fear of abandonment and an experience of many different professionals can lead to a very real reluctance to open up to someone who will be leaving in a few months. If these issues are not addressed, it can be difficult for service users to engage with students, leading to unsatisfactory placements where the work never really gets off the ground. In this sense, managing the time-limited nature of the work actually allows the work to begin.

It can be difficult for social workers to acknowledge the strength of feeling aroused by the social work relationship. Student social workers in particular have a tendency to minimise their importance to the service user. It is not always comfortable to be on the receiving end of such charged feelings and projections or to be so significant in a client's life, especially when you know you will be leaving in a few months time. Yet this is often the reality, even when the contact has been short as in the case of social work placements. It is important to acknowledge the significance of the social work relationship in order to take on board the profound effect that an ending can have.

The impact of loss and change

We are accustomed to thinking about endings as a time of resolution, when work has been completed to a desired outcome and aims satisfactorily met. However, even in this ideal situation the endings process can be painful and difficult, evoking powerful feelings of loss.

In recent years a lot of work has been done on bereavement and the mourning process. The 'worry work' first described by Freud in 1917 and later developed by Bowlby (1979), Murray Parkes (1972) and others includes common stages of: numbness and denial when the person staves off acknowledgement of the loss; intense and painful emotions as the denial breaks down, including feelings of pining and anger; a period of depression and withdrawal; finally reaching some form of acceptance and ability to re-invest emotional energy into new people or projects.

People who have a strong sense of self-worth and positive early experiences of attachment have internal resources that help them survive the powerful feelings of anger, sadness and disappointment that are a natural part of the mourning process. Those people whose emotional and physical needs have not always been adequately met are more likely to find those feelings intolerable and develop defence mechanisms to repress the pain. Although this works in the short term, the 'worry work' never gets completed and the person is hampered from fully coming to terms with the loss.

Freud suggested that many mental health problems are a result of 'pathological mourning' and this has been supported by other research (Bowlby 1979). For example, Brown and Harris (1978) found that early loss of a mother figure (amongst other factors) predisposes women to depression, when precipitated by an event such as a present loss or change.

It is often such losses that bring service users to our attention and their importance cannot be under-estimated. The important point here is that loss is not only relevant in the context of bereavement. It has been broadened to include many other sorts of losses that mean a significant adjustment, such as divorce, moving house, getting older, losing a limb and so on. This has been well explored by many theorists including Marris (1986) and Salzberger-Wittenberg (1970).

It follows that the ending of the client–social worker relationship can also be experienced as a significant loss for service users. However, the flavour and significance of each individual ending will depend on the investment in the relationship, the nature and extent of the transference and the individual's learned responses to loss and change.

How endings can affect the clients of student social workers

In any social work setting, service users may well be allocated a number of different social workers over a period of time, with each experience influencing the expectations that they bring to the next social work relationship. We have probably all had to work with client mistrust and frustration at having to repeat their story many times or with clients who make favourable or unfavourable comparisons with previous workers.

This is one of the reasons why facilitating positive endings with service users is always important in social work relationships, but never more so than on social work placements, where the time-limited nature of the work is a known factor and where there may be other issues for the service user concerning the student status of the worker.

So what are the feelings that can be raised for the service user? Even where closure is planned and agreed between worker and client, there may be a very similar range of feelings to those in the mourning process: denial that the ending is in sight, anger at being left, worries about how to cope without the person, sadness at the loss, relief that the relationship is over, guilt at these feelings and so on. The importance of allowing service users to acknowledge and work through these feelings, that is, to carry out the 'worry work' that will enable them to disinvest from the relationship successfully, is a crucial element in the practice learning curriculum. Bywaters (1975b) discusses the importance of this from his research into endings. In my own experience as a practice teacher, I too have known service users to show a wide range of emotions when the student placement is coming to an end and to need skilful intervention on behalf of the social work student to manage the situation.

In one example, a service user, Rose, wrote to me as the manager of a mental health project, six weeks before the student was leaving, to request a new worker. She expressed a complete lack of confidence in the student, 'we just don't get on, I feel like she doesn't understand me'. When I explored this with Rose, she was unable to be any clearer about what the problems were but reiterated her feelings of dislike for the student and suggested that she was not very competent in her role.

It was only after we had talked it through for some time that Rose started to say things like 'well, she'll be leaving soon anyway' and it became clear how affected she was by this imminent loss. She then started talking about a previous worker that she'd been very attached to but who had 'let her down badly' and her early experiences of abandonment as a child.

This is a clear example of how the client's concerns about the ending, combined with strong transferential feelings, can endanger the social work relationship. In this case, Rose responded to her feelings by rejecting the student in a bid to 'get in first' and maintain a sense of control. It is easy to sympathise with why service users might do this. However, if unaddressed, the client is left with yet another experience of failure, even greater reluctance to trust someone else and without access to the necessary support.

In this situation, exploring the issues helped Rose to recognise to some extent the process that was taking place and she agreed, albeit reluctantly, to carry on with the student until she left. They used this time to talk about endings and Rose's experience of them. The crisis became an opportunity for growth, with Rose opening up in a way she never previously had. When the student finally left and Rose was taken on by one of the permanent workers, everyone in the team was amazed by how positively she now viewed her relationship with the student!

Rose's extreme reaction made it fairly easy for me to identify the processes that were taking place, but often the signs are a lot more subtle. It may be that the service user appears very accepting of the situation or adopts a 'don't care' attitude. However, where the client is known to have developed a significant relationship with the social worker who is leaving, it is important to be aware that there may be much more going on under the surface than at first appears.

In the mental health projects that I manage I have often seen service users respond in a very dismissive way about someone leaving, 'it doesn't make any difference to me', but there then follows a period of acute distress and anger, sometimes leading to a full relapse. When this happens, it is rare for the client to make the link themselves that they are affected by their worker leaving, although they may talk about feelings such as no one caring for them or mention people who have left them in the past.

This is where understanding the role of defence mechanisms is so useful, in that it makes sense of behaviour that would otherwise make little sense. For example, when students have a Christmas or Easter break, it is not unusual for service users to fail to turn up for their sessions the following week, to be unusually critical of the student on their return or to make flippant comments about the fact that students have something better to do than see them. Understanding this behaviour in terms of the client defending against the pain of loss allows the student to respond therapeutically and not collusively or punitively.

Another common response to loss from service users is to become more vulnerable and needy as the ending date gets nearer. This can be very distressing for the student, raising feelings of guilt and anxiety. At this point the student may need additional support in not being drawn out of role. For example, service users have sometimes asked whether the student will still keep in touch once they have left or if they could become friends. Maintaining the professional boundary at this time can feel uncomfortable and withholding for the student. Discussion in supervision about the common responses to closure can help students feel more comfortable with their role at this time.

How endings can affect the student social worker

One of the most important arguments in this chapter is that the ideas about loss are as relevant to the student social worker and practice teacher as they are to the client. Although it is hoped that workers are not in a state of crisis and have the resources to manage their lives, they too will have developed various defence mechanisms over the years to help them cope with the painful feelings evoked by endings and may well have unresolved issues to do with loss and change or events in the present such as a divorce or a bereavement that are bringing these issues to the fore.

In addition to personal factors, there are a number of relevant issues to do with change that arise from being on a social work course. Students are in a learning role, where their habitual views and working practices are being challenged. In the placement, they talk much about feeling 'deskilled' by this spotlight on their practice. They are also having to face a fast turnover of beginnings and endings with fellow students, placement colleagues and clients within a two-year timescale.

So the student social worker is already likely to be sensitised, to varying degrees, to issues of loss and change. In addition to this, we have seen how endings are likely to provoke some powerful feelings in the service user, many of which will be negative. Expressions of aggression, passive withdrawal or 'rubbishing' of the work or worker are all ways in which the service user may deal with the ending.

In the example I have given above, the student was devastated when Rose rejected her. She blamed herself and struggled with questions of her own competence. She also felt extremely angry and betrayed by Rose. She needed additional support during this time to process her own feelings, expressing her bewilderment and outrage. She was then able to separate out her feelings of personal rejection and respond to the client in a professional way, allowing the worry work to take place.

Because helping a service user express their feelings about the approaching ending often means hearing anger, despair or criticism, it is no wonder that the student will often avoid opening up these discussions. They would much rather hear that they have been helpful, liked and effective! This is especially relevant in the context of their placement being evaluated and fears about failure and performance anxiety.

If the preparatory worry work is not given plenty of time, then the client's negative feelings may dominate at the time of closure and the final assessment, raising doubts for the student about their role and effectiveness. This has appeared to be the case among highly competent qualified social workers (Fox *et al.* 1969), let alone student social workers at the point of assessment.

Student social workers need support and encouragement from their practice teachers to open up the subject of endings with their service users in plenty of time and to see it through, even though it may be difficult.

How endings can affect the practice teacher

If student placements are challenging for the student, then they are equally so for the practice teacher who has a responsibility for ensuring that the placement works for the student, the service users and other team members. The task of balancing the different roles of teaching, supporting and assessment is a complex one, especially when students, in particular first-years, often bring high levels of anxiety with them.

For the practice teacher who has no management experience it can be particularly hard to feel comfortable with the assessment process and the use of personal authority that it entails. This, together with the inevitable last-minute rush to ensure every part of the practice curriculum is covered and evidence collected, can add to the experience of the ending as a challenging time. While the student social worker may feel that the spotlight is solely on their practice, the practice teacher is only too aware of their own responsibilities in ensuring a successful placement and sufficient evidence for any decisions they make. Have they been available enough to the student? Were the cases they allocated the student suitable? Have they done enough direct observation? All these kind of concerns can preoccupy the practice teacher as they seek to be as fair as possible in the assessment they make.

To respond effectively to endings, it is important that the practice teacher encourages the student to talk openly about the processes that are taking place. This means reassuring the student that any negative feelings expressed by the client in the worry work will not adversely affect their assessment. One of the difficulties here of course is that criticism of the student can easily raise doubts for the practice teacher about the student's level of performance, especially where direct observation of practice is difficult. It is essential, therefore, to have sufficient means of gaining evidence from several sources and not to leave the gathering of evidence for assessment to the end of the placement.

In addition to the assessment task, the ending for the practice teacher will be influenced by the quality of the relationship they have built up with the student. The nature of the practice teaching role and the frequency of contact can make it a significant and sometimes highly charged relationship for both parties. Where a strong bond has been built up in a successful placement, there can be a great sense of loss at the ending. In the case of a borderline or failing student, the practice teacher may have to deal with strong feelings of failure, guilt or pity.

The practice teacher's own present and past experiences of loss and change and the organisational culture in which they work will also play a part in how equipped they feel to deal effectively with the ending of the placement. Where the practice teacher has unresolved issues to do with loss or is currently experiencing a relationship break-up or bereavement, or works in a highly stressful environment where no credence is given to working with emotional issues, then it becomes much harder to contain the strong feelings raised by the endings process on the part of the student and the service users. In this situation, there is a higher likelihood that the endings process will be neglected, with the practice teacher colluding with the student's denial or perhaps 'forgetting' to arrange a leaving do for the student.

This process is not limited to practice teachers, however. Endings are generally difficult for most people and social workers are no exception. Taking a broader view, it could be argued that there is a national tendency towards the 'stiff upper lip' and the denial of expressing feelings around loss. It has been suggested that this is why the termination process is such a neglected area in social work training (Fox *et al.* 1969).

It is clear that regular, good quality supervision for all practice teachers must be a key element in helping them explore and understand their own responses to the ending of the student placement. This allows them better to facilitate the student's ending within the placement and with the service users.

The benefits of good practice in regard to endings on placement

Because endings can evoke such painful feelings, it is easy to see this as a negative phase of the work, especially when the closure is governed by the placement dates rather than the service user's needs. Yet, like much bereavement work, the 'crisis' of the ending of the social work relationship can also have a positive side, if well handled.

This idea of seeing the ending as a potentially therapeutic tool has been explored by Winnicott (1964) among others. The main thrust of the theory is that by providing an opportunity for the client to express their feelings of anger and sadness at the ending, the worker helps the client resolve some of the feelings from past losses that have never been addressed. By handling the intense and difficult emotions of anger and sorrow, the social worker shows that such feelings can be contained, modelling a positive way of dealing with the frustrations and limitations of life. Bywaters points out that in this way, time-limited work makes a virtue out of a necessity:

> Closure therefore has unique possibilities for exploring with the client the acceptance of limits, the move towards greater independence and the survival of loss...providing the possibility for learning how to handle negative feelings towards others. (Bywaters 1975b, p.337)

Given all the evidence for the significance of loss in many of our clients' lives, the importance of the acquisition of transferable skills and the therapeutic effects of well-handled endings should not be under-estimated.

Moreover, an ending that is carefully and thoughtfully managed will improve the degree to which gains from the work are internalised and maintained, while a mishandled ending can lead to the discounting of productive work. A service user who feels safe and free to express their feelings and fears will feel empowered and more confident in managing alone.

Conversely, a bad ending fails our clients. If the many and complex issues are not worked with, a service user can feel rejected and worthless, carrying around repressed feelings that they have not had a chance to explore or understand. For many vulnerable clients this can be a devastating experience, and one which is likely to affect future contact with social workers. A good ending is therefore just as important in the case of a transfer to a new worker, if that relationship is not to be sabotaged due to unfinished business with the last.

In the case example of Rose, the ability of the student social worker to 'survive' Rose's rejection and criticism and not respond defensively herself was an essential part of maintaining the relationship. It meant that Rose had an opportunity to explore her own responses to endings in a safe environment. Paradoxically, although this meant she was in touch with her sad feelings about the loss of the student relationship, it also meant that she was able to approach her next social work relationship with a degree of trust and openness.

Guidelines for practice teachers in helping students manage endings

From the exploration of the issues around endings, some obvious indications for good practice emerge.

- Think carefully about which cases to pass to the student. Is there a time-limited piece of work that could be finished in the duration of the placement? Have the clients allocated to the student had many workers passing through or have they developed a significant rapport with a particular worker? What issues are raised for individual service users from having a student social worker with a time-limited placement?

- Raise the issue about the ending right at the beginning of the student's placement, encouraging them to think about it as a factor that may influence the nature of the client's engagement with them.

- Ensure that the student has been explicit about the time-limited nature of the placement with all their clients from the beginning. As this is likely to go hand in hand with exploration of their student status, which can raise issues about the student's perceived competency and lead to challenges by the service user, this may well be something that the student baulks at. Thoroughly discussing the issues in supervision helps the student explore their fears so that they can address the issues with the client confidently and assertively.

- Help the student explore their client's reactions to their holidays as a useful rehearsal of the leaving process. Encourage them to notice overt or covert signs that the client is preoccupied with loss or feelings of abandonment. The information that such reactions provide is very useful in understanding how the person copes with loss and change and in working with this in time for the actual ending.

- Use the available opportunities to discuss theories of loss and change with the student, helping them to integrate theory and practice. Knowledge of the common stages of the mourning process can help alleviate feelings of guilt and anxiety about leaving.

- Ensure that the student starts addressing the endings process explicitly in plenty of time. You may have to be proactive in raising the subject and prepare the student for a range of negative responses from their clients. Keep it on the agenda for every supervision in the final month so that it cannot be forgotten or neglected.

- Encourage the student to explore their own feelings about the ending process, their habitual responses to loss, any feelings about leaving the placement, colleagues and clients. Give permission for a range of feelings, including bad ones, and help them explore any difficulties.

- Where assertiveness may be an issue, give the student an opportunity to practise in supervision how they would respond to possible boundary testing by the client, for example to questions such as 'Will you write to me and let me know how you are getting on?'

- Be very clear with the student about the assessment process: what your criteria will be and how you will apply them. This will help the student be confident in encouraging the client to express any negative feelings raised by the endings process without fear of this prejudicing their assessment.

- Use your own supervision to explore your own responses to loss and change and to check that you are not yourself defending against the pain of managing the ending or colluding with the student's or client's denial.

- Where a service user is to be transferred to another worker, consider the transfer process carefully to maximise the sense of safety and containment for the service user. Consider introducing the new worker a couple of weeks before the student leaves, but not in the last session which needs to be free for the final goodbyes.

- Check that no aspect of the endings process has been neglected in the placement. For example, has the student's leaving been planned for and acknowledged by the team? The more attention paid to leaving within the culture of the team, the better the student's own ending is facilitated.

Conclusion

Endings are usually difficult. This is why people will go to great lengths to avoid the distress and discomfort that they provoke. This certainly applies to our clients, but social work students and practice teachers are no strangers to the process either. In fact, social work generally tends to neglect this crucial dimension of the work. Fox, Nelson and Bolman go so far as to suggest that social workers' lack of awareness of the importance of managing endings successfully represents 'an important public health problem' (1969, p.54). Whether or not this is the case, it is certainly true that defensive avoidance and denial of the significance of endings do not work in the best interests of our service users. We need to help clients with the worry work, however difficult this may be, so that the ending becomes a positive, enabling experience.

Practice teachers have a responsibility to address the issue of endings with their social work students, both to ensure successful practice placements and to model good social work practice. If the importance of this phase of the work is stressed in social work education, there is a good chance that it will become standard practice among social work practitioners in the future.

References

Bamford, T. (1989) 'Discretion and managerialism.' In S. Shardlow (ed) *The Values of Change in Social Work*. London: Tavistock/Routledge.

Bowlby, J. (1979) *The Making and Breaking of Affectional Bonds*. London: Tavistock.

Brown, G. and Harris, T. (1978) *Social Origins of Depression*. London: Tavistock.

Bywaters, P. (1975a) 'Ending casework relationships (1).' *Social Work Today 6*, 10, 301–304.

Bywaters, P. (1975b) 'Ending casework relationships (2).' *Social Work Today 6*, 11, 336–338.

Egan, G. (1975) *The Skilled Helper*. Monteroy: Brooks/Cole..

Fox, E., Nelson M. and Bolman, W. (1969) 'The termination process: a neglected dimension.' *Social Work: Journal of the National Association of Social Workers 14*, 4, 59–63.

Marris, P. (1986) *Loss and Change* (Revised Edition) London: Routledge.

Parkes, C.M. (1972) *Bereavement*. London: Tavistock.

Salzberger-Wittenberg, I. (1970) *Psycho-Analytical Insights and Relationships*. London: Routledge.

Winnicott, D. (1964) *The Child, the Family and the Outside World*. Harmondsworth: Penguin.

Further reading

Brearley, J. (1995) *Counselling and Social Work*. Milton Keynes: Open University Press.

Danbury, H. (1994) *Teaching Practical Social Work*. Aldershot: Arena.

Doel, M., Shardlow, S., Sawdon, C. and Sawdon, D. (1996) *Teaching Social Work Practice*. Aldershot: Arena.

CHAPTER 9

What Works

Essential Knowledge and Skills
for the Probation Student

Corinne Pearce

Introduction

The probation service nationally is in the grip of financial cutbacks, a severe erosion in the social work professional training base and is beset with doubts as to the effectiveness of its practice. Government thinking which is set on a course of punishment-based programmes is at odds with recent research findings which show that rehabilitation programmes which contain certain features can reduce recidivism. The focus of this chapter is to review some of the research that has taken place over the past 20 years in determining the most effective ways of reducing recidivism, the 'what works' debate. My aims in writing this chapter are threefold: first, to provide an overview of the 'what works' theory base which has had so much impact on practice, policy and research in criminal justice up to the current time; second, to provide an outline of current effective intervention with offenders; and third, to consider the relevance of these issues for a probation student who through the practice teaching role can be taught to apply cognitive behavioural and structural casework approaches in practice with offenders.

For the past 30 years at least, a debate has taken place amongst academics and professionals as to the most effective ways of reducing crime and rehabilitating offenders. This has veered from a social work based, person-centred approach to a far more punitive belief that rehabilitation does not work and that the best way to reduce crime is by punishment and determent. During the 1970s particularly, probation officers were largely informed by social work values which emphasised the importance of the therapeutic relationship, where trust could be developed, the person nurtured and positive change result. However, a series of large-scale research reviews were conducted in the United States and Britain during the 1970s and 1980s which sought to draw together all the evidence then existing from treatment outcome studies in work with offenders. This research suggested that the psychodynamic casework approach, whilst very valuable with certain groups, was ineffective in reducing recidivism.

'Nothing works'

The belief that 'nothing works' in the rehabilitation of offenders originated from research conducted in both Britain and the USA in the 1970s. Researchers found that studies based on poor research methodology and design made conclusions difficult and, in studies that were rigorous enough, there was still no evidence that anything worked to reduce reoffending.

Robert Martinson (1974) in the USA concluded from his review of criminal rehabilitation literature and a survey of research on correctional treatments that: 'in the rehabilitation of offenders almost nothing works'.

In his work (1974 and in 1975 with Lipton and Wilks) he reviewed 231 studies carried out in the United States which involved interventions with both juvenile and adult offenders. His influential conclusion was that: 'with few isolated exceptions the rehabilitative efforts that have been reported so far have had no appreciable effect on recidivism'.

In Britain, Stephen Brody (1976) reached the same conclusion from a similar review: '...reviewers of research into the effectiveness of different sentences or ways of treating or training offenders have unanimously agreed that the results so far offered little hope that a reliable and simple remedy for recidivism can easily be found... Studies which have produced positive results have been isolated, inconsistent in their evidence and open to so much methodological criticism that they must remain unconvincing'.

Martinson and Brody's findings came at a critical time when penal policy had shifted from the old medical model of deviance to the justice model, with decriminalisation and diversion all growing in importance. The 'nothing works' assertion acquired increased status in the 1970s and 1980s influencing and undermining rehabilitation work with offenders. This resulted in a decreased confidence in the effectiveness of probation policies and practices among politicians, probation workers and the general public.

Since this time research has demonstrated that the 'nothing works' notion was flawed. Studies carried out on the work of Martinson and others found validity and reliability errors cast doubts on earlier findings (Martinson 1974). The use of meta analysis since the 1980s has shown that recidivism can be reduced. Meta analysis, a statistical methodology, allowed evidence from different studies to be combined and analysed. Furthermore, the increased use of cognitive/behavioural or task-centred methods which involve structured interventions with explicit aims and time limits has facilitated more accurate evaluation.

'Some things do work'

There is now substantial evidence that it is possible to reduce rates of reoffending and it is with this research that a probation student should be familiar. A number of meta analyses studies have been conducted since the 1980s and have demonstrated far more optimistic conclusions with net reduction rates in offending of between 10 per cent and 12 per cent. However, in order to identify which factors affect recidivism rates it is necessary to review what meta analyses revealed about ineffective interventions. First, there is little evidence that classical psychotherapeutic models are effective. This is also true of individual casework counselling (Fischer 1973; 1978) although more recent research by Russell (1990) reveals that more structured casework, such as task-centred or cognitive behavioural based methods, can be effective. Furthermore, interventions based on medical models lacking in psychosocial components have not been shown to have any lasting impact in reducing reoffending. Correctional and punitive measures which are perhaps more popular with the general public have also been found to be ineffective and indeed exacerbate recidivism. Lipsey (1995) for example found that punitive programmes such as shock incarceration, boot camps and similar approaches on average resulted in a 25 per cent increase in reoffending rates when compared with control groups.

The growing belief that some interventions do work has received more interest during the late 1980s and 1990s. Andrews *et al.* (1990) and Lipsey (1995) have carried out the largest-scale meta analyses to date, with Lipsey conducting 397 studies. Both reached positive and encouraging conclusions, Andrews stating: 'positively we predict that appropriate treatment – treatment that is delivered to higher risk cases that target criminogenic need, and that is matched with the learning styles of offenders – will reduce recidivism'.

Lipsey (1995) argues that: '…the more structured and focused treatments (e.g. behavioural, skill orientated) and multi-modal treatments seem to be more effective than the less structured and focused approaches, e.g. counsel-ling'.

Although this research does not claim that there is a unitary approach that will alone reduce recidivism, the reviews do give some clear guidelines about the factors that identify effective programmes.

It was found that higher-risk offenders require more intensive supervision with the focus of supervision being on criminogenic needs as opposed to non-criminogenic need. Examples of criminogenic factors are a pro-criminal attitude, little victim empathy and weak problem solving. A community-based, structured multi-modal programme employing a skills-orientated, cognitive behavioural approach with clearly monitored and evaluated aims are also deemed important factors in effectiveness. Programmes should match the needs and learning styles of the individuals and programme con-tent and delivery should be sensitive to issues such as culture, race, gender, sexuality and disability.

The cognitive behavioural approach

The use of cognitive behavioural methods in probation supervision of offenders in both one-to-one supervision and groupwork provision is increasing. In light of the 'what works' findings it is vitally important that probation students have an understanding of the cognitive behavioural approach to working with offenders. The cognitive behavioural approach is a composition of two positions in psychology. The radical behavioural model maintains that patterns of extrinsic reinforcement and punishment must be understood in order to predict and change behaviour. The cognitive position on the other hand stresses the role of mental processes in understanding behaviour such as thoughts, memory and language and places emphasis on intrinsic rather than extrinsic determinants of behaviour. Cognitive behav-ioural techniques therefore focus on both cognition and behaviour as the primary change areas. One of the most important features of the cognitive behavioural approach is the teaching of coping skills which empowers the offender, reduces and prevents relapse and avoids the fostering of depend-ence on the worker.

Cognitive behavioural techniques are time limited, applicable to a wide variety of problem areas, highly structured, relatively easily acquired and can be employed on a group or individual basis. My experience is that probation students on even a relatively short placement can become proficient in employing cognitive behavioural techniques in working with offenders.

Ways of teaching and familiarising the student with the concepts and techniques would include reading material about the theoretical base and particular methods of intervention, for example, motivational interviewing. A practical working knowledge of how the techniques may be employed can be gained through direct observation and case discussion and the practice and refinement of skills can be achieved through role play in supervision.

Introducing the 'what works' debate and teaching the cognitive behavioural approach to students

I believe that teaching a student about the 'what works' debate and cognitive behavioural techniques of intervention is a crucial role of a probation practice teacher. It would seem that the only way forward for the probation service is to demonstrate its effectiveness constantly by understanding the 'what works' theory base and applying cognitive behavioural and structured casework approaches in practice. I shall now consider how I, as a practice teacher, could effectively engage a student in this learning process and assess the student's effectiveness as a practitioner. My approach and expectations of the student would, however, differ depending on whether they were a first or second-year student. I would certainly introduce the 'what works' principles and cognitive behavioural approach to a first-year student and encourage them to employ cognitive behavioural techniques with offenders on an individual basis, in the same way as I would a second-year student. However, with regard to groupwork it is more usual for a first-year student in my local probation service to have very limited groupwork involvement, and it would be more observational in nature than participative. This would, however, give the student some insight and understanding of the approach and techniques employed in a group context.

A second-year student on placement with my local probation service would be required to supervise offenders on both an individual basis and within a group context. Two examples of how I would familiarise the student with the cognitive behavioural approach would be by teaching the student to use the motivational interviewing technique with a client on an individual basis and, in respect of a second-year student, by co-working the reasoning and rehabilitation groupwork programme.

Motivational interviewing

I will start by briefly outlining the two methods of working. Motivational interviewing uses a series of counselling techniques to help people acknowledge and do something about their present or potential problems. The worker's overall goal is to increase the offender's motivation so that change arises from within rather than being imposed from without. In order for this to occur emphasis is placed on increasing the client's self-esteem and self-efficacy so that they believe they have the ability to change. It also focuses on increasing the client's level of concern about their offending behaviour, eliciting self-motivational statements, that is, intrinsic reasons for change. Counselling techniques with which the student will be familiar, such as open-ended questioning, summarising, affirmation and selective reflective listening are used to prompt the client towards change. To assess a client's motivation to change, the Prochaska and DiClemente (1984) model of stages of change is used. This cycle recognises six stages through which a person undertaking personal change may pass: pre-contemplation, contemplation, decision to change, active changes, maintenance when the change is consolidated, and relapse, when the client resorts to the previous pattern of behaviour. One of the most productive stages at which to use motivational interviewing is the contemplation stage. It aims to increase cognitive dissonance and enables the client to identify intrinsic motivation to change. Hence when this approach is done properly it is the client who presents the arguments for change rather than the worker, at the point when the client sees their offending behaviour as incompatible with their view of themselves.

Reasoning and Rehabilitation programme

A growing number of probation areas, including my local area, use the Reasoning and Rehabilitation groupwork programme. This programme was developed by two Canadian psychologists, Ross and Fabiano (1990). The Reasoning and Rehabilitation programme was devised as a result of a research project into rehabilitation programmes for offenders undertaken in North America between 1973 and 1978. Ross and Fabiano had discovered reductions in recidivism ranging from 30 per cent to 74 per cent. In comparing the successful groupwork programmes with those that had failed they discovered that what was different about the successful programmes was that they concentrated on people's thinking.

In its pure form the programme comprises of 35, two-hour sessions and contains a series of cognitive training methods and exercises. Although it is fair to say that it has attracted a series of criticisms for its prescriptiveness, Americanisms and sexist assumptions, I am aware that many probation areas have eradicated the concerns and criticisms about the programme by adapting and rewording much of the material. The programme is process, not content orientated, and consists of nine interrelated modules: problem solving, social skills, negotiation skills, the management of emotions, creative thinking, values enhancement, critical reasoning, skills in review and cognitive exercises. The fundamental premise of the programme is that the way people think affects the way that they feel, and that the way that they feel influences the way that they behave. Therefore, a limited ability to think through a situation can cause considerable behavioural difficulties. Teaching methods include role play, brainstorm, discussion and a series of lateral thinking exercises. The programme has a manual and a planned 'building block' approach. A successful atmosphere for delivering the programme is informal, task orientated, thought provoking, frustrating/stimulating, lively, debating, emotional and briskly paced. I have had some experience of teaching the concepts and presentation style to students. The paper *Time to Think: A Cognitive Model of Offender Rehabilitation and Delinquency Prevention* (1990) written by Ross and Fabiano is a useful introductory text to the concepts of the programme for a student. My observations would suggest that a student can quite quickly acquire the concepts, and with supervision and practice learn to deliver the programme effectively. Since 1991 the Mid Glamorgan Probation Service has used this programme and research by Raynor and Vanstone (1994) revealed that those who successfully completed the programme had lower re-conviction rates than comparable offenders receiving custodial sentences.

The teaching curriculum

The curriculum I have developed to teach the student about the research and methods outlined in this chapter are informed by my understanding of adult learning theory and the recognised learning style and needs of the individual student. On the basis of this a learning curriculum may take the following form. In the first month of the placement I would provide the student with information about the key 'what works' research material which is in written and audio/visual form. Discussion in supervision would seek to assist the student to pull out the main principles from the research material and to ascertain whether the student had grasped a basic understanding of the main theoretical principles. The process of then relating theory to practice becomes important. I would envisage that the student's involvement in groupwork would come later in the placement as the core skills of a probation officer, for example, report writing, case supervision and court work would initially be the main priority. A probation student, whether first or second-year, is initially allocated about three cases and from these it would be possible for the student to select a case on which the techniques of motivational interviewing could be employed. It is likely that there will be times when the student will encounter difficulties in engaging the offender, who may present as resistant, hostile, unmotivated and coerced. This can be anxiety provoking, frustrating and undermining for the student. Motivational interviewing can be a useful model to overcome such difficulties as it requires the worker to enter the offender's frame of reference for it is the offender who must express concerns and the arguments for change.

Through reading, discussion and role play in supervision and direct observation of motivational interviewing techniques the student should quite early on in the placement reach a stage at which they feel confident to try out the techniques. Supervision of this by the practice teacher from the outset would be crucial. The linking of theory to practice, encouragement and support of the student's work and an opportunity for reflective learning and discussion of practical ideas for consolidating and furthering the work with the offender will be key issues for supervision. Also as the work progresses critical evaluation by the student of their work is important and this would include the impact of the work on the student. I request the student to produce process recordings and audio/visual recordings of their work in order for a thorough assessment of the student's knowledge, skills and feelings about the work to be made.

The very nature of groupwork makes it high profile, both to the client group and colleagues. This can be a daunting experience for a student and understandably is likely to raise some anxieties. The Reasoning and Rehabilitation programme in my local area is targeted on serious, high-risk offenders as an alternative to a custodial sentence. The sessions are of three hours in duration and held once a week in the evening. Levels of client energy, interest and co-operation, motivation and ability differ which makes it difficult for a group-leader always to get it right. This can feel particularly pertinent for a student who is being assessed. I believe that co-worker and practice teacher support, encouragement and direct, honest feedback is vital if a student is to begin to feel confident as a groupworker in a probation setting where authority and boundaries are frequently challenged. A benefit of starting the groupwork experience later in the placement is that the student will have begun to consolidate skills learnt and feel more confident in the role of the probation officer. The gender and ethnic origin of the student/co-worker is also worth considering here. Probation group members in my local area tend to be predominantly white and male and it is likely that a female or black worker may be the only woman and/or black person in the group. It would be important to explore this with the student and to encourage the student to recognise and acknowledge the impact of this on them. Although being the only woman in a group of men can feel particularly pertinent when working with perpetrators of sexual offences, my experience is that issues are just as likely to surface in other groups. There are different, but equally important, gender issues for a male worker, for example, male co-leaders may be drawn into colluding with some group members' sexist, discriminatory attitudes and comments. This can cause internal conflict, as the male worker seeks to empathise and get 'alongside' group members, whilst adequately supporting a female co-worker and promoting anti-discriminatory practice. It would be important for a black student working in a predominantly white area with a white practice teacher to have access, if desired, to an organisation such as the National Association of Black Probation Officers.

Prior to joining the group I would expect the student to have demonstrated an ability to apply cognitive behavioural and structural casework approaches in individual work, and to have read and obtained a working knowledge of the concepts and programme material in the reasoning and rehabilitation programme. Initially, I would propose that the student join the group as an observer/participator. This would enable the student to meet and begin to build a relationship with what is likely to be an established group and become familiar with the programme style of delivery and distinct atmosphere. Gradually the student would be encouraged to present some of the material to the group and as time passes increasingly assume the role of co-leader. In my experience it is difficult to predict how long this process might take as the student's previous experience of groupwork, confidence and abilities vary. However, I would hope that by the end of the placement the student would feel confident as a qualified worker to run groups, an expanding area of work in the probation service. As a groupworker it is likely that I would have an opportunity to directly observe the student in a groupwork role and/or co-lead a group. I would also use video recordings of sessions to enable the student to reflect on their practice and in supervision discuss with the student their progress and areas for further learning and development.

Conclusion

In a climate of efficiency savings and a search for evaluation effectiveness the Home Office and the probation service are increasingly expecting staff to develop a practitioner evaluation culture. Whilst the Home Office and a growing band of academics appreciate the value of 'what works' evidence, government thinking seeks greater use of custody and longer prison sentences. It would seem that the only way forward for the probation service in these troubled times is to demonstrate its effectiveness constantly by understanding the 'what works' theory base and applying cognitive behavioural and structural casework approaches in practice. In order to be able to apply theory to practice it is vital that students become familiar with the concepts involved and through both university and practice-based learning develop the required skills. I believe that the role of practice teacher is crucial in this process if students are to leave training courses equipped with the knowledge and practical skills to effectively challenge offending behaviour and reduce recidivism.

References

Andrews *et al.* (1990) 'Does correctional treatment work? A clinically relevant and psychologically informed meta analysis.' *Criminology 28*, 369–404.

Brody, S. (1976) *The Effectiveness of Sentencing*. Home Office Research Study No. 35. London: HMSO.

Fischer, J. (1973) 'Is casework effective? A review.' *Social Work 18*, 5–20.

Fischer, J. (1978) 'Does anything work?' *Journal of Social Service Research 3*, 213–243.

Lipsey, M.W. (1995) 'What do we learn from 400 research studies on the effectiveness of treatment with juvenile delinquents?' In J. Maguire (ed) *What Works? – Effective Methods to Reduce Re-Offending*. Chichester: J. Wiley and Sons.

Lipton, D. *et al.* (1975) *The Effectiveness of Correctional Treatment: A Survey of Treatment Evaluation Studies*. New York: Praeger.

Martinson, R. (1974) 'What works? – questions and answers about prison reform.' *The Public Interest 10*, 22–54.

Prochaska, J.O. and Di Clemente, C.C. (1984) *The Trans-Theoretical Approach: Crossing Traditional Boundaries of Therapy*. Homewood, IL: Dow-Jones.

Raynor, P. and Vanstone, M. (1994) *Straight Thinking on Probation: Third Interim Report*. Bridgend: Mid Glamorgan Probation Service.

Ross, R. and Fabiano, E. (1990) *Time to Think: A Cognitive Model of Offender Rehabilitation and Delinquency Prevention*. Johnson City: Institute of Social Sciences and Arts.

Russell, M.N. (1990) *Clinical Social Work*. Newbury Park: Sage Publications.

Further reading

Bochel, D. (1976) *Probation and After Care*. Edinburgh: Scottish Academic Press Ltd.

Ford, K. and Jones, A. (1987) *Student Supervision*. Basingstoke: Macmillan.

Hawkins, P. and Shohet, R. (1989) *Supervision in the Helping Professions: An Individual Group and Organisational Approach*. Milton Keynes: OU Press.

Lishman, J. (ed) (1994) *Handbook of Theory for Practice Teachers in Social Work*. London: Jessica Kingsley Publishers.

Maguire, J. (1994) *The Principles of What Works* . Notes of the Greater Manchester Probation Service Staff Conference.

Maguire, J. (1995) *What Works: Reducing Reoffending: Guidelines from Research and Practice*. Chichester: John Wiley.

Raynor, P. *et al.* (1994) *Effective Probation Practice*. Basingstoke: BASW, Macmillan.

Walker, H. and Beaumont, B. (1988) *Working with Offenders*. Basingstoke: BASW, Macmillan.

CHAPTER 10

Student Placements in Agencies Undergoing Significant Change

Challenges and Learning Opportunities

Tina Cox

Introduction

My first thought when asked to take a student on placement was that this was completely the wrong time. It followed a period of significant change involving the merger of two teams, the appointment of two new local managers, a change of office and associated loss of contact with colleagues in adult services who had previously shared accommodation. Individual workers experienced each change differently but all had felt loss in some way.

My second thought, however, was that the new team appeared to be working well and amicably, that change is inevitable in the current climate and that an essential aspect of social work is helping clients come to terms with change. Perhaps there was a way of capitalising on what was happening in the team and making it a part of a student's learning. I started therefore to look at the wider aspects of change and to relate them to the factors that make a successful student placement and how this might match up to CCETSW's competence framework for the qualifying social worker.

Since local authority social services departments were set up in 1970 following the Seebohm report (1968) change has been an almost continuous feature within the profession, starting with the first steps towards a mixed economy of welfare under Labour in the late 1970s and intensifying under the Conservative governments of the 1980s (Langan 1993).

Pressure has come from above in the form of legislation, most notably the Children Act 1989 and the 1990 NHS and Community Care Act. These introduced the ideas of a purchaser/provider split, specialised services for each client group and multi-disciplinary working. At the same time a new culture has developed with an emphasis on 'good housekeeping' brought in from the private sector. The result has been a relatively small number of specialist workers undertaking assessments while a larger number provide packages of care (Langan 1993).

Pressure from within and below has come from radical social workers positing that deviant behaviour is socially determined and social work is part of state oppression (Corrigan and Leonard 1978; Bolger *et al.* 1981; Jones 1983) and from collective action through community, trade union and political organisations representing a variety of oppressed and minority groups. A number of their findings have been influential in the development of the concept of anti-discriminatory practice.

Demand for social work has increased with the rise in homelessness, poverty, family breakdown, racial attacks and so on but local governments' powers to respond have been curtailed through, for example, ratecapping and the ban on using proceeds of council house sales to build replacements (Langan 1993).

All this has been set against the background of public perception and tabloid newspaper coverage portraying social workers as 'wimps or bullies' with the latter predominating as child sexual abuse has become increasingly visible, and in particular following the removal from home of a large number of children in Cleveland in 1987 (Langan 1993).

Today's students will therefore inevitably need to learn how to cope within an ever changing organisational context.

The changes in my organisation were structural only. The work itself did not change and the effect on clients was indirect, for example time spent moving office led to unfortunate delays in casework. In other placement settings students may find the nature of the work itself has changed from what they were expecting – or, in some cases, prepared for. For example some students have felt confused, or even cheated, when the placement team's focus on longer-term therapeutic work has shifted to short-term assessment and ongoing work is transferred elsewhere.

Finally, although this chapter looks at constructive ways of managing and learning from change, it should be remembered that some proposed changes will be detrimental, whether to users or workers or both. Such change should *not* be accepted or accommodated and should be resisted, if necessary via a trade union, tribunal, user group or professional body. The ability to recognise when the limit has been reached and the resolve to carry out appropriate action form a crucial part of a social worker's development of professional competence.

Implementing change

All change starts with someone identifying a problem or an improvement. While even self-selected and life-enhancing change is stressful and involves loss at some level, factors such as who makes the initial identification, when and why and which model of change is used, all determine whether change will be implemented and if so whether it will be successful.

Within social work the initiative could come from national government, the employer (whether local government or a private organisation) or internally from managers or workers, and problems fall largely into two areas: shortcomings or suggested improvements in practice, and budgetary considerations.

Models of change are broadly similar but with differing emphases on particular stages. Dyer (1977) focuses on the tasks for those proposing change. An ongoing circular process occurs involving identification of a problem, data gathering, diagnosis, planning, implementation and evaluation leading to identification of a new problem and so on. Young (1986) explores further the degree, nature and timing of consultation varying in stages from the proposer making a sole decision which others accept, through to a joint decision by the proposer and others. Dryden and Hill's (1993) adaptation of Prochaska and DiClemente's (1986) model for organisational change highlights how to maximise employee involvement and counter resistance by precontemplation (gathering data from employees); contemplation (presenting, discussing and analysing data); determination (assessing support for change); action (developing a plan for change and a measure for progress); maintenance (encouraging discussion and monitoring) and relapse (studying and learning from inevitable setbacks).

Whichever model is selected, certain factors will maximise the chances of successful implementation. Social services are still in general arranged in a hierarchy of senior managers, intermediate managers, 'frontline' workers and service users. The position of those within each level, their individual style, previous knowledge of the change and degree of opportunity to influence it will all have a trickle-down effect on those below them in the hierarchy.

Hughes and Pengelly (1997) describe a 'triangle of tension' for senior managers who have to make decisions in relation to service users on behalf of the electorate, with both groups having needs, rights and wants. The three constraints are political (policy and finance); professional (assessed needs and statutory duties); and financial (actual budget and resources). Each organisation has its boundary with external influences including politics, finance, law, society and media, professions, pressure groups and other agencies, while internally there is its own particular hierarchy.

The further up the hierarchy change is proposed, the greater will be the need for consultation with intermediate managers and 'frontline' staff. Intermediate managers will need to be able to convince staff that the change was necessary and that all other possible courses of action were ruled out before arriving at the particular decision. If, however, intermediate managers have had change imposed on them it is vital that they acknowledge and accept their feelings about this.

The more open managers can be with staff below them, the more frontline staff will feel their own feelings and reactions are given validity. They will then be more likely to own the need for change, will be committed to implementing the change and will be able to take into account factors which affect their daily work but which may not be known to those at the top of the structure. Even if it is not possible for staff to have any choice in the decision itself then they need to be involved as much as possible in the details of the implementation.

Students are in theory outside the formal hierarchy of the organisation. In practice, in terms of power and influence, unless they are unusually confident they are probably at a level below basic grade workers and above clients and users. The student's ability to utilise the learning opportunities will depend on the position in the hierarchy of their practice teacher; the practice teacher's influence on and/or accommodation of the change; the practice teacher's ability to draw on their own feelings to enrich theoretical discussions with the student and facilitate learning about change; and the timing of the student's arrival, whether before, during or after the change and the effect this has on their opportunity to influence the change.

Coping with change

In order to understand fully the effects of changes in working practices or environments it is helpful to look at why people work and in particular why people choose social work.

Woodcock and Francis (1984) identified six areas of motivation for workers: working environment; remuneration; security; personal development; involvement; and interest and challenge.

In a 1994 survey, *Community Care Magazine* asked social workers why they had chosen social work. Sixty-six per cent said it suited their talents and skills, 53 per cent desired to help oppressed or disadvantaged people, 40 per cent were attracted by the perceived job satisfaction and 21 per cent wanted to express their political or religious beliefs in practice. Only 7 per cent were attracted by career prospects and 2 per cent by the financial rewards.

Students in particular begin their placements with high expectations of being able to help their clients. The discrepancy between these high expectations and the reality of limited resources has to be managed sensitively by the practice teacher.

Changes that are based in ideology, for example those which are led by the wish to improve service delivery to clients or increase opportunity for workers' personal development are most likely to win support from workers whereas those which are imposed because of financial restraints will be hardest for workers to accept.

Marris (1974) describes three types of change: incremental or substitutional changes which pursue the same purposes as previously; changes that involve growth; and those that represent loss. Individuals will ascribe change to a category depending on the meaning they attribute to it. Workers at different levels within the organisation may ascribe roles to each other of 'Persecutor, Rescuer and Victim' and become entrenched in these positions (Karpman 1968) or fall into two camps: the 'old breed', who may experience more loss, identify strongly with the past and find it difficult to move on, and the 'new breed' who may experience some loss but find enough positive aspects in the change to enable them to look to the future. Those in either camp may still experience 'survivor guilt' following the redundancies of colleagues (Hughes and Pengelly 1997).

In addition to the above factors relating to a specific change, an individual's response to change will be influenced by their personality, how they react to stress in general and their life experiences.

People react to stress in different ways and may experience extremes of emotions. Some people are able to express these emotions openly and assertively and this provides a healthy and positive outlet. On the other hand, unfocused and uncontrolled anger over a period of time could be damaging. Others might show reduced levels of emotion or adopt a strategy of 'wait and see' which might be an assertive choice initially, but a suppression of deeply held feelings may be damaging in the longer term.

In addition a person's attitude to change will be based on other experiences during their lifespan. Rutter (1981) would argue that the quality of early relationships and subsequent experiences of separation and loss have a profound effect on how change is experienced. Other factors will include the level of personal resilience at the start of each change; the number and variety of changes; the extent to which they were able to express their feelings about each change and receive appropriate support; how previous changes were experienced; the extent to which previous changes have been resolved; and their personal style, for example the meaning they attach to work and authority.

Despite these differences in individual perception the experience of change follows common patterns for all individuals across a wide range of situations.

Dryden and Hill (1993) describe resistance to change as 'a normal outgrowth or consequence of an individual's thinking and not as some kind of psychological aberration' and stress the need for those affected by change to be part of the process in order to foster 'psychological commitment' to its implementation and success.

Different individuals within an organisation may have their own perceptions about its purpose and role and these perceptions may be similar or divergent depending on the levels of internal communication. Lawrence (1977) differentiated between the 'normative primary task' (the official task), the 'existential primary task' (what staff believe they are doing) and the 'phenomenal primary task' (what staff can actually be observed to be doing). In times of frequent or repeated change, the opportunities are greatly increased for misunderstandings and disagreements around these categories.

Workers who remain unconvinced of the necessity for change, who feel that managers could have done more to resist change, and those who suffer a real or perceived loss, may react in a similar way, although usually to a lesser degree, to those suffering loss or bereavement in their personal lives, passing through certain classic stages. These stages, which are passed through at different speeds and with some revisiting, are shock and denial, yearning, despair, and acceptance (Lishman 1994). A good practice teacher will be aware of the stage they have reached and will recognise when might, or might not, be a good time to have a student.

The loss or perceived loss can take many forms: loss of work with a particular client group; specific skills with that group; variety in the work; colleagues previously worked with; the workplace; local amenities; a manager; the ability to help clients if resources are rationalised; a sense of value if the worker's feelings and wishes have been ignored.

Lack of meaningful input into the decision-making process and implementation of change is not just counter-productive in terms of the way it affects service delivery to clients and the difficulties it causes for management and management/staff relations; it is also harmful to workers' health. Research has shown that workers' participation in decision making and goal setting leads to feelings of acceptance and commitment and, ultimately, enhanced performance and productivity. Dissatisfaction with working conditions and feeling under-valued was the factor most closely related to depression, escapist drinking, overall poor physical health and shortened life expectancy (Pfeiffer and Goodstein 1984).

A team is likely to come through change stronger and better able to offer a good student placement if they accept the need for change, feel that senior management has done all it could to resist the change, have been fully consulted about its implementation and have been given a chance to monitor the outcome of the change.

Having said this, a team that has had a negative experience of change may still be able to offer a successful placement if it has pulled together in solidarity against other forces and is able to be welcoming and democratic rather than afraid and closed.

The practice teacher

An essential task of the practice teacher if they are to ensure a successful placement despite the instability of the team in which it is located, is to pick the 'right' student! In reality of course practice teachers are not able to choose their student and attempts to match students to placements are often hampered by organisational constraints and shortages of student placements. Where possible, however, careful consideration should be given to the personality, learning style and stage of learning of a student considering a placement in an agency where there is or has been significant change. The student's feelings about this placement and their general level of resilience will be particularly influenced by their experience in any previous placement, their expectations of the proposed placement including how much real choice they had in accepting or refusing it, the extent of their prior knowledge of or contact with the agency and whether they arrive before, during or after a change. A pre-placement meeting could begin to explore these issues before the final decision is made as to whether or not to proceed.

In reflecting on whether placements undergoing significant change can work, it is crucial to consider the skills and attributes of the practice teacher themselves. What makes an effective practice teacher, given the recent shift in perspective regarding this role, and what type of practice teacher is most likely to be able to come through a period of significant change with sufficient energy and enthusiasm to offer a placement and help a student maximise the learning experience?

The most prominent teachers in the ancient world were teachers of adults and learning was seen as an active process with the student being jointly responsible. Many different cultures followed this method for some centuries. In seventh-century Europe, however, boys' religious schools were set up which discouraged independent enquiry in favour of acceptance of Christian doctrines and beliefs. This educational model of 'pedagogy' (from the Greek for 'leader of children') persisted in this country until after World War I when ideas began to emerge about adult learning and how this differs from the ways in which children learn.

Knowles (1990) developed the themes first put forward by Lindeman (1926): in general adults are motivated to learn by their needs and interests; their orientation to learning is life-centred; their learning is based in their experiences; they need to be self-directing and to engage in mutual enquiry with the teacher; and they have individual preferences relating to age, style, time, place and pace of learning.

There has been a parallel shift in social work education away from the model of the student as an apprentice learning from a supervisor, towards the worker as practice teacher responsible for managing and facilitating a learning experience. The practice teacher needs to have a high level of self-awareness of their own values, strengths and weaknesses, to be committed to their own continuing self-development and to be able to facilitate the student's learning rather than act as an 'expert' passing on pearls of wisdom.

In Neil Thompson's (1990) 'H5W' framework (how, who, what, where, when, why), responsibility for learning is shared primarily between practice teacher and student but also with colleagues and clients. Learning takes place everywhere, linking theory and practice with the student's personal life, knowledge, experience and values. Students should be helped to link the experiences of the team undergoing change to their own personal experiences as well as their clients' situation. Practice teaching is necessary, according to Thompson, because it brings theory to life, it provides a protected environment for ideas to be tried out and for values and beliefs to be explored and challenged, and students can learn how to use effective supervision to begin the process of self-evaluation and development that should continue throughout their career.

The balancing act to which Hughes and Pengelly (1997) liken the supervisory task, 'a balancing act...between checking through every case and detailed discussion of one or two...between ensuring agency policies are followed and attending to workers' emotional responses to the work', becomes more critical in times of change. It may be extremely difficult for the permanent team members to give proper weight to both process and task and even more so for a student who lacks part or all of the information, knowledge, experience and perspective of colleagues. It falls to the practice teacher to provide a level of 'containment' (Bion 1970) for the student to enable the coherent thought to take place which will lead to both personal learning and constructive work with clients. The work of Schön also has relevance here. He identified four professional roles: the expert (knowledge-based), managerial (involved in planning and allocation), practical (oriented to problem solving) and the reflective practitioner. This latter is someone who 'recognises the limits of professional knowledge and action, builds in a cycle of critical reflection to maximise the capacity for critical thought' (Schön 1988). While his original work was directed towards worker–client relationships it has relevance on a number of levels within the practice teaching context. Enabling the development of the student's reflective practice is a key practice teaching task.

In times of change the practice teacher more than ever needs to be clear about their authority. Sawdon and Sawdon (1995) refer to the work of both Pettes (1967) who categorised authority as administrative authority, authority based in knowledge and that derived from personality, and Payne and Scott (1982) who developed this theme of authority (here in the context of worker and client) as administrative (legalistic), sapiental (derived from wisdom or experience) and the authority of relevance (arising from the possession of knowledge relevant to the client's own feeling of well-being). Just as the use of authority is central to the duties of the social worker in the protection of vulnerable clients, so it is an essential aspect of the practice teacher role. It ensures the learning programme is well planned and thoroughly undertaken. An understanding and acceptance of the authority role by the practice teacher provides the student with some stability in what might be an unstable learning environment and ensures a clarity of roles. The constructive use of authority is crucial in fostering the student's self-development and self-management.

A worker who has undergone recent changes at work and is considering offering a student placement will need to consider their current situation and carefully examine their motives giving particular regard to issues of confidence, power and the general relationships within the team.

Someone who has recently been involved in planning, implementing and monitoring change and who has regarded change as positive or resolved any negative feelings is likely to be mentally prepared to examine their own working practices and those of a student. On the other hand, someone who feels that change has been imposed, regards it negatively or retains feelings of resentment may feel under-valued and lack the confidence, energy and detachment to be an effective practice teacher until these feelings have been dealt with. They may feel that their way of working is the only certainty they have left and try to pass this on to a student in a dogmatic way. They may perceive the change as a loss of power and offer to take a student as a way of regaining this power. The worker's own supervisor should be involved in facilitating this self-analysis and in the final decision as to whether or not to offer a student placement.

The relationship between the practice teacher, colleagues and managers after the change is crucial if a placement is to succeed. Good relationships will mean the practice teacher feels secure in their own position within the team. The student will not be caught up in negative team dynamics and the practice teacher will not be tempted to be precious about 'my student' or use the student as an ally against the rest of the team. It will also mean that the student feels at ease consulting and learning from all members of the team and is not over-dependent on the practice teacher.

A key element of the social work task lies in helping people to identify problems and use their own resources to change, with outside help if necessary. The practice teacher will need to be able to help the student to use what they learn from any change, whether initiated by the student or imposed, to increase their own confidence and professional competence and to guide clients through the same process.

Learning opportunities

In *Assuring Quality in the Diploma in Social Work: 1* (1996) CCETSW recognises that 'Social workers practice in a society of complexity, change and diversity...' (p.16) and lists six core competences which encompass the necessary knowledge, values and skills essential to effective practice and which the student must satisfactorily demonstrate in order to pass the placement. These competences – communicate and engage; promote and enable; assess and plan; intervene and provide services; work in organisations; develop professional competence – in many ways reflect the skills needed to work effectively in the different stages of the change process – identification of problem; data gathering; diagnosis; planning; implementation; evaluation. This is because working with change lies at the heart of social work practice. Social workers work with clients and service users at times of crisis both to cope with, and to effect, change. The nature of social work itself, and the organisations within which it is located, have changed as they respond to fundamental political, economic and legislative changes in the wider society.

If we are effectively to prepare students for practice, then we must prepare them for working with change in all its aspects. Where the practice teacher and team have worked through many of the issues already discussed within this chapter, a placement located in a setting undergoing change has the potential to provide excellent learning opportunities to understand and work with the change process, and to help the student become an effective change agent in both direct work with service users and within the organisation.

The range of learning opportunities the placement affords will depend on the current phase of the change process. Where the team is involved in early stages of problem identification and information gathering, the student will be able to participate in discussions around the problem, whether it is in fact a problem and whether the problem in question or a different problem should have priority for attention. There will be many opportunities to 'communicate and engage' with key members of the organisation itself (often one positive effect of turbulence is increased communication between colleagues), other agencies and service users, to obtain information regarding the proposed changes and to discuss potential effects on different groups both in the organisations and in the community. The results of those communications will then be used to 'assess and plan'.

Social auditing and community profiling are increasingly being used in relation to the planning and delivery of services and this is reflected in CCETSW's Practice Requirements. A phrase such as 'identify and evaluate the key economic...cultural...environmental and political factors which impact on the service and its users' lends itself to the need to engage in work which has a wider remit than individual casework affords. 'Communicating effectively' and 'networking relationships' are phrases which invite the student social worker to consider a range of methods of communication to generate information about the needs of the community: telephone surveys, written questionnaires and exercises, group discussions, inter-agency meetings and consultations with users each requiring different levels of complexity and formality. Where a student is encouraged to be a part of the early stages of the change process, then many learning opportunities for liaising with, and understanding the differing needs of, a range of sectors of society are opened up.

Underlying all the work done by the student will be the need to demonstrate anti-discriminatory practice, and there are learning opportunities in this area throughout the whole process of change. Past and present institutionalised inequalities, for instance around race, gender, sexuality, age and disability, have influenced which people are currently in positions of power and therefore able to initiate change. Within minority or oppressed groups issues of gender, age, language and poverty may affect who receives information about proposed change and therefore who has an input to decisions about whether change occurs and if so how it is implemented. The impact of any imposed change will be disproportionately felt by those who are already disadvantaged and whole communities may feel themselves to be outside the sphere of influence. The practice teacher, student and clients may have particular needs depending on their individual circumstances and these needs may conflict and will need to be explicitly addressed in supervision.

Within the competence 'Intervene and provide services' CCETSW highlights the importance of supporting individuals through the process of change. This entails assisting them to 'express their emotional needs through the process of change', providing 'emotional support to sustain' them through the change, and helping them manage conflicts which may occur between them and other parts of their family or community. Working effectively with people undergoing change also calls for regular review and evaluation.

The most powerful method of teaching how to help clients through change is by the practice teacher modelling an enabling role where the process of change is openly on the agenda and feelings are acknowledged and validated. The practice teacher may draw on examples from their own practice or from their own response to, and feelings generated by, the change to facilitate an exploration of student feelings. This may include unforeseen consequences of working in a team undergoing change which were not addressed in pre-placement meetings and which may include, for example, discomfort the student is experiencing because of holding different views about the change from those in the team or from the practice teacher.

The practice teacher may be in a dilemma, trying to model a way of working with change that is not being modelled in the organisation as a whole. Too often practitioners feel that they have not been a part of the initial phases of change and that changes have been imposed with insufficient consultation with those who will be most affected, the practitioners themselves and the service users. Minimal attention may be paid to the feelings and experiences of those at the sharp end of the changes.

CCETSW is clear that a competent worker is one who 'promote[s] opportunities for people to use their own strengths and expertise to enable them to meet responsibilities, secure rights and achieve change' (Core Competence Promote and Enable). An important element of this is assisting users to 'participate in decision-making'. Key social work principles of partnership and empowerment must underpin all work with clients. The practice teacher will strive to ensure these principles are a part of the practice teaching relationship and would hope that such principles have been applied within the organisation itself. Whether or not this is the case, a skilled practice teacher will be able to help the student make connections between the student's involvement in the change process in the organisation and the effects this has on the student's work with the client, for example how far the client is being empowered to function and fully participate in the decision-making process.

Making the connections between the student's world and the client's world generates opportunities to consider whether feelings of negativity and powerlessness are unconsciously being transferred onto the client or whether parallels induce empathy and stimulate the student's renewed attempts to involve the client as fully as possible in any change. The student should be invited to draw parallels between the problem-solving strategies being adopted by the team and those that may be relevant in their clients' lives while at the same time demonstrating an ability to separate their own experience and feelings from those of their clients.

The role of the practice teacher will also be to ensure the student is familiar with the stages of change and the loss and grief process and to integrate this theoretical material into discussions of the experiences of the team and the student as well as their clients.

The competence identified by CCETSW as 'contribute to the work of the organisation' involves student social workers being able to demonstrate capacity to work as an accountable and effective member of the organisation and contributing to the planning, monitoring and control of resources as well as the evaluation of their effectiveness. The latter is achieved by 'seeking feedback' from colleagues, other agencies and service users. Where change has already been implemented students could be encouraged to evaluate and review the changes. When seeking feedback from those within the agency students should ask specifically about colleagues' feelings about the change, whether it was comparable to other changes they have experienced and in what ways, how the change could have been handled differently, and what strategies for coping with change were found to be most effective. In this way a tremendous amount of learning about change can be gleaned.

Students are also expected to 'facilitate [service users] to make suggestions about improvements to services'. Where changes to service delivery have occurred that service users have not found sympathetic to their needs this may entail helping the client use the complaints procedures. The practice teaching sessions may be the vehicle for ensuring the student is not only clear about the client's rights and procedures to make challenges and complaints, but also their and their colleagues' own channels for addressing concern about the process and outcomes of change.

Developing 'Professional competence', CCETSW's sixth core competence, is measured in the way the student social worker conducts themselves in the work with service users, within supervision, in the team, and within the wider organisation. Time management and stress management, two essential skills CCETSW identifies, may be particularly put to the test in times of change and unrest. The practice teacher will need to address these explicitly within supervision. Students should be encouraged to identify their own strengths and resources to counteract the effects of stress, as well as being made aware of counselling services offered by the agency or educational establishment.

However, I would argue that preparing student social workers for social work in the new millennium demands more than helping them 'cope' with change. It requires helping them learn how to influence that change. Ensuring they are given the means – team meeting minutes, internal memoranda and even highlights of the organisational gossip (often a powerful influence on proceedings!) – to participate fully in team discussions is important. Students who work on placement only a portion of the week are, like part-time workers, apt to miss out on vital new events or information and practice teachers need to be mindful of this to ensure students are not marginalised.

But there is still a wider understanding of the changing nature of society and social work that is essential if student social workers are to be enabled to engage in and inform the public, political and professional debates about social work and its future which are shaping services at a local level. Being located in a team which is experiencing the ramifications of these wider shifts in public and political perceptions of the welfare state's response to need gives an excellent opportunity to debate the issues in the practice teaching sessions, within the team and at other levels including Council Committees. The practice teacher should encourage the student to make use of resources held in the educational establishment to further this wider exploration of political debate.

Conclusion

A student even in the most stable of placements needs to be able to live with uncertainty, accept that no one knows all the answers, have the confidence to weigh up all the different opinions, look below the surface of a situation and form their own judgement. A student who is not yet at this level of ability might well perform badly in any placement but it would be unfair to load the dice against them from the start and these uncertainties may well be multiplied considerably in an agency which is undergoing or has recently undergone significant change.

Even if a student is capable of critical analysis and forming an independent judgement, their confidence to express these openly may be stifled in a team with 'unfinished business' arising from change and where there may be an atmosphere of resentment.

I would suggest that a student placement during, or immediately after, a time of change is most likely to succeed if:

- the change has been well managed, that is, it was brought in after due consultation, the reason was understood by staff, and staff were involved in the implementation

- staff viewed the change as positive or had the opportunity to express any negative reactions

- the change contributed to team building and resulted in a welcoming and democratic atmosphere

- the practice teacher is at ease in the role of facilitator, has resolved any issues arising from the change and is committed to drawing out the specific learning opportunities available

- the student is able to cope with uncertainty and to accept joint responsibility for their own learning experience and is relatively mature and self-confident

- the change is viewed in its wider context of structural, political and organisational change, is explicitly addressed and used in the placement as a learning opportunity to engage in wider debates about social work in the new millennium.

References

Bion, W.R. (1970) *Attention and Interpretation.* London: Tavistock.

Bolger, S. *et al.* (1981) *Towards Socialist Welfare Work.* Basingstoke: Macmillan.

CCETSW (1996) *Assuring Quality in the Diploma in Social Work: 1.* London: CCETSW.

Community Care Magazine (issue no. 1054, 9–15 February 1995) *Social Worker Survey 1994.*

Corrigan, P. and Leonard, P. (1978) *Social Work Practice Under Capitalism: A Marxist Approach.* Basingstoke: Macmillan.

Dryden, W. and Hill, L. (1993) *Innovations in Rational-Emotive Therapy.* Sage Publications.

Dyer, W. (1977) *Team Building: Issues and Alternatives.* Newbury Park, CA: Addison-Wesley Publishing.

Hughes, L. and Pengelly, P. (1997) *Staff Supervision in a Turbulent Environment: Managing Process and Task in Front-Line Services.* London: Jessica Kingsley Publishers.

Jones, C. (1983) *State Social Work and the Working Class.* Basingstoke: Macmillan.

Karpman, S. (1968) 'Fairy tales and script drama analysis' *TAB 7*, 26, 39.

Knowles, M. (1990) *The Adult Learner: A Neglected Species.* Houston: Follett Publishing Co.

Langan, M. (1993) In J. Clarke (ed) *A Crisis in Care?* London: Sage/OUP.

Lawrence, W. (1977) 'Management development...some ideals, images and realities.' In A. Colman and M. Geller (eds) (1985) *Group Relations Reader 2.* Washington DC: The A.K. Rice Institute.

Lindeman, E. (1926) *The Meaning of Adult Education.* New York: New Republic.

Lishman, J. (ed) (1994) *Handbook of Theory for Practice Teachers in Social Work.* London: Jessica Kingsley Publishers.

Marris, P. (1974) *Loss and Change.* London: Routledge and Kegan Paul.

Payne, C. and Scott, T. (1982) *Developing Supervision of Teams in Field and Residential Work.*

Pettes, D. (1967) *Supervision in Social Work.* London: Allen and Unwin.

Pfeiffer, J. and Goodstein, L. (1984) *The 1984 Annual Developing Human Resources.* San Diego, CA: University Associates Inc.

Prochaska, J.O. and Di Clemente, C.C. (1986) 'Toward a comprehensive model of change.' In W.R. Miller and N. Heather (eds) *Treating Addictive Behaviour: Processes of Change.* New York: Plenum.

Rutter, M. (1981) *Maternal Deprivation Reassessed* (Second Edition). Harmondsworth: Penguin.

Sawdon, C. and Sawdon, D. (1995) 'The supervision partnership – a whole greater than the sum of its parts.' In J. Pritchard (ed) *Good Practice in Supervision.* London: Jessica Kingsley Publishers.

Schön, D. (1988) *Educating the Reflective Practitioner.* London: Jossey Bass.

Seebohm Report, The (1968) *Report of the Committee on Local Authority and Allied Personal Social Services,* Cmnd 3703. London: HMSO.

Thompson, N. (1990) 'More than a supervisor – the developing role of the practice teacher.' *Journal of Training and Development.*

Woodcock, M. and Francis, D. (1984) *The Unblocked Manager: A Practical Guide to Self-Development.* Aldershot: Gower.

Young, A. (1986) *The Managers Handbook: The Practical Guide to Successful Management.* Sphere Books.

CHAPTER 11

'On Shifting Sands'

Student Social Workers' Experiences of Working in Multi-Disciplinary Medical Teams

Andy Mantell

Introduction

Recent developments in health and social care policy following legislation such as the National Health Service and Community Care Act 1990 have had enormous impact on the roles and responsibilities of social workers working within adult services. New multi-disciplinary teams have been created in an endeavour to co-ordinate the assessment and provision of services to local communities. Existing teams have had to accommodate changes as care management has called for changes of role and shifting emphases of social work practice. In the hospital setting in which I worked, for example, there has been a shift away from more 'traditional social casework' to assessment and effecting discharge arrangements. The changing nature of social work itself, taking place within a new context of health and social services reforms can feel like working on shifting sands. The task for the practice teacher working with a student in this setting is providing an anchor for them, and using the opportunities the placement affords to their full advantage.

One central opportunity for the student is to learn about effective inter-disciplinary working. Recent legislation (Children Act 1989, NHS Community Care Act 1990) has been underpinned by the principle of effective inter-agency collaboration and joint working. A recent CCETSW publication has addressed the importance of interprofessional learning as a basis for effective joint working, and has also identified some of the barriers that need to be overcome if different disciplines are to work together successfully. CCETSW states that the history of collaboration between social workers and medical workers has been marked by difficulties, inequality, mistrust and tension since the turn of the century when lady almoner social workers began working in hospitals and were often seen as the doctors' handmaidens.

Drawing on Huntingdon's work CCETSW continues:

> Collaboration between the two professions is further complicated by cultural and organisational differences. The longer history and higher social status and prestige of medicine and the greater numerical size of the profession makes the development of an equal working relationship between the two difficult. (Huntingdon 1981 in CCETSW 1996, p.4)

Jo Connolly, however, robustly argues that such fear of medical domination over social work is outdated: 'The risk of being regarded as medical "handmaidens" in hospital discharge planning must have receded apace with the introduction of reforms in health and welfare policy' (1997, p.299).

Within this chapter I have endeavoured to use the concepts of role and status to unravel some of the difficulties social workers – and student social workers in particular – encounter working within multi-disciplinary medical settings. I have drawn on the comments of a small sample of social work students in a variety of multi-disciplinary medical settings who responded to my questionnaire regarding their perceived role and status in the organisations within which they were placed.

Students need to negotiate a position within a variety of systems whilst on placement. In the hospital setting, for example, social workers work alongside occupational therapists, physiotherapists, nurses and doctors who each have their own systems based on professional culture and practices. The 'role' and 'status' that student social workers are assigned within each system will significantly affect their performance. I will describe the students' experiences within these contexts and use them to identify ways in which practice teachers, tutors and other members of these systems can help them develop firm foundations within these 'shifting sands'.

Role and status

Multi-disciplinary medical teams tend to be complex hierarchically structured systems. An appreciation of the concepts of role and status provides insight into their construction and the interactions between their component members.

A person's role is the 'expected behaviour associated with a particular social position' (Banton 1989, p.714). Their status can be seen as the positive or negative values, privileges and/or rights which are assigned to that social position. Thus the level of someone's status only gains meaning in relation to the status of someone else within that social grouping from whom they demand or give a deferential response (Weber 1922). The assignment of status can be considered to be dependent on a person's position within a social structure (Linton 1936) or negotiated between an individual and his/her audience, with personal characteristics playing an important role (Gerth and Mills 1953).

However, Garfinkel (1956) identified that it is the audience who has the critical role in assigning status. Wolf (1989) also differentiated between 'ascribed' status, for example, race, and 'achieved' status, for example, through educational attainment, although it could be argued that the constantly evolving nature of society blurs such distinctions.

Medical and social perspectives of care in the hospital

Hospitals are examples of environments containing many same-status individuals. Bensman (1972) has noted how such individuals may align in 'status communities' to protect and develop their privileges. Over time these medical status communities have become achievement based at the entry level and have developed what Freidson (1973) termed 'occupational control', enabling them to dictate and self-regulate the roles which they undertake. Medical status communities developed their own natural science orientated culture which has guided the way in which they undertake their roles. This approach concentrated on the treatment of the organic causes of illness and became known as the 'biomedical' or simply, the 'medical' model.

Medical training feeds this approach. Although there is evidence of change, medical education has 'emphasised the teaching of science, biophysical functioning, pathology and an individual clinical approach' (CCETSW 1996, p.4). Teaching methods used are largely didactic and reinforce an approach to patients (and other professionals) which Cunningham and Davis (1985) termed the 'expert model'. This approach assumes that the clinician is the expert in terms of diagnosis and treatment and implicitly that the patient has little to contribute. Davis and Fallowfield (1991) warn that this under-estimation of the patients' input may lead to them being patronised by the clinician. It could be argued that some clinicians also adopt the same approach with professionals from disciplines with different value bases.

Social work education, by contrast, emphasises understanding of human behaviour and the importance of partnership and empowerment models of intervention.

Many students anticipate the different professional perspectives before embarking on their placement and it may lead to additional anxiety. One student social worker noted that:

> I was informed of the possible 'tensions' and conflicts between medical, nursing staff and social workers in terms of their philosophy and values and…the need to have social workers in hospital settings.

Occupational, physio-, speech and language therapy, although sharing the medical and scientific status of doctors and nurses, are too new for their status also to be assigned by their position within the hospital structure. Instead it could be argued that their status corresponds more closely to Gerth and Mills' (1953) concept. Their status is partly a product of their position within the hospital hierarchy but also dependent on the ward's (audience's) perception of their individual attributes and role performance. Their greater dependence on their audience may be a disincentive to their adopting an expert view.

Some clinicians have become increasingly aware of the weaknesses of the 'expert' and 'medical' approaches to illness through their training and practice. Many have been actively pursuing the bio-psycho-social model propounded by Engel (1990), in which the illness is considered not in isolation but instead within the person's psychological and social context. Connolly argues that the current health and social care reforms provide an excellent climate for hospital social workers, 'through regular contact and communication, to educate and influence health care colleagues about the social meaning of health' (1997, p.300). Practice teachers need to capitalise on this changing climate to find ways of developing this educating role.

Changing climate of social work and shifting roles

The Conservative government's 'new culture' based on efficiency, effectiveness and value for money (Yelloly and Henkel 1995) has placed health and social care professions under scrutiny and challenged their occupational control. Yelloly and Henkel argue that 'Social work is one of the most political of all professions. Indeed, it has virtually no role, no identity outside the welfare institutions where it is located' (1995, p.9). Social work is shaped by political ideas and government policies. The impact of the NHS and Community Care

Act 1990 on hospital social work demonstrates well how the role of the social worker shifts with the changing tides of government reform. Younghusband (1981) contends that social work has had a history of rapid change and this affects its sense of boundary and direction. It also lacks an established status community and occupational control, possibly because the élitism inherent in these concepts is at odds with the profession's values of equality and empowerment.

In many authorities the NHS and Community Care Act 1990 has resulted in a change of emphasis in the role of the hospital social worker, away from the counselling role identified by Barclay (1982) and towards that of the social care planner. Where counselling is a legitimate activity in the discharge-planning process it still remains part of the social work role, but longer-term counselling as a discrete piece of work is now seen by many hospital social workers as falling within the remit of 'provider services' and to be contracted out. This may both reflect and reinforce the counselling profession's development of its own status community and occupational control.

The hospital social workers' status is assigned by the ward (audience) on the basis of how they present and their role performance (after Garfinkel 1956). The ward may see the social worker's role differently from that prescribed for them by government statutes. The lack of clarity of role may result in dissonance between patient and other health workers' expectations and social workers' performance. Connolly (1995) noted how much of the social worker's role is a matter of negotiation between the nurses and the social worker. It could be argued that the social worker's basis for negotiation is dependent on the flexibility that s/he is allowed by his/her employer and the status that the ward has assigned to the worker. However, 'the medical imperative for early discharge' (Connolly 1997) and concern about bed-blocking puts pressure on the whole multi-disciplinary team. Social workers can find themselves downplaying social work values and processes and focusing only on the practical tasks necessary to expedite discharge, no longer the social worker but the 'bed clearer'. Pressure to fulfil this role may come from other members of the multi-disciplinary team and/or from management. Pietroni (1995) has highlighted the problems of individual workers and teams being pitted against managers in the organisation. She argues that the quality of team leadership is crucial in the standard of practice that is established: sometimes quality of thought and judgment survives, but commonly individual and team mentally join forces against the management of the organisation who, since quality and inspection units have been introduced, are often seen as part of a general 'more for less' climate rather than the protectors of good practice (1995, p.39).

This represents another interface at which the social work role has to be debated and negotiated. However, a change of role does not necessarily imply a change of status and students need help to own and, working with the team, shape, the new role.

The assessment process pivotal to care management requires an empowering, sensitive approach to all patients, their families and support systems in the planning of their future. New information and procedures can only be grafted onto traditional social work skills, not substituted for them. Jo Connolly (1997) believes care management/discharge planning with clear objectives gives a rigour to social work which may have been lacking. She writes:

> The challenge of 'managing care' instead of cases is significant, linking the critical task of assessing need with the right of the person being assessed to contribute to that assessment and to be involved in decisions about the services to be delivered. It embodies social work principles but widens the resources. (1997, p.298)

The students' experience in multi-disciplinary settings: role

Before undertaking their placement the student social workers will already have developed a notion of the role of the hospital social worker based on their previous experiences and shaped by the teachings of the university. Some of the respondents to my survey were aware that changes in the role of the hospital social worker had taken place, but were unsure of the nature of those changes before their placement began. Their understanding of what to expect ranged from 'foggy' and 'very little' to 'that it would include assessment work, counselling, benefits advice and general social work'.

From their various starting points the students then had to reconcile their understanding with that held by the hospital social work team. Two thirds considered that their perception of their role changed once placement commenced. 'With the onset of community care the focus of the work was assessment of older people which became monotonous with little patient contact, but much paper and telephone work'. Another wrote: 'Although I was able to undertake a variety of tasks it appears that the social work aspect of the role is being eroded in favour of an assessor role'. A practice teacher whose student separates out the assessment role in this way should seize the opportunity to discuss ways of holding on to essential social work values and skills despite changing tasks.

Just over half considered that their role was different from that of the qualified social worker working in the same team. This mainly related to the students having less responsibility and more opportunities to do different types of work, such as counselling and groupwork that were no longer considered to be part of the social worker's role. It must create a disturbing paradox for students to engage in work which they see that their qualified colleagues are not given the opportunity to undertake anymore and I would argue that practice teachers should recognise that a hospital setting now offers different – but equally valuable – learning opportunities such as the skills involved in assessment and interdisciplinary working rather than hanging on to more traditional notions of 'what to give the student'.

The students' experience in multi-disciplinary setting: status

The students' perceived status is critical in the negotiation of their role on the different wards. The students were concerned with the status of social workers generally within the hospital setting, and also their student social work status. One student was surprised at the qualified social worker's ability to prevent the discharge of a patient and another at a psychiatrist's willingness to listen to their (student) opinion. Most students felt that they had the same or more status than social work assistants but less than qualified social workers, yet over half of the students found that ward staff treated them the same as qualified social workers. Those who were treated differently found:

> Once I had spent time on placement, ward staff did begin to be more helpful – but, initially, when I felt unsure of my position, they often kept me waiting and did not readily offer information.

> Ward staff were sometimes less able to discuss serious diagnosis/death/emotionally overwhelming information [with me].

This second statement highlights the ambiguity that wards often feel towards the student until they have 'proved themselves', perhaps by demonstrating an ability to handle issues of death and illness, and negotiated a role within the team.

When the student respondents were asked to rank their status compared to other ward staff they placed themselves below doctors and senior therapists and above student nurses and student occupational therapists. This gives an important indication of the kinds of attitudes and self-perceptions that students bring with them into the hospital placement and practice teachers need to be sensitive to these issues to be able to help their students make effective contributions to multi-disciplinary decision making. Working in a culture where a medical model of illness and treatment dominates, student social workers may feel unsure of the credibility of their value base. An important early learning objective must be the understanding of, and confidence in, social work values which include the consideration of social issues in the causation and treatment of illness, empowerment models of intervention and the rights of individuals to choice and participation in decision making. The practice teacher has a crucial role in helping the student understand and value the contribution these perspectives can have on treatment and rehabilitation. As the placement progresses the practice teacher will be able to help the student take this understanding further, by helping them explain and argue their perspectives within the team. This develops a climate of mutual learning and understanding which must enhance multi-disciplinary working.

Status, then, can be achieved through knowledge and confidence. To help the student through early days of the placement when these attributes are in short supply, the practice teacher should make links with the experience (both personal and work) and resources the student brings to the placement with them. Valuing these skills and facilitating the transferability of learning are essential first practice teaching tasks.

'The informal process of sizing up': the effects of public perceptions, personal experiences and presentation

A number of factors affect what one respondent referred to as the 'informal process of sizing up' and which may be seen as the dialectic by which status is assigned to the student social worker by each ward with whom they work. It is affected by the ward's perception of students generally: hospitals provide an essential training ground for students from both health and social care disciplines. Students are seen as part of the system and provide energy and labour to stretched hospital resources and a supply of staff to replace staff losses. It is also affected by the ward's perception of student social workers in particular, and of social work itself. This will be influenced by individual workers' past experiences and wider societal views of social work. Media 'moral panics' (Cohen 1973) such as the press reporting on the Cleveland situation (Campbell 1988) are likely to have a detrimental impact and undermine the trust of other workers in social workers.

Similarly two thirds of the students considered that their previous experiences of hospitals and medical professionals affected how they presented themselves. Three of the students had previous experience as health professionals. Two of these found this helpful. One said that 'this enabled me to understand the hierarchical structure that exists in the health service' and the other felt 'very comfortable on the wards and with staff'. Relevant qualifications were also found to have been helpful in providing an understanding of illnesses and medications. Busy ward staff can assume that the other multi-disciplinary members already have this knowledge and do not always have time to give explanations to student social workers.

However, such qualifications created other difficulties for students. For example an ex-nurse stated: 'I was aware that I had to adopt a new role and that the familiar role of nurse was inappropriate. At times it proved problematic and confusing'.

Other students who, as recipients of health services in the past, had found medical professionals intimidating and inhibiting also found that these experiences had a negative impact on how they now interacted with these professions: 'subservience to male doctors, minimising emotional concerns and feelings, ideas that you are wasting time, i.e. their time'.

Almost half of the respondents considered that their age and gender had influenced the way in which they were treated. One student stated that 'as a woman it was easier for me to assimilate into an all female team'. Others experienced discriminatory attitudes relating to their age and gender and connected this to wider societal power imbalances: 'Some consultants and doctors were discriminatory in their views of female roles. This is perhaps best understood in the context of an organisation that historically has mainly men in senior posts and mainly females do the "hands on" caring, cleaning etc.'.

One tenth of the respondents also considered class to be important. For example, one respondent found that 'being older and from a professional background (I was previously a teacher) helped in that the consultant listened to me (and the others followed his lead)'. This comment highlights the important role that the consultant can play in the allocation of status.

The discrimination experienced by these respondents demonstrates how in medical teams the worker is faced by the discriminations prevalent in the wider society. However in this context the discrimination may also generate generalisations from the 'expert model', which are then used to judge the value of the students' contributions.

In my small sample none of the respondents considered race, ethnicity, religion, sexuality, or disability as being relevant to how they were treated and this may be because the practice teachers in this sample have been unsuccessful in explicitly linking the relevance of these other issues to the students' personal experiences. In many cases, of course, such attributes will play a crucial role in how the student social worker is perceived and will need to be explicitly addressed in practice teaching sessions.

How the student dressed was also considered relevant to how they were treated. For example, one respondent considered that it was 'Very important to present as a professional (and dress accordingly) if you wish to be listened to by consultants etc. (impressions matter here!)'.

How can the practice teacher help?

Some ways in which the practice teacher can help the student social worker carve an effective role within the multi-disciplinary team have already been addressed. In the early stages of placement in this new environment and role good supervision is crucial: the student should feel 'contained' with clear support, boundaries and permission to explore feelings generated by the work. My research indicated that students often felt quite overwhelmed when first on placement and that more pre-placement preparation might have helped ease them into the role:

> There is a lot of information to gain in a hospital setting – not only social work and how social services operates in this setting but also medical hierarchies, different illnesses and their effects, plus medical terminology. Practice teachers need to be aware of this.

Several of the respondents emphasised the need for the practice teacher to spend time with the student in the first week to familiarise them with expectations of the student social worker's role in that particular multi-disciplinary team. 'Accompanying students on initial ward/patient visits and explaining systems of information gathering – also introduction to the ward staff' were considered to be important. Flow charts and checklists were suggested as helpful ways of enabling the student to gain more detailed knowledge of systems and procedures. These should be supplemented by information about the wider political system so that students are helped to contextualise changes within the social work role. This could all be contained within a practice curriculum of useful information and learning objectives.

Co-working cases with the student was also suggested by one respondent. This would supply the student with a role model and also provide the practice teacher with an early opportunity to observe the student's practice.

Use of self is essential to the social work role and to how the students present themselves to the wards. Some respondents felt dismissed and disempowered as students, whilst others were enabled to use their student status to ask questions and explore their role. It is important that the practice teacher helps to nurture their self-confidence. One student noted: 'My contributions to ward rounds were acknowledged but when my practice teacher was present then her contributions were given more weight (obviously)'. Co-working, then, can be both containing and disempowering, and the timing of such work needs to be discussed with the student.

Initially providing the students with simple pieces of work will enhance their confidence and provide the ward with positive first impressions. Students in any placement must be helped to find their authority, but this can be more difficult in multi-disciplinary teams for the reasons already outlined. The ability to communicate confidently and assertively is essential and assertiveness training was identified as having an important place in all student social work learning.

The practice teacher must provide an anchoring point for the student in the 'shifting sands'. They need to ensure that the placement provides the student with the opportunities to apply their previously gained skills and theory from the university/college whilst learning the actual social work role that is undertaken in that placement. This will necessitate helping the student to come to terms with the rapidly changing nature of the social worker's role, whilst instilling a sense of social work identity, based upon the key aspects and competences of social work and its value base.

The team

The respondents clearly valued the role of the team in enabling them to learn. For example: 'The staff team were clear about my role and were supportive in encouraging me to experience a range of opportunities in casework situations. They ensured that I had the opportunity to work with them and understand how the different wards and social workers functioned'.

Others valued being given the opportunity to shadow workers, consider examples from other workers' caseloads or simply having 'time to raise concerns and questions about their role and any difficulties they may have'.

University/College

Whilst the practice teacher needs to balance the demands of the placement with ensuring that the student learns the core competences of social work, the tutor must perform a similar role at the university/college. They need to constantly monitor that their courses provide the students with the skills to meet the changing demands of the workplace. In these 'shifting sands' of demand they also need to ensure that they continue to teach the key aspects and competences central to social work practice.

They must also consider the structure of the course and its ability to continue to meet the demands placed on the students. Two thirds of the respondents felt that the length of the placement (which ranged from six to ten months) was appropriate. However, almost a quarter suggested that due to the brief nature of the work, more days or even a block placement would be best for this type of placement. As one respondent stated:

> I am enjoying the placement, but for me personally I feel that full weeks spent at the hospital would be more beneficial from a learning perspective, therefore enabling me to have a fuller, overall view of what my clients' needs are and I could be involved in them first hand rather than leaving work to be picked up by another worker on the two days I'm at college.

The increased patient turnover in hospitals does, indeed, mean that students can find it is rare to see a piece of work through, and team members must be willing to provide cover for students' cases when they are not on placement.

One tenth of the respondents also considered the specialist nature of these placements to be more suited to second-year students.

Conclusion

The student social worker can be seen as being 'on shifting sands' in having to adapt and respond to a whole new range of systems and their demands. Those systems can all help bolster the student's resources and gradually enable them to establish sound foundations. The practice teacher and personal tutor can be seen as having the key roles in facilitating this process. If they are successful then the student may share the experience of the respondent who stated 'I knew the role would be part of a multi-disciplinary role but I was pleasantly surprised by how integrated the role was'. If, however, they are not successful then the student is more likely to be left feeling that:

'It wasn't a useful social work experience for me…because of…fundamental issues about multi-disciplinary working practices'.

The link between the breakdown in trust and co-ordination between professionals and service failures has been well documented. The Department of Health (1996) advocates that members of multi-disciplinary mental health teams should train together to develop trust, a better understanding of the other professions and a shared approach to the key worker role. Some initiatives such as the MAANI (Management of the Adult with an Acquired Neurological Impairment) programme have already effected this interdisciplinary approach to service provision and training with good results.

Students placed in multi-disciplinary settings are in a prime position to break down cultural stereotypes, gain an understanding of other disciplines, and work together to provide a coherent service to the client. The concepts of role and status help us to understand the complexity of this process and the challenges that the student may face.

Within this chapter I have demonstrated the importance of making explicit issues of status and power within the multi-disciplinary team (often brought into sharp relief by disparities in salary!) and consider this important for two reasons. Firstly, it begins a dialogue which strikes at the heart of the barriers to effective joint working, and secondly, it generates wider considerations of power relations in society. Such understanding is crucial in effective health and social care policy and practice.

I have also tried to use social work students' own words to articulate some of the factors which have affected the way they have managed to find their authority in the team. Practice teachers need to be aware that many students will feel unprepared for, and overwhelmed by, the amount of new information a multi-disciplinary team demands. The students' previous experiences as well as their current self-perceptions will influence their abilities and need to be explored within supervision. The programme of work should be carefully managed, and it should be the same kind of work other social workers in the team are engaged in. Every opportunity – including formal and informal meetings – should be taken for the mutual sharing and learning about different disciplines' skills and value bases.

In this challenging climate in which social work is undergoing a 'starburst' of titles describing new, more specialist roles (Niven 1997) Niven advocates that we ground social work as the core professional title and use the British Association of Social Workers as the unifying organisation to 'claim and reclaim core areas of social work'. Within this chapter I have argued that the multi-disciplinary medical setting offers excellent opportunities for the student to gain an understanding of the evolving role of the social worker and students should be engaged in, and helped to influence, those debates. Some authors, for example Connolly, argue that the introduction of care management has given the impetus to a helpful re-negotiation of professional roles. Others believe 'the role of social workers as counsellors will need to be reintroduced and highlighted if all needs are to be met' (Phillips 1996, p.150). However, it is only through maintaining and developing the key aspects and competences in social work, firmly grounded in social work values, that social workers will be able to sustain and enhance the role of social work within inter-disciplinary teams.

The practice teacher plays a crucial role, anchoring the core elements of social work in these shifting sands.

References

Banton, M. (1989) 'Role.' In A. Kuper and J. Kuper *The Social Sciences Encyclopaedia*. London: Routledge.

Barclay, P. (1982) *Social Workers: Their Role and Tasks*. London: Bedford Square Press.

Bensman, J. (1972) *Status Communities in an Urban Society: The Musical Community*. Cited in Wolf, C. (1989) 'Status.' In A. Kuper and J. Kuper (eds) *The Social Sciences Encyclopaedia*. London: Routledge.

Campbell, B. (1988) *Unofficial Secrets: Child Sexual Abuse, The Cleveland Case*. London: Virago.

CCETSW (1996) *A Report for Social Work Educators Developing Shared Learning with Medical Students and General Practitioners*. London.

Cohen, S. (1973) *Folk Devils and Moral Panic*. London: Paladin.

Connolly, J. (1995) 'What do nurses want from social workers?' *Nursing Times 91*, 46, 38–39.

Connolly, J. (1997) 'The hospital.' In M. Davies (ed) *The Blackwell Companion to Social Work*. Oxford: Blackwell.

Cooper, T. (1997) 'It was an exhausting, exhilarating time.' In *Twenty Five Years of the British Association of Social Workers, A Professional Social Work Supplement*. Birmingham: BASW.

Cunningham, C. and Davis, H. (1985) *Working with Parents: Frameworks for Collaboration*. Cited in H. Davis and L. Fallowfield (eds) (1991) *Counselling and Communication in Health Care*. Chichester: Wiley.

Davis, H. and Fallowfield, L. (eds) (1991) *Counselling and Communication in Health Care*. Chichester: Wiley.

Department of Health (1996) *Building Bridges: A Guide to Arrangements for Inter-Agency Working for the Care and Protection of Severely Mentally Ill People*. London: HMSO.

Engel, G. (1990) *The Essence of the Biopsychosocial Model: From 17th to 20th Century Science*. Cited in H. Davis and L. Fallowfield (1991) *Counselling and Communication in Health Care*. Chichester: Wiley.

Freidson, E. (1973) *The Professions and their Prospects*. London: Sage.

Garfinkel, H. (1956) 'Conditions of successful degradation ceremonies.' *American Journal of Sociology 61*.

Gerth, H. and Mills, C. (1953) *Character and Social Structure*. Cited in Wolf, C. (1989) 'Status.' In A. Kuper and J. Kuper (eds) *The Social Sciences Encyclopaedia*. London: Routledge.

Linton, R. (1936) *The Study Of Man.* Cited in Wolf, C. (1989) 'Status.' In A. Kuper and J. Kuper (eds) *The Social Sciences Encyclopaedia.* London: Routledge.

Niven, D. (1997) 'The voice of social work – yesterday, today, tomorrow.' In *Twenty Five Years of Social Work, A Professional Social Work Supplement.* Birmingham: BASW.

Pietroni, M. (1995) 'The nature and aims of professional education for social workers.' In M. Yelloly and M. Henkel *Learning and Teaching in Social Work.* London: Jessica Kingsley Publishers.

Phillips, J. (1996) 'The future of social work with older people in a changing world.' In N. Parton (ed) *Social Theory, Social Change and Social Work.* London: Routledge.

Weber, M. (1922) *Economy and Society, I and II.* Cited in Wolf, C. (1989) 'Status.' In A. Kuper and J. Kuper (eds) *The Social Sciences Encylopaedia.* London: Routledge.

Wolf, C. (1989) 'Status.' In A. Kuper and J. Kuper (eds) *The Social Sciences Encylopaedia.* London: Routledge.

Yelloly, M. and Henkel, M. (eds) (1995) *Learning and Teaching in Social Work: Towards Reflective Practice.* London: Jessica Kingsley Publishers.

Younghusband, E. (1981) *The Newest Profession: A Short History of Social Work.* London: Community Care/IPC Business Press.

Further reading

Frith, S. (1985) 'The sociology of youth.' In M. Haralambos (ed) *Sociology: New Directions.* London: Causeway.

Jones, S. and Joss, R. (1995) 'Models of professionalism.' In M. Yelloly and M. Henkel (eds) *Learning and Teaching in Social Work: Towards Reflective Practice.* London: Jessica Kingsley Publishers.

Kuper, A. and Kuper, J. (eds) (1989) *The Social Sciences Encyclopaedia.* London: Routledge.

Maguire, P. (1984) *Communication Skills and Patient Care.* Cited in H. Davis and L. Fallowfield (1991) *Counselling and Communication in Health Care.* Chichester: Wiley.

Underwood, P., Owen, A. and Winkler, R. (1986) *Replacing the Clockwork Model of Medicine.* Cited in H. Davis and L. Fallowfield (1991) *Counselling and Communication in Health Care.* Chichester: Wiley.

CHAPTER 12

Reconciling the Act and the Actor

Probation Practice Teaching, Pre-Sentence Reports, and Anti-Oppressive Practice

Carole Ballardie

'The Probation Service is still oppressed by National Standards.' (Graham Smith CBE, Chief Inspector, Her Majesty's Inspectorate, speaking at a staff conference of East Sussex Probation Service, 22nd January 1997)

National Standards are not new for the probation service. They arrived in the late 1980s, initially in Community Service. National Standards covering the majority of probation activities were introduced in October 1992, to coincide with the implementation of the Criminal Justice Act 1991. These standards were the result of extensive and wide-ranging consultation between the Home Office and probation organisations, and this is reflected within the 1992 National Standards, which show an understanding of the complexity of the task, the varied nature of probation clients, and of probation officers' concerns to engage and work effectively with their clients.

The swing toward a harsher, more punitive political climate followed quickly upon the heels of the Criminal Justice Act 1991. Within five months of its implementation, in early 1993, the Home Secretary announced fundamental changes to those parts of the Act which had turned out to be politically unpopular – notably, the Unit Fines system, anathema to some rich (and influential) offenders; and further announced the introduction of a secure training order for persistent young offenders. In October 1993 at the Conservative party conference Michael Howard, the new Home Secretary, declared: 'Prison works... We shall no longer judge the success of our system of justice by a fall in our prison population'. The Probation Service, having been declared 'centre stage' in the criminal justice system by the new Act, found itself shuffled ignominiously into the wings.

One direct effect of this punitive climate on probation practice has been the replacement of the 1992 National Standards by the 1995 National Standards, the latter reflecting Home Office concern that probation officers may be 'soft on crime'. The struggle faced by practitioners trying to meet the organisational demands resulting from the 1995 National Standards while maintaining good standards of practice are most clearly encapsulated within the practice teacher/student relationship. This chapter will examine some of the issues faced by practice teachers in the current climate.

The 1995 National Standards

The 1995 National Standards are, as indeed they are intended to be, precise and rigorous. The emphasis upon the offence rather than the offender implied by the 'just deserts' principles underlying the Criminal Justice Act 1991 is clearly delineated throughout the standard for pre-sentence reports – in fact, the standard suggests that a report prepared without benefit of an interview with the defendant will do (Para 2.4). A requirement that the report be produced within 15 working days implies that enquiries will need to be quickly 'processed'. These requirements do not lend themselves to a carefully considered assessment enhanced by full and careful contact with the individual defendant – yet this is what we would commonly acknowledge to be a base-line for good practice. The challenge then must be to make the 1995 National Standards work for us, and not against us. The oppressive potential is there, but so too are the tools by which we may resist it.

Know your standards

This may seem so obvious as to be hardly worth saying. However, often local service guidelines will be held to suffice for day-to-day working requirements, and in my experience these tend to be heavy on requirements, and light on anti-discriminatory practice. Yet if we look to the 1995 National Standards for direction to practise in an anti-discriminatory way, we will find it. Although the reference to equal opportunities has been relegated from a fulsome paragraph of 15 lines in the introduction to the 1992 standards to five lines tucked away at the bottom of page five in the 1995 standards, it is still there.

It is useful to ask students to scrutinise the National Standards carefully, and list every requirement which offers the opportunity for anti-discriminatory practice. This is a productive exercise which has the effect of acquainting students with the minutiae of the standards, and enabling them to realise that although the language is formal, and some of the requirements stringent, the anti-discriminatory potential remains. For example in the introduction, the permission to depart from the standard is described in paragraph 1.3; the practitioner is enabled to exercise his/her professional judgement in paragraph 1.5, and in that same paragraph is required to deliver supervision 'fairly, consistently and without improper discrimination'. Local discretion and initiative are encouraged in paragraph 1.11, and the equal opportunities statement in paragraph 1.16 specifically refers to the 'duty not to discriminate' established in section 95 of the Criminal Justice Act 1991. All these statements are made within a framework of agency accountability, and students should be encouraged to develop advocacy skills in making their client's case for departure from the standard. This process also allows the practice teacher to assess whether the client has been properly listened to, and the client's voice 'heard'.

There is, however, also oppressive potential in these standards. Knowing exactly what they say, and how they can be used, is not always enough. Local probation services have individual cultures, and a service with a bureaucratic and managerial culture may well reflect this in the manner that the National Standards are monitored, and shortcomings in meeting the standards communicated to their staff. Service managers may be supportive to staff, but it is also their job to make sure that objectives are set, and targets met. If colleagues feel oppressed by meeting the requirements of the standards, this will soon reach the potentially most vulnerable member of the team – the practice student. Students who experience a culture where colleagues seem to be driven by the standards, rather than taking control of the standards so that they work for them and their clients, are going to have difficulty in finding the confidence necessary to uphold their case in departing from the standard on behalf of their client. There are no easy answers to this, although careful consideration of these issues within supervision can ameliorate the worst aspects, and this has to start with practice teachers being aware of the situation, and understanding the impact of organisational pressure upon our own practice.

National Standards: who is oppressing whom?

Turning to less tangible aspects of National Standards, it is helpful, when considering matters of oppression, to set the scene in its wider context. It is generally accepted that the changes to report format brought about by the more prescribed format of the 1992 and 1995 National Standards, together with a formalising of quality assurance procedures, have led to an improved document:

> PSRs [pre-sentence reports] at the beginning of the 1990s were probably better – more focused, more relevant to their purposes – than 10 years earlier. (Smith 1996, p.146)

However, as the opening quote from the Chief Inspector suggests, oppressive aspects prevail. This is hardly the fault of the standards themselves, nor is it a phenomenon restricted to probation work:

> ...in these new political and cultural contexts many of social work's theories and practices have become analytically more shallow and increasingly performance oriented (Howe 1996, p.77)

Howe examines the history and development of social work from a postmodern perspective, and concludes:

> Within a radical liberal perspective, actions are judged more by their results and consequences...behaviour is no longer analysed in an attempt to explain it. Rather it is assessed in terms of administrative procedures, political expectations and legal obligations. Social workers now ask what clients do rather than why they do it, switch from causation to counting, from explanation to audit. (p.88)

In the probation context this change was circumscribed by the Criminal Justice 1991 concept of 'just deserts' requiring a shift of focus from the actor to the act, from the offender to the offence. Such re-focusing may cause us some apprehension, but in other respects the changes to reports required by National Standards have been positive. It is hard to imagine that we used to write reports without the benefit of prosecution information, thus risking a weakly critical (at best) version of the defendant's own account. Similarly, incorporation of the victim perspective into reports is long overdue, and it is possibly a reflection of probation's apparent inability to present its practice in creditable terms that, in this respect at least, the Home Office had to force the agenda.

Thus, in many respects, report-writing practice has improved, but in other respects it has not.

Harris, writing in the same volume as Howe, reflects upon 'the post-modern condition of probation'. He suggests that probation:

> oddly straddles the modern and the post-modern, its political discourse being modern, thus acknowledging a political expectation that contemporary problems of law and order can be 'solved in a manner appropriate to the laboratory experiment' – and, of course, evaluated and shown to work in a systematic way. (Harris 1996, p.116)

It is helpful to reaffirm that while current discourse within probation is politically led, it has not always been so. Today's depiction of crime and offenders belongs to the media, to the tabloids, and the law and order debate is high on the political agenda. Any notions of the usefulness of rehabilitation are lost amidst a fear of being seen to be 'soft on crime'. It is hardly surprising if we see probation staff 'buying in' to all this and defending their position as one of punisher, restricter of liberty, manager of risk, and so on. Yet Harris invites the service again to 'engage with its narrative self' and recall the traditional role to: 'Advise, assist, befriend' – responses we still offer (though it is unpopular to say so) to offenders as people, and to their general moral behaviour, rather than to a specific crime.

Writing two years on from the production of the 1995 National Standards, we see that the responses of services have been various, with some embracing them wholeheartedly – with little thought as to the possible consequences of acting with unnecessary haste – and others taking a more cautious approach.

> Emphasis on control, scrutiny and quality as a checking mechanism may only serve to reinforce the managerial attitude that performance is enhanced by issuing prescriptive rules and standards, and that the main managerial objective is to seek strict adherence to them. In this scenario, innovation is stifled and commitment of staff is diminished. (Kemshall 1993, p.123)

Kemshall suggests that such an approach will prompt mediocrity; it can also maximise oppression, creating anxiety among staff and students alike.

As a teacher of social work and probation students I want to see students engage with probation clients as the 'whole person'. Yet as a probation officer I am similarly concerned to engage a student with agency accountability and correct observation of National Standards. In terms of the pre-sentence report, this is to answer the requirements of National Standards whilst also engaging with Harris's 'narrative self'.

> Good reports were also ones which managed to convey to the sentencer something about the defendant as a person. (Gelsthorpe and Raynor 1995, p.196)

My experience is that the types of checklist that National Standards monitoring tends to generate can cause considerable anxiety. An anxious student cannot be creative or imaginative, let alone reflective. It is also the case that at the start of a probation placement – or any statutory placement for that matter – formal report writing commonly seems to cause more anxiety than any other task.

I will now offer some suggestions from my own experience which I have found helpful in facilitating the learning and practising of good report writing.

Preparation

The greater the preparation, the less the anxiety. This may seem an obvious point, but I make no apologies for it because it is one I must constantly remind myself of in a busy working life. When I first started probation teaching, I found that there was plenty of material around about how to *write* a pre-sentence report; however I could find little about how to conduct the enquiry, that is, the interview process. Indeed after many years of report writing it was an aspect of practice which had become routine. I decided to write my own 'guide to a PSR enquiry' based on local guidelines and my own practice – somewhat to my surprise by the time I finished it had grown to more than 2000 words in 23 paragraphs! I describe this as an indication of how we, as busy practitioners, tend to forget just how much there is to address within an enquiry. I hasten to add that I do not wish to be too prescriptive about the process – local guidance and procedures vary, as does individual practice. However for a new student, struggling to attend to the form-filling, whilst not forgetting to engage appropriately with the defendant, or remember all they have learned about anti-discriminatory practice, preparation prior to the interview does help.

A further pressure introduced by the 1995 National Standards has been the requirement to submit reports within 15 days (Para 2.51). Indeed in the Crown Court, where 'reports should be available for the sentencing judge by 1.00pm on the day before sentence' (Para 2.46) the time may be even less.

Many defendants are now seen only once for the enquiry. I believe it is essential for students to see the defendant more than once – partly in the interests of good practice, but also to facilitate the lessening of anxiety. However given the constraints of time, it is helpful to encourage students to complete enquiries as far as possible in the first interview, so that a draft of the report can be completed before the second interview. This has the further advantage of prompting the writer to write *for the defendant* as well as for the Court – any doubts about how the defendant's account should be represented can then be checked out with her/him.

How to conduct the interview

An interview is not an interrogation, yet it is easy to slip into interrogating when we feel anxious, pressured, or short of time. I encourage students to develop interviewing techniques based upon some of the theoretical approaches underpinning motivational interviewing (Miller and Rollnick 1991). Although some amount of direct questioning is inevitable during the enquiry process, as far as possible a non-directive approach should be used. Motivational interviewing suggests that confrontation need not necessarily imply heavy-handed or coercive tactics, and can be achieved by raising awareness, so that one can understand and accept reality, thus enabling an understanding of the possibilities for change.

I am not however proposing that a full motivational interviewing session should take place during the pre-sentence report interview. Rather, I suggest that the enquiry can be facilitated by some of the more general aspects of the motivational interviewing process, with the added advantage that they may initiate a train of thought which leads to contemplation of change. These are strategies derived largely from client-centred counselling, upon which motivational interviewing is based (Miller and Rollnick, p.64).

1. An opening structure

> Given the socio-political status of the Probation Service, it would be a naive offender who did not regard the probation office as an antechamber to a less pleasant locus for punishment; yet this gloomy perception is only half the truth, for the probation office is simultaneously a place of warmth, support and confession. (Harris 1996, p.118)

Defendants come to the probation office with widely varying expectations, and often with some apprehension. A good structuring statement can put their mind at rest, help them to feel comfortable, and get the interview off to a good start. This might include:

- the amount of time set aside for the interview
- an explanation of the probation officer's role
- the reason why the defendant has been asked to attend
- the details that must be attended to
- an open-ended question, such as 'Maybe you could tell me what happened in your own words...'.

2. Open-ended questions

These are questions which cannot easily be answered with a brief reply, and are intended to encourage the defendant to do most of the talking. Obviously some direct questions are necessary, but in order to facilitate the defendant's participation as fully as possible it is helpful to keep them to a minimum.

3. Reflective listening

Reflective listening is more than keeping quiet and hearing what someone has to say. The crucial element is *how* the listener responds to what is said. Thomas Gordon (1970, cited in Miller and Rollnick 1991, p.73) outlines some responses that are *not* listening:

warning, giving advice, making suggestions, providing solutions, telling people what they should do, interpreting, questioning...

Such responses are termed 'roadblocks' because they get in the interviewee's way by interrupting a train of thought. The essence of reflective listening is rather to try and guess what the defendant actually means, and to reflect this in a statement which checks out what you think the defendant means, rather than assuming that you know.

4. Summarising

Summary statements are useful to link together the material that has been discussed in the interview. Other information available in the interview can be linked into a summary, for example:

'Let me try and pull together what we've talked about so far... You've said these things to me about how the offence happened...this is what the prosecution papers say...then again this is what your former Probation Officer said about your offending in the last report…it seems to me that you're feeling rather hopeless about getting into trouble again, but at the same time it sounds as though you're beginning to think about how things might be different…does what I'm saying sound like a fair summary so far? Or are there things that I've missed out?'

It is useful in embarking on a major summary such as this to make a prefacing comment of what is to follow: it is the defendant's turn to hear your version of what has been said between you, which will form the basis of the report. The final comment is also important – the defendant is invited to augment or clarify your understanding of events.

Practising

These techniques look easier on paper than they are to practise in the interview situation, and it is helpful to employ some basic motivational interviewing exercises which can be tried in individual supervision, or in group learning. I have made some adaptations to suit the context of the pre-sentence interview.

1. 'How not to do it'

The purpose of this exercise is to enable understanding of why a directly confrontational approach is unlikely to be helpful:

> In pairs, for five minutes: one student plays a man or woman who has been directed by the Court to attend the Community Alcohol Project about their heavy drinking. S/he is interviewed by Big Nurse, whose task is to tell her patient that it is time s/he faced up to reality and learned what is good for them.
>
> Feedback: how does the defendant feel (stuck, angry, defiant, disempowered, needs a drink…)?

It can be useful to return to this exercise later, when some different techniques have been tried out. The same situation can then be explored using the more facilitative approach: how does the defendant feel this time?

2. Accurate listening and understanding

The purpose of this exercise is to enhance an understanding of the importance of checking out with the defendant exactly what they mean, rather than assuming we understand. The process of reflective listening is one that checks the listener's perceived meaning against the speaker's own meaning.

> In pairs: *Speaker*: 'One thing I like about myself is…' (this should be a statement concerning a fairly abstract characteristic e.g. 'I am friendly', rather than a concrete attribute e.g. 'I have brown eyes').

> *Respondent*: 'Do you mean that…?'

This response can be tried out a number of times. The speaker should reply only 'yes' or 'no'. A 'no' reply will indicate a mistakenly assumed meaning, rather than a true meaning for the person making the statement. This raises a number of questions: how often do we check out with our clients that we truly understand what they tell us? How does it feel only to answer 'yes' or 'no'? Often we very much want to elaborate and explain – to 'put it right' with the respondent: do we always allow our clients the space to do that?

3. Understanding roadblocks

There is nothing intrinsically wrong with roadblocks, and they have their place in our communications with our clients. However they will obstruct the specific process of reflective listening. An examination of the list previously described will enable any of us to quickly identify the ones that we are particularly good at!

> In pairs: *Speaker*: describe 'something I feel two ways about' (e.g. smoking, exercising), and try and explain the dilemmas to the listener (3–5 minutes only).

> *Listener*: In response, fit in as many 'roadblocks' as possible.

> Then change places.

In feedback, identify the feelings raised by roadblock responses and having to deal with them – what underlying messages do they communicate? How much information does the listener gain from the speaker in the face of the roadblocks?

4. Forming reflections

Reflective listening statements are similar to the 'do you mean' questions in that they offer a hypothesis, but different in that the hypothesis is presented as a statement rather than as a question. The speaker must also beware of a 'questioning' inflection – raising the voice at the end of the statement will introduce an interrogatory influence. Some sample sentence beginnings can be useful:

It sounds like you...

You're feeling...

It seems to you that...

So you...

Then try these out. One person should offer a 'change statement', such as 'One thing I would like to change about myself...'. As before the statement will work best if the speaker is able to avoid concrete attributes, such as 'my curly hair'.

Respondents should reply in a similar way to the 'do you mean' exercise, but with a reflective statement. The speaker may then reply with a statement which probably includes 'yes' or 'no', but also offers some elaboration. The next reflective statement should build upon that new information. This is not as easy as it sounds, and it takes practice.

I will now explain how these techniques can effectively inform the pre-sentence report, particularly the Offence Analysis.

The Offence Analysis

The 1995 National Standards state clearly what is required in this section of the pre-sentence report (2.12–16), and the direction 'assist the Court's understanding of *why the offender committed this offence at this time*' (National Standards emphasis) is helpful in understanding what is expected.

'How to do it/write it' is not prescribed. I struggled with this myself after the introduction of the 1995 National Standards. I tended to drift into learned habits and present the 'offender's version versus the prosecution version' account of the incident. Interestingly, students writing reports for the first time tend to do this also. The issue then is: how to overcome it?

One of the main purposes of the exercises described above is to encourage defendants to talk, and open up. They are also intended to encourage defendants to talk about how they *feel*: this is why the exercises are best tried out in a group setting, as feedback is crucial in enabling the participants to identify how they feel as part of the process. An understanding of how an offender feels at the time of the offence, as well as immediately afterwards, and again at the time of the interview for the report, is essential for an offence analysis.

Therefore it is necessary to pursue discussion of these feelings during the interview, and facilitate the defendant in his/her exploration of them.

A note of caution. It can be uncomfortable for any of us to maintain a dialogue which may entail hearing from the defendant about their positive feelings about offending – particularly if we ourselves find the offence/s distasteful or repugnant. Yet any prospect of change is going to involve ambivalence – the offender will need to contemplate gains and losses before s/he can make a decision to change. If we are to help in this process, we will need to know what these gains and losses are. It is important to practice 'stickability' – staying with what the defendant is saying, managing our own discomfort, enduring the silences, keeping on the same track and so on. I have been encouraged by observing that once the technique has been grasped, learning moves on, and because this is an approach that 'works', students take it enthusiastically into their practice and consolidate expertise.

Back to the 'feeling' words. Students can brainstorm the 'feeling' words that they have elicited from the defendant in interview. They then select three or four of these words that best portray their view of what this defendant's offending was about, and, as nearly as possible, put each of these words into a sentence which describes the offence. Because we are focusing on feelings, we are able to avoid offering a simplistic straightforward account of the defendant's story, and move more toward what an analysis is supposed to be about – 'why the offender committed this offence at this time' (Home Office 1995, 2.12). Having approached the construction of the analysis from the 'feeling' end rather than the 'fact' end, it is then relatively easy to embellish the account with such facts as are necessary.

An example:

> Mr X says he committed this theft in order to gain money to buy drugs. He further says that he *feels completely despondent* about his drug dependency. He is *at a loss to understand* why, in spite of several spells in hospital for detoxification, he continually returns to drug use. Mr X left his accommodation and became homeless only weeks before he was to be offered a housing association flat. Probation records confirm that Mr X *seems to offend when he has something to lose*, and in interview Mr X was able to *identify self-destructive tendencies*, although he remains *bewildered* by them at this present time. However Mr X is *ashamed and embarrassed* by his behaviour, particularly as *he feels he should know better* at his age. Accordingly *he does wish to offer an apology* to the Court.

The importance of irrelevant information

> However politically expedient it may be to do so and however unfash-
> ionable to do otherwise, it is not self-evidently progressive or wise to
> unravel complexity when a *terrible simplification* is likely to result. This is
> not to argue for obfuscation – there has been too much of that already in
> probation's history – but for a clear exposition of complex reality.
> (Harris 1996, p.133)

Harris urges us away from the 'simplistic story telling which currently enjoys
hegemonic status'.

If narrowly interpreted, National Standards may encourage a focus away
from the defendant as a unique individual. However they do not say that probation work has to be conducted accordingly, and students, albeit anxious to
acknowledge agency procedures, should be encouraged to develop a wider
view. I believe that we have drifted into a culture of 'if in doubt, leave it out' –
a culture which stifles our clients' stories. This leads me to the importance of
'irrelevant information'.

Students need to be clear that the pre-sentence report interview should
not be constrained by the requirements of National Standards, but should be
used to gather as much information as possible. Until we have this fuller picture, how can we say with any authority what may be relevant and what may
not be? Until we understand how the offending fits with the client's whole
story, how are we going to see how we might best help them change?

The 'test of relevance' has endured over time as an effective tool of anti-
discriminatory practice. My recollection of the early days of 'gatekeeping' is
that it was effective in weeding out discriminatory and stereotypical statements which had no direct bearing on the defendant's current situation and
the offence with which s/he was charged. It still fulfils this essential function,
albeit most of us have learned to avoid the worst vagaries of stereotyping.
However there may also be a place in a pre-sentence report for information
which is, perhaps, 'less relevant', but not irrelevant, and, as long as this information is not in any way discriminatory, it can enhance the report by offering
a more lively picture of the defendant, and a less simplistic discussion.

National Standards do not inhibit this train of thought.

> ...the report should also provide a *balanced* picture of the offender, set-
> ting out both strengths and weaknesses. (Home Office 1995, 2.21)

I encourage students, rather than restricting themselves in writing a 'relevant information' section, to write a fuller account of the defendant, which can be edited later. This gives rise to useful discussion about definitions of relevance for the court report purpose, and offers an opportunity to rehearse arguments in support of the information included.

This has been part of my own practice, and I have been surprised to find that although I have rehearsed the arguments, I have not had to use them. Indeed on a number of occasions, gatekeepers have commended the report. This leads me to believe that, with due thought, and care, it is possible to tell our clients' stories, and thereby revive our talents for narrative. Thus we can return the offender to the offence, the actor to the act.

> The case materials available to probation officers are social problems in action, moral mazes which, when articulated by reference to personal experience, do not lend themselves to the flip, unthinkingly punitive solutions to which so much contemporary debate has degenerated. (Harris, 1996, p.132)

Conclusion

Writing this chapter has prompted me to revisit both the 1992 and the 1995 National Standards, and I am reassured by what I find. There is no doubt in my mind that the 1992 standards are superior, revealing attention and thought to good practice and the central place of social work skills (and far more sensible contact requirements!) but it is still possible to practise professionally and effectively within the 1995 National Standards. Discretion and the exercise of professional judgement still pertain within the framework of agency accountability. Thus National Standards may be only as oppressive as the agency determines – so that if you are a practice teacher in a heavy-handed agency, then you and your students have some extra work to do, some extra links to make.

The last couple of years have been fraught times for probation training. At the time of writing this chapter, the future is less than clear. A separation for probation training from social work training is proposed, yet the different skills that a trainee probation officer should supposedly acquire remain a mystery.

I have been reassured and encouraged by my probation officer colleagues and students, who, despite every discouragement within and without the agency, continue to work in a client-centred way, and to demonstrate good social work practice. I believe it is essential that we hold on to a training which will enable our skills of perception, assessment, enabling, and narrative to continue. I am reminded again of the words of the Chief Inspector, as he urged us to maintain our 'fugitive' – our casework – skills, with the warning: 'If you don't use them, you may lose them'. Thus far there seems little chance of this happening. It is up to us to keep it that way.

References

Ballardie, C. (1995) 'Some notes on conducting pre-sentence report interviews.' Unpublished seminar presentation.

Gelsthorpe, L. and Raynor, P. (1995) 'Quality and effectiveness in probation officers' reports to sentencers.' *British Journal of Criminology 35*, 2, 188–200.

Harris, R. (1996) 'Probation in the contemporary social formation.' In N. Parton (ed) *Social Theory, Social Change and Social Work*. London: Routledge.

Howe, D. (1996) 'Surface and depth in social work practice.' In N. Parton (ed) *Social Theory, Social Change and Social Work*. London: Routledge.

Home Office (1992) *National Standards for the Supervision of Offenders in the Community*. London: HMSO.

Home Office (1995) *National Standards for the Supervision of Offenders in the Community*. London: HMSO.

Kemshall, H. (1993) 'Quality: friend or foe?' *Probation Journal 40*, 3, 122–126. NAPPO.

Miller, W. and Rollnick, S. (1991) *Motivational Interviewing: Preparing People to Change Addictive Behaviour*. New York: Guilford Press.

Smith, D. (1996) 'Pre-sentence reports.' In T. May and A. Vass (eds) *Working with Offenders*. London: Sage.

Smith, G. (1997) *What Works: Conference Proceedings 1997*. East Sussex: East Sussex Probation Service.

CHAPTER 13

Teaching Social Work
Law to Students

Polly Hoad

Teaching social work law to students is often the last subject on a practice teacher's mind. It is tempting to leave this subject to the confines of the class-room for a number of reasons. Social work law is a complex subject, raising many practice dilemmas, and social workers are frequently uncertain of the correct use of the law. The idea of practice teachers tackling the subject of law with their students, in addition to all the other demands laid upon them, can be panic inducing. Recent research studies have shown that for the practitio-ner, the legal framework underpinning their roles and tasks contributes significantly to stress. Keeping abreast of legislative change, appearing in court and feeling uncertain about policies and procedures appear to correlate with anxiety and depression (Davies and Brandon 1988; Jones *et al.* 1991). The courts are often perceived by social workers as a frightening and even hostile environment. Lawyers are seen as coming from a distinct professional position which may not be sympathetic to the concerns and interests of social work and its clients; magistrates and judges wield considerable decision-making powers, the exercise of which may support the aims and values of social work, but equally may frustrate them (Vernon 1993).

Social workers' knowledge and use of the law have been the subject of a great deal of public criticism, most of which has been contradictory and so has simply added to the confusion. For example the Blom Cooper reports into the Beckford and Carlile cases (London Borough of Brent 1985; Lon-don Borough of Greenwich 1987) stated: 'We are conscious that social workers do not always take readily or kindly to legal intervention in the prac-tice of social work'. The reverse view was later expressed in Cleveland where public perception was of an over-zealous use of legal powers by social workers, doctors and other welfare professionals (Preston-Shoot 1993). Not only is it suggested that social workers do not know the law but that they also resort too readily to it, leaving social workers feeling that they are in a 'no win' situation.

A CCETSW research paper (Vernon, Harris and Ball 1990) suggests that the teaching of law had been marginalised on many social work training courses partly due to a view that somehow law and social work were uncomfortable bedmates. Law, according to Vernon *et al.* is about power, enforcement, compulsion and formality, whereas social work is about liberation, freedom and growth. In preparing the Law Report (Ball *et al.* 1988) the researchers highlighted the importance of law to social work:

> With few exceptions the fact that social work in the UK was a state activity which derived its authority from statute had been ignored. Social work involved implementing social policies and existed within an accountable political structure. Only a minority of social work clients were entirely voluntary; in many cases 'confidentiality' was actively undesirable. Use of the law was central to practice, whether the law was being used to enforce a client's rights or to impose control. In this sense, law was at the heart of practice: it defined the powers and duties of the social workers and the rights and duties of the clients, and it guided many of the interactions between workers and clients. (Vernon, Harris and Ball 1990)

The use of the law in social work practice raises other dilemmas such as the conflicts between needs and resources, which have clearly emerged in relation to practice under the Children Act 1989 and the NHS and Community Care Act 1990. Trying to balance the social work values of anti-discriminatory practice and user-led services, and government interpretation of the purposes and scope of community care services and ever tightening budgets, can be a difficult juggling act for social workers.

The practice teacher needs to be aware that these conflicting demands are met by student social workers as soon as they commence qualifying training. Students are required (CCETSW 1996) to work in partnership with service users and to promote anti-oppressive policies. Yet they must act within organisational and legal structures and understand the social (controlling) functions of the law, even though these may contribute to the oppressions experienced by service users (Braye and Preston-Shoot 1992). Social workers are expected not only to promote choice but also to work within available budgets and organisational decision-making processes which may limit service user participation in the definition of need and the package of services to address it (*ibid.*). Braye and Preston-Shoot (1992) point out the familiar practice dilemmas that students must negotiate and the questions they raise:

1. Care versus control – what values and principles should we operate?

2. Needs versus resources – are services needs-led or provider-led?

3. Welfare versus justice – what criteria should determine the intervention?

4. Humanitarianism versus economics – are considerations of cost or effectiveness to predominate?

5. Agency versus professionalism – to whom are practitioners accountable?

These are useful points and it may be helpful for practice teachers to use them in discussion with their students.

Braye and Preston-Shoot (1992) also point out that the requirement to work in accordance with statutory powers and duties can be difficult to reconcile with social work's commitment to anti-discriminatory practice when it is realised that some major legal enactments either fail to remove discrimination and provide redress, or promote dominant societal values and discriminate against people in the areas of ethnicity, gender, disability, sexuality and age. How should social workers intervene, in what should they be competent, and what should trainers teach, when practitioners are required to work in a context of conflicting legal and social work dilemmas and concerns? For practice teachers teaching the practice of social work law, the question is how much emphasis should be given to the implementation of legal powers and duties and how much to challenging and enabling students and their clients to challenge law and procedures (*ibid.*).

For many aspiring social workers, as well as for their qualified counterparts, the price of apparent 'failure' remains high. Although some recognition has been given to the adverse effect on practice outcomes of cuts in service (Fox Report 1990), there remains a powerful tendency to blame practitioners when tragedies occur. The dilemmas and constraints of practising social work are ignored, with emphasis given instead to the competent use of knowledge and procedures. It is not surprising, therefore, when practitioners adopt a defensive 'safety first' approach (Harris 1987) or that they experience their statutory duties as stressful (Preston-Shoot 1983).

The task of the practice teacher is to guide the student through this minefield to enable them to reach a good understanding of the legal role and competence in carrying out legal duties, whilst recognising the associated value dilemmas.

Teaching law at college versus placement

Recent research (Hogg, Kent and Ward 1992) concluded that practice teachers did not know what was expected of them in terms of teaching law. Many did not know what law was being taught at college and what place in the timetable specific pieces of law took. Practice teachers did not know what was expected of them in terms of measuring a student's knowledge of, understanding of, and ability to use the law in a social work context. On the other hand, the researchers found that students, in spite of receiving lectures and seminars on law in college, had the perception that, when they started their placement, they did not know any relevant social work law. Students were also reported as saying that they learnt the law on placement, not at college, and yet most of the formal teaching they received on the subject was in college, not on placement. The problem, according to Hogg *et al.* (1992), is that the theory (law, as taught in college) is not sufficiently related to practice. It is clearly important for practice teachers to have some understanding of the actual content and timing of the law taught at college, to enable them to complement and enhance college-based learning by helping the student to relate theory to practice. It is also important that practice teachers are aware of the overlapping roles between the law taught at college and that taught in placement and that efforts are made to integrate these, for example, by ensuring that college assignments are discussed or used as a basis for developing learning.

As well as needing to know what to teach, it is very useful if practice teachers have some knowledge of how to teach particularly when tackling such a complex, value-laden subject as social work law. However, before considering how best to teach students, it is worthwhile reminding practice teachers what it is they are required to teach. A recent report, published by CCETSW in October 1995 under the title *Law for Social Workers in England and Wales* is highly relevant. The original report (now revised) has been described as, in many respects, providing a curriculum checklist or specification for law teaching on Diploma in Social Work courses (Vernon 1993). A section of the 1995 report is attached as an appendix for ease of reference.

Building student competence in social work law

Building the student's competence in social work law is difficult for practice teachers, given that students are not expected to take on direct case responsibility in cases which will provide the necessary experience. Before tackling this task, however, it is helpful if the practice teacher has some awareness of the student's learning process, including any preconceived myths about the law, in addition to the practice dilemmas outlined above.

Despite gaining a theoretical understanding of the complexity of the relationship between law and social work, students often welcome with a sense of relief the law's contribution to the social work task: 'here at last is something that will tell us what to do'. In their very helpful book, *Practising Social Work Law*, Braye and Preston-Shoot (1992a) consider that this view is also held by the wider society, which holds a number of myths about the law in relation to social work. According to Braye and Preston-Shoot, these myths include:

1. The myth that the law provides clarity. However the legal framework does not inform social workers as to what they ought to do, only as to what they *can* do (Howe 1980); therefore social workers need to decide what constitutes sufficient grounds to act (e.g. when is harm significant?).

2. The myth that the law is helpful, which could be challenged by those who have been compulsorily detained under the Mental Health Act or those who have sought legal protection from domestic violence.

3. The myth that the law is neutral, but people are not equal before it, since it could be said to perpetuate oppression by lending its more coercive and punitive aspects to, for instance, the racist oppression of black people by the mental health system or the disproportionate numbers of black children in the care system.

4. The myth that the law provides good and right solutions, when we have to look no further than the events in Cleveland, which took place in an identical legal context to the one in which Jasmine Beckford and Kimberley Carlile died, to realise that the solutions

provided by the law are only as good or as right as judgement can allow.

It is too simplistic to assume that the only problem is social workers' ignorance of the law and that all would be well if only they would use it appropriately (Braye and Preston-Shoot 1992a).

In addition to being aware of any preconceived myths which may be held by the student (or indeed, by the practice teacher), it is helpful if the practice teacher is able to recognise blocks to learning on the one hand and incentives to learning on the other. The practice teacher needs to develop an understanding of how the student learns, the styles and patterns of learning the student adopts. What is required, therefore, is a basic understanding of how adults learn in general – the common patterns – and how the student on placement learns in particular.

Adult learning can be seen as significantly different from conventional school-based learning; therefore much of the established literature on education is not applicable. The behaviourist approach to learning is probably the most familiar to social workers and is the basis for a major approach to social work (Sheldon 1982). The term 'learning theory' is strongly associated with the behavioural perspective and is, in fact, more or less synonymous with it The main tenets – stimulus response, reinforcement, etc. – the idea that someone's behaviour is likely to reoccur if it is positively rewarded – are now so widely accepted in social work they are almost regarded as common sense.

The basic concepts of the behavioural approach can be of significant value to the practice teacher, but the literature of adult learning shows this approach to be one small part of a complex whole. Of the many accounts of adult learning, one which can be helpful to practice teachers is that of D. A. Kolb, who regards learning as an intrinsic and therefore continuous aspect of human experience (Kolb et al. 1971).

Kolb's approach has been clearly detailed by Thompson, Osada and Anderson (1990), and addresses the issue of 'problem solving', a process Kolb sees as being a key dimension of learning, which takes place continually, throughout our lives, for the simple reason that each day we are faced with new problems to tackle. Kolb argues that problem solving can be linked to a process involving four stages and the potential for learning can be enhanced or diminished at each stage (ibid.).

In summary, Kolb's four stages of learning are: Concrete Experience which can be reading a book, a lecture or day-to-day experiences; Reflective Observation which is making sense of it; Abstract Conceptualisation, linking the experience to other experiences to integrate it into one's overall life experiences; and Active Experimentation, where the hypotheses formed at the previous stage are tested out in practice. These four stages complete the first cycle. However, according to Thompson *et al.* (1990), Kolb's model is not a linear, static one, it is dynamic and continuous, for as one cycle ends another begins. The active experimentation of one cycle of learning is the basis of the concrete experience stage of the next cycle, and so what we have learnt and put into practice leads on to further learning. Kolb's model is a simplified version. We do not go through one cycle at a time in a neat and orderly fashion but may be going through a number of cycles simultaneously. The model does, nonetheless, offer a valuable tool for understanding the way adults learn and, equally importantly, the way adults may fail to learn.

Thompson *et al.* (1990) helpfully show that identifying problems of learning by reference to the learning cycle can enable practice teachers to tackle such blocks to learning. Problems may occur, for example, at the concrete experience stage. If the student has difficulty in getting started on a task, avoids taking on work or fails to tackle issues in an interview, it is doubtful that learning will take place as the cycle will not have begun.

At Stage Two, students may fail to obtain sufficient or appropriate information, or may misinterpret so that they are unable to gain a sufficiently clear experience to reflect upon.

Abstract conceptualisation is the stage at which the integration of theory and practice is a crucial issue. The student may avoid conceptualisation perhaps because of an inadequate knowledge base to draw from or an anti-intellectual rejection of theory. They may prefer action to thinking. We cannot learn effectively, argues Kolb, without thinking about our experiences, and theories give us the conceptual framework with which to do this.

In order for learning to be confirmed and consolidated, it is necessary to experiment with it, to put it into practice. Students may experience difficulties if they are unwilling or unable to put their ideas into practice, possibly due to lack of confidence or excessive caution or shyness. Whatever the underlying reason, this creates a significant block to learning.

According to Thompson *et al.* (1990), to be an effective learner it is necessary to be reasonably competent at all four stages. If the student is failing to learn, or finding the work very difficult, the practice teacher is likely to gain some very significant clues about the remedial steps to take if s/he is able to identify the stage or stages at which the student struggles. Appropriate assistance can then be offered to boost the student's skills, confidence and capabilities in that area or areas. Anxiety can be a major stumbling block at any or all of the stages, and, as I have argued, using the law can be particularly anxiety provoking, therefore calming, reassuring and supporting can be an important part of the practice teacher's skills (Thompson *et al.* 1990).

Practice learning and practice teaching

Recognising, understanding and negotiating the dilemmas of practice are at the root of practice teaching and learning. As we have seen from Kolb's learning model, it is a cyclical process – beginning competence raises awareness of dilemmas, tackling them builds competence, bringing the student to further and more complex dilemmas, and so on. The competence requirements in relation to practice dilemmas will therefore vary from first to second-year placements (Braye 1993).

The Law Improvement Project Group Report published by CCETSW in October 1991 (Ball *et al.* 1991) emphasises two points which are helpful to practice teachers. The first is that practice teachers and colleges must work together and the second is that second-year competence must build on the first year and that the second year is about more depth as opposed to more law (Gwenlan 1993).

The first point is achievable if there is good partnership and communication between the college and the practice teacher. My own experience, however, is that it is almost impossible to sit down with the college tutors to devise sample exercises to be used in placement which test out and extend the teaching given at college or university. One is left with the course handbook for guidance on the areas covered at college and past experience from previous students on the same course. The research has highlighted very clearly the importance of the placement experience in creating and providing learning experiences for the students in social work law (Hogg, Kent and Ward 1992). However, it has also highlighted the variation and inconsistency in what the practice teachers provide. This is not surprising, according to the researchers, given their lack of consistency in what they think the colleges expect and require from them, and their lack of knowledge of what law is being taught in college, when it is being taught in relation to placements, and how.

The researchers concluded that without clarification of expectations between college and practice teacher, college and student, and student and practice teachers, the input from the practice teachers on placements is likely to be inconsistent and patchy. If colleges were able to provide practice teachers with the timetable, content and method of teaching of law on their courses, this would be a start towards helping them to understand what is being expected of them. The research suggests that the placement is central to the student's learning. We know teaching of basic theory is taking place at college and therefore we need to enable the practice teacher to link that teaching to the reality, as experienced in practice, in order for the learning of a theory of social work legal practice to take place (*ibid.*). The use of place-ment contracts and planning between the student, tutor and practice teacher at an early stage in the placement can be effective in ensuring that the stu-dent's individual needs are met, as far as possible, within the placement. Where practice teachers have managed to establish close links with the tutors, it has made practice teachers more aware that it is not enough to depend on live case material in a relatively short placement that may not yield an age mix, gender mix, or ethnic mix in the caseload. It is this area, of assessing the student's competence in social work law and building competence, that is the major challenge for practice teachers.

It has been argued that social workers are not, and should not try to be, mini lawyers (Wilson and James 1989). Law is merely one resource for achieving their central concerns – the core from which all other tasks are derived – the care and protection of the client (Ward and Hogg 1993). David Carson (1989) took the view that meeting the objectives laid out in *The Law Report* (Ball *et al.* 1988) would oblige social work students to follow a more taxing course than considered appropriate for law students. It is impossible for any student to have all the material in *Teaching, Learning and Assessing Social Work Law* (Ball *et al.* 1991) at their fingertips. They should, however, be exposed to this material on their course.

It is a basic requirement of CCETSW that: 'students need to know the substantive law relevant to social work practice, its nature and sources' (CCETSW 1995). According to Braye and Preston-Shoot (1991) every social work student (whether they eventually work in Child Protection or not) should be aware of Emergency Protection Orders (EPOs) and know that the legislation is found in the Children Act 1989. That an application for dis-charge of an EPO cannot be heard by a court until 72 hours have elapsed (S45(9)) does not have to be known: whether it is 48 hours or 72 hours can be looked up. We should be assessing whether students confronted by a case study have sufficient confidence to know their way round the Act and find this kind of detail if it is relevant to the case study (Mather 1993). A basic working knowledge would at least avoid the undesirable fame accorded to one local authority social worker whose ignorance of the law was high-lighted in a recent judgement in the High Court, following an appeal by the mother after the guardian *ad Litem* had recommended that the court make a Care Order when the local authority applied to extend a Supervision Order:

> The guardian *ad Litem* attended court and recommended that a care or-der should be made in place of the supervision order. This was resisted by the mother and at that time by the local authority in the mistaken be-lief that they would not be able to leave the child with her mother if a care order was made. (Butler-Sloss 1995)

Some ideas for practice teachers to provide learning experiences for students

To gain a wider variety of experience of the law relating to social work, in addition to the actual live experience offered by the placement, the practice teacher can use the following methods.

Exercises and questions

Excellent examples of these can be found in the final chapter of *Practising Social Work Law* (Braye and Preston-Shoot 1992a). These are useful in that they can be selected by practice teachers to illustrate a certain point and can be discussed during supervision with the student. They are also helpful for the practice teacher to reflect on his/her own practice dilemmas from using social work law.

Case studies

These have the advantage that students clearly understand the relevance of the task as it can be related closely to their future work. Writing them can be a problem, often practice teachers use an anonymised case that is familiar to them, which can give the advantage of being able to tell the student what the final outcome was. A complex case can be broken down into several scenar-ios, leading the student through the various stages of the case, rather than swamping them with an excess of information at the beginning. It is useful for students to become accustomed to thinking through case studies as in my own experience they are often used during appointment interviews.

Role play

Role plays must be familiar to any social worker who has undertaken training, since they are frequently used on social work courses. Role play, known
as 'mooting', has been a voluntary activity in law school for many years.
Moots are legal debates in a hypothetical court room setting in which students play the roles of counsel and present legal arguments based on a
fictitious legal action. For example, a fictitious case study on child abuse
could be written, with students playing the roles of the local authority applying for an EPO, of the parents opposing the order and of the legal
representatives for or against an order. If there are not enough students at a
placement this may be difficult for the practice teacher to set up, unless willing team members can be enlisted to play a part. Role plays can be adapted
for use between the student and practice teacher, for example, if the student
has a difficult visit with a client the student could practice with the practice
teacher playing the role of the client. This can give inexperienced students
the confidence to face real situations, even such basic situations as introducing themselves and explaining their role to clients.

Live case material

One of the most 'real' ways of widening students' knowledge of legal situations in social work is to use live case material, either from the practice
teacher's own caseload, or from within the team. This has the advantage that
the student can follow a case through, reading relevant court reports, attending court hearings and case conferences as an observer. It is vital that students
are given the opportunity to attend court as an observer before they become
key workers in court proceedings. I know from my own experience how
unnerving it can be to find yourself in court for the first time giving evidence
in heavily contested care proceedings. By observing the workings of a complex case, the student can gain a deeper understanding of the issues than
would be available to them in direct experience on their own restricted
caseload.

Conclusion

It is important for social workers to have an understanding of the legal system
and of the nature of the law in different parts of the UK. This applies not just
to those with a statutory role, such as local authority field workers, approved
social workers and probation officers, but to all social workers who may
come into contact with the law through their professional practice with

clients. An understanding of the legal system should therefore be an essential element of professional competency within social work. The needs of many clients will include the need for preliminary informed advice about the law and the legal system that can only be provided by a social worker who is familiar with the nature of the law and the operation of the legal system (Vernon 1993).

Research has shown that it is helpful for social work students to receive some legal input prior to their first placement, since this provides a grounding to enable students to ask pertinent questions (Hogg *et al.* 1992). However, it must be borne in mind that there is clear evidence that learning about legal duties in classroom situations has not been retained in practice (DHSS 1982; Beckford Report 1985; Carlile Report 1987), and that loss of learning occurs almost immediately between academic courses and arrival on placement (Hogg *et al.* 1992). It has been suggested that this is because academic learning is insufficiently linked to practice. It may also be because for knowledge to stick, social work law teaching must promote understanding of the connections between the law and social work, and students must be actively engaged on a personal level within the context of what they are learning (Braye and Preston-Shoot 1992).

These findings are of great relevance to practice teachers and indicate that use of 'live' case material and 'learning from doing' are more beneficial to the student than a more theoretical mode. This argument has been applied to social work training in general (Braye and Preston-Shoot 1992).

Research has also found that student-centred approaches are more empowering, since they promote responsibility, understanding and transfer learning. They encourage learning in depth, based on critical, reflective and conceptual ability, active experimentation and a wide use of resources (people and knowledge) which is more likely to be retained and re-employed. This closely fits Kolb's pattern of adult learning, outlined earlier.

The aim of this chapter has been to encourage practice teachers to consider the subject of social work law and how it should be taught in placements; with all its dilemmas and demands it remains at the core of social work practice. The major tension in the practice of social work law has been highlighted by Braye and Preston-Shoot (1992a):

> The more practitioners emphasise a legal role, the more they are likely to incur user displeasure; the more they emphasise social action, the more they risk government or agency displeasure. To hold the middle ground, and to avoid a continuing dive in credibility, requires that social

workers, individually and collectively, implement strategies which make empowerment and anti-discriminatory practice a reality in the statutory context; develop a political awareness which connects the individual and the social, and raises consciousness about the law, about unmet needs, about inadequate resources and structural inequalities; make sense of and promote that understanding of social work's position and engage in debate about social work's mandate. (p.19)

A deeper understanding of social work law will surely help all social workers, practice teachers and students to 'hold the middle ground' in this most complex and challenging of tasks.

Appendix: A Section of *Law for Social Workers in England and Wales*. (CCETSW 1995)

Knowledge

Students need to understand:

(i)   that the law gives social workers their mandate to practise:

    (a) as employees of statutory bodies (when, for example, employed as a local authority social worker); or officers of the court (when employed, for example, as a probation officer)

    (b) by defining the various groups of people in respect of whom social workers have duties and powers

    (c) by defining a social worker's legal functions in relation to each client group;

(ii) that legally accountable powers, when appropriately used, can promote and encourage good social work practice: e.g. by emphasising the importance of prevention and rehabilitation; by setting out the conditions upon which compulsory intervention is permissible; by ensuring that compulsory intervention with a person's rights takes place in accordance with proper legal safeguards, such as due process of law and adherence to principles of natural justice;

(iii) that the exercise of legal powers may be oppressive or discriminatory if not used in ways that avoid discrimination and respect client's rights; and that social and legal institutions and processes, such as the court system, to which social worker practice must often relate, are frequently identified as discriminatory and racist in operation and practice.

Students need to know:

(i)   the substantive law which is relevant to social work practice, and its nature and sources;

(ii) the relationship between local authority and probation policy and the law;

(iii) the structures and processes of the relevant court and tribunal systems.

Values

Students need to have commitment to:

(i)   social justice, equality and anti-oppressive practice;

(ii) the right of individuals to receive care/treatment and control in the context of:

- the least restrictive alternative,
- normalisation/non-stigmatisation,
- ethnic/cultural/language needs, with access to appeal and choice, as far as possible;

(iii) social order: e.g. the right of society to protection from significant risk, danger or harm; the recognition of the rights of significant others e.g. victims.

Issues of oppression and civil rights are intrinsic to these values/aims, and social work law courses will need to consider them regularly and routinely as they affect social work practice and social work provision.

Skills

These should include:

(i)   cognitive, interpersonal, decision-making and administrative skills, e.g. ability to assess, to plan, to communicate, to provide support for clients, their families and carers;

(ii) ability to use correct and appropriate knowledge and values in the interest of the client, the agency, the courts and society;

(iii) ability to conduct him/herself appropriately in adult and youth criminal courts, and family proceedings courts. Ability to prepare and present evidence;

(iv) development of appropriate report writing techniques;

(v) ability to work in a multidisciplinary setting, e.g. with lawyers, doctors and health visitors;

(vi) ability to use legal processes, including emergency procedures, appropriately in relation to client groups with whom they work in their assessed practice experiences.

References

Ball, C., Harris, R., Roberts, G. and Vernon, S. (1988) *The Law Report: Teaching and Assessment of Law in Social Work Education* (Paper 4.1). London: CCETSW.

Ball, C., Roberts, G., Trench, S. and Vernon, S. (1991) *Teaching, Learning and Assessing Social Work Law*. London: CCETSW.

Blom-Cooper Report, The (1985) *A Child in Trust*. London: London Borough of Brent.

Braye, S. (1993) 'Building competence in social work law for the Diploma in Social Work.' In M. Preston-Shoot (ed) *Assessment of Competence in Social Work Law*. Social Work Education Special Publication. London: Whiting and Birch.

Braye, S. and Preston-Shoot, M. (1991) 'On acquiring law competence for social work: teaching, practice and assessment.' *Social Work Education 10*, 1, 12–29.

Braye, S. and Preston-Shoot, M. (1992a) *Practising Social Work Law*. London: Macmillan (Second edition published 1997.)

Braye, S. and Preston-Shoot, M. (1992b) 'Honourable intentions: partnership and written agreements in welfare law.' *Journal of Social Welfare and Family Law 6*, 511–28.

Butler-Sloss, L.J. (1995) Re A (Supervision Order: Extension) CA 1995 1 Family Law Reports.

Carlile Report, The (1987) *A Child in Mind. Report of the Commission of Inquiry into the Circumstances Surrounding the Death of Kimberly Carlile*. London: London Borough of Greenwich.

Carson, D. (1989) 'Learning the use of legal skills.' *Social Work Today* 20 July.

CCETSW (1995) *Law for Social Workers in England and Wales*. London: Central Council for Education and Training in Social Work.

CCETSW (1996) *Assuring Quality in the Diploma in Social Work: 1. Rules and Requirements for the DipSW*. London: CCETSW.

Cleveland (1988) *Report of Inquiry into Child Abuse in Cleveland Cm 412*. London: HMSO.

Davies, M. and Brandon, M. (1988) 'The summer of '88.' *Community Care 733*, 16–18.

DHSS (1982) *Child Abuse: A Study of Inquiry Reports 1973–1981*. London: HMSO.

Fox Report (1990) *Report into the Death of Stephanie Fox*. For the London Borough of Wandsworth. London: London Borough of Wandsworth.

Gwenlan, C. (1993) 'Law teaching, learning outside the college and assessment.' In M. Preston-Shoot (ed) *Assessment of Competence in Social Work Law*. Social Work Education Special Publication. London: Whiting and Birch.

Harris, N. (1987) 'Defensive social work.' *British Journal of Social Work 17*, 1, 61–9.

Hogg, B., Kent, P. and Ward, D. (1992) *Teaching of Law in Practice Placements*. University of Nottingham.

Howe, D. (1980) 'Inflated states and empty theories in social work.' *British Journal of Social Work 10*, 3, 317–40.

Jones, F., Fletcher, B. and Ibbetson, K. (1991) 'Stressors and strains amongst social workers: demands, supports, constraints and psychological health.' *British Journal of Social Work 21*, 5, 443–69.

Mather, V. (1993) 'College based assessment of competency in social work law.' In M. Preston-Shoot (ed) *Assessment of Competence in Social Work Law*. Social Work Education Special Publication. London: Whiting and Birch.

Preston-Shoot, M. (1993) 'Whither social work law? Future questions on the teaching and assessment of law to social workers.' In *Assessment of Competence in Social Work Law*. Social Work Education Special Publication. London: Whiting and Birch.

Sheldon, B. (1982) *Behaviour Modification: Theory, Practice and Philosophy*. London: Tavistock.

Thompson, Osada and Anderson (1990) *Practice Teaching in Social Work*. Pepar.

Vernon, S. (1993) *Social Work and the Law*. London: Butterworth.

Vernon, S., Harris, R. and Ball, C. (1990) *Towards Social Work Law – Legally Competent Professional Practice* (Paper 4.2). London: CCETSW.

Ward, D. and Hogg, B. (1993) 'An integrated approach to the teaching of social work law.' In M. Preston-Shoot (ed) *Assessment of Competence in Social Work Law*. Social Work Education Special Publication. London: Whiting and Birch.

Wilson, K. and James, A. (1989) 'Looking into the Law Report: a two dimensional affair.' *Social Work Today 20*, 27, 12–13.

Further reading

Braye, S., Preston-Shoot, M. and Wasik, M. (1993) 'A painful silence.' *Community Care 959*, 22–23.

Butler, B. and Elliott, D. (1985) *Teaching and Learning for Practice*. Aldershot: Gower.

CCETSW (1989) *Requirements and Regulations for the Diploma in Social Work*. (Paper 30). London: Central Council for Education and Training in Social Work.

CCETSW (1991) *Rules and Requirements for the Diploma in Social Work* (2nd edition) (Paper 30). London: Central Council for Education and Training in Social Work.

CHAPTER 14

Practice Teaching and Violence

Carol Kedward

This chapter sets out to offer practice teacher and student a framework for dealing with violence in the workplace. It reviews the development of the profession's awareness of the problem and the present stage reached in attempts to handle it. The most significant written sources are noted and some indicators on prevention, management and post-incident debriefing and support are suggested. It makes a case for the handling of challenging and violent behaviour to be treated as an integral part of student learning, prepared for, continuously addressed during and assessed at the end of placement in concert with the student's other competences. I believe that good practice in relation to violence cannot be separated from the wider issue of staff care and support. This relates to all levels: while it is obvious that a management culture which values staff is much more likely to take safety seriously than one which does not, similarly, workers, practice teachers and students who take proper care of themselves at work are better placed to make sound decisions when it comes to violence.

Violence against social workers: a résumé

There are now an increasing number of references covering various aspects of violence; there is only space here to trace the major events. Those seeking a fuller account might wish to consult *Violence Against Social Workers: The Implications for Practice* (Norris with Kedward 1990) which brought together all the research available at the time on incidence rates, definitions, explanations, risk factors and agency response and made wide-ranging recommendations on good practice. Stanley Bute's beautifully crafted chapter, 'Violence to social workers', in *Violence and Health Care Professionals* (Wykes 1994) provides a briefer, classic summary.

Concerns were first expressed in the late 1970s and early 1980s. One of the first contributors was Stanley Bute. His letter and two subsequent articles in *Social Work Today*, 'An Indictment upon Us for Failing to Learn' (1979a), 'The Threat of Violence in Close Encounters with Clients' (1979b) and 'Guidelines for Coping with Violence by Clients' (1979c), evoked a widespread response from social workers and may be considered landmarks in the field. Bute, whose interest was first triggered by his own experience of being taken hostage by a client, carried out the first piece of large-scale research: his 1979 postal survey of social workers in the Hampshire area finally appeared in 1986 as *Social Workers at Risk: The Prevention and Management of Violence* (Brown, Bute and Ford 1986) and provided the first solid evidence that previous thinking on the matter was seriously flawed. Of those surveyed, 22 per cent of field, 44 per cent of residential and 50 per cent of day-care workers had been attacked or threatened in the previous three years. This was a vastly greater proportion than anyone had foreseen and gave the lie to the notion that violent or threatening incidents were rare events which befell only the unfortunate or incompetent worker or those working in stigmatised inner-city areas.

Subsequent studies not only confirmed the findings of the 'Wessex Study' as it became known, but added to them. Colin Rowett sent questionnaires to every social worker in one Shire county and followed them up with interviews. In *Violence in Social Work* (Rowett 1986), he showed that whereas senior management using their own records estimated that one worker in 259 would be sufficiently assaulted to need medical help in a five-year period, his questionnaires suggested the figure was one in four. While 76 per cent of all assaults were minor (cuts and bruises), 18 per cent were moderate (recognisable but non-permanent damage such as broken bones) and 6 per cent severe (untreatable injuries such as blindness). Twenty-four per cent of injuries were therefore serious, and all social workers were at risk, residential workers particularly so.

Further studies followed throughout the 1980s (*see* References), by which time clear patterns were visible despite the range of definitions, methodologies, sample size and geographical area represented. Many of the early findings continue to be reinforced both in published studies and in agencies' own unpublished monitoring and this chapter will attempt to cover some of the most relevant to the practice setting. Others are conflicting, unclear or inadequately researched but also need pointing out, since lack of information is a potential risk factor in itself. Before moving on to this, however, two further points need to be made.

It is now beyond dispute that in public, professional and domestic settings, wherever proper records are kept, the incidence of violence and threatening behaviour is much higher than in the profile presented prior to monitoring. While it is likely that in all these cases, some of the increase can be accounted for by improved reporting and recording, there is considerable evidence in the professional sphere that there is also a real increase. An example of this for social work is Norris's 'Nova' study (Norris with Kedward 1990): while admittedly a small sample (38 workers), consistency with previous studies and social workers' personal accounts suggest its reliability. Workers reported an average of 5.6 attacks as a career total and 2.6 in the last year while threats ran at 5.1 for career total and 2.6 in the last year; unless workers have forgotten earlier events, which seems unlikely, this represents a significant increase.

One of the most disquieting findings to emerge from virtually all the early research was the generally poor response of management and other colleagues to social workers when attacked and threatened and the consequent under-reporting of incidents as a result. Social workers complained not just of lack of support but of being held responsible for violence; they therefore concealed incidents for fear of being labelled incompetent and coped, or

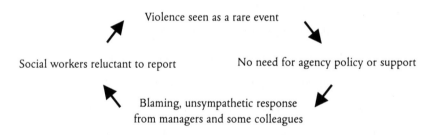

Violence seen as a rare event

Social workers reluctant to report   No need for agency policy or support

Blaming, unsympathetic response
from managers and some colleagues

Figure 14.1

failed to cope, alone or with the help of family and friends. A classic negative cycle was therefore identified:
Faced with this unhelpful situation, social workers tended to blame themselves. This is particularly ironic when, at the same time, the profession was working hard to alert an unwilling public to the structural nature and extent of violence in society, child and partner abuse in particular, and to enable

victims/survivors to free themselves from self-blaming behaviour. Their own professional situation directly mirrored that of their clients.

The severity and deeply unpleasant nature of most threats and actual incidents is nevertheless quite clear from the start and replicated in every study, small or large-scale from Bute to the present: a dismal litany of injuries from cuts and bruises to irreparable damage, a similarly alarming list of weapons and projectiles and an equal variety of abusive language including threats to workers' own families have become increasingly familiar over the years. The implications, however, were painfully slow to register despite the fact that the first recorded death, that of Fred Gray, social worker with deaf persons, occurred as early as 1979. The 'unthinkable' nature of such an event and the consequent failure to take precautions allowed the toll to rise to a completely unacceptable six murders by 1990, sadly justifying Stanley Bute's castigation of the profession for its failure to learn.

Contexts

The contexts in which violence occurs have been established as:

1.   disciplining or advising of clients

2.   the witholding of goods or services

3.   the removal of children from families through court proceedings or perceived threat of it

4.   the compulsory admission of clients to psychiatric hospital

5.   the worker acting as intermediary between warring client or users

6.   interviewing new clients or those about whom little is known

7.   working with clients known to the worker for six months or more.

The first five are easily understood, have been well publicised and in many cases incorporated into thinking about good practice. The last two have proved more problematic and merit some consideration since they are as likely to affect students as workers, and, more fundamentally, the failure to take account of them seems indicative of core concepts, attitudes and values which bedevil the profession's whole approach to the subject.

In the first place, the social work task is to advise, assist, befriend and empower the client and while the exercise of statutory responsibilities is accepted as an integral part of the work it is usually the least popular. To go still further and think of clients as possible assailants, therefore, is too conflicting to be borne and so is avoided. This underlying tension is further exacerbated in different ways by the two contexts under discussion.

As far as the first is concerned, it particularly runs counter to traditional social work values to be cautious about new or little-known clients since it is the social worker who is meant to keep an open mind, listen and understand the world view of someone who has usually had a raw deal from everyone else in life both private and public.

The second strikes at the heart of the social worker's existence, namely the ability to form relationships. Social workers usually enter the profession in the belief that they are 'good with people' and their training leads them to see the worker/client relationship as a key element through which all else is mediated. On the face of it, therefore, attack by a long-standing client implies either a failure of a fundamental nature or a betrayal by someone in whom a great deal has been invested or both, all adding to the traumatic nature of the event. One explanation which might prove useful here, both because awareness might help prevent such attacks as well as draw some of the 'sting' from them when they do occur, is that of transference. This process, whereby attributes and behaviour from early experience are 'transferred' onto authority figures and situations in later life, is well documented and immediately recognisable to teachers, doctors, police etc., even those sceptical of or hostile to the Freudian theories in which it originated. While it is useful for all those in authority to be aware of it, those who, like social workers, deal with people whose early experience has often been painful and abusive, need to be especially attuned since the effects are likely to be negative; young and inexperienced workers should be clear that it is a consequence of role and they are therefore as likely to be affected as older, more senior staff. What seems to have happened here is that the proper development of a wide range of social work methods and the consequent decrease in significance of formerly dominant psychodynamic models have allowed important learning to fade with them: not so much a failure to learn as a loss of learning we once had.

The length of time workers spend with clients is also central to the issue of context of violence since length of exposure tends to increase the risk, particularly where client groups are known to present challenging behaviour. What is striking here, however, is that different studies reach different conclusions about which groups present the highest risk. It is impossible to say whether this reflects policy, practice, 'real' difference in population or simply variable methodology and reporting. What is clear is that all client groups traditionally in receipt of institutional care – children, young people, those with learning and physical disability, mental health service users, older people and the elderly mentally infirm – all score significantly on some-body's list and are all capable of violent and threatening behaviour. (Initially there was some surprise at how frequently EMI residents were prominently featured in reports.) The point to register, therefore, is that there is no such thing as a 'safe' group.

The venues in which attacks other than those in institutional settings take place are varied, and again the hierarchy of risk depends on area and study. Attacks take place wherever social workers and clients find themselves together, in clients' homes, social work offices, reception areas, office car parks, cars and transport vehicles: all figure frequently as might be expected. A more unexpected finding, less commonplace but perhaps more alarming, is that a number of attacks occur away from the workplace in the street or shops, or outside workers' homes, some due to chance sightings while others represent deliberate targeting of workers. In general it is thought safer to conduct potentially dangerous interviews at the social work office (provided of course that this is itself in a safe building with properly maintained alarm systems etc.), which allows for careful planning of everything from reception to departure, should encourage the client to observe formal behavioural boundaries and has reinforcements near at hand if the worst should happen. Some clients however may feel more angered or threatened by office sur-roundings or refuse to attend when statute demands they be seen, in which case much care has to be taken to plan a safe home visit, or some neutral set-ting may be preferred. Working alone in a building is to be avoided, and home visits or car journeys should only be taken alone after careful consid-eration and when the worker feels fully confident. While working in twos is recommended, it is not in itself a panacea as, sadly, many pairs have been attacked. Cautious and careful planning, sensitive and skilful use of worker and reliable back-up are the crucial factors.

There are a number of other areas where the sparse or conflicting nature of the evidence leads to the conclusion that each case must be carefully con-sidered on its merits. As regards gender and risk, for example, early studies suggested that male workers were more at risk than female; among the hypotheses were that women were less aggressive, better at spotting and defusing violence, that men were allocated or called in to deal with the most difficult cases or that some perpetrators were less likely to attack women. Some later studies reinforce the finding; others run counter to it. Regardless of who is more at risk, however, it is clear that women are subject to the full range of abusive behaviour up to and including brutal killing; in some cases it also seems that some male perpetrators are more likely to attack women, particularly if they feel themselves threatened by women in positions of power.

Levels of abuse against workers who are from structurally disadvantaged groups for reasons of disability, race or sexuality, and levels of sexual harassment are impossible to determine since only a tiny minority of authorities monitored such factors in the early stages, many still do not, and there is no coherent overall picture. A certain number of authorities do now have a clear policy on the unacceptability of discriminatory behaviour and a considerable history of collecting information. From the evidence available and from personal accounts, it is clear that workers are subject to all these forms of harassment, and that this should be borne in mind when planning work or debriefing staff or students. We also need to avoid stereotypical thinking: for example, what evidence we have suggests that male workers are subject to more sexual harassment from female clients than might have been anticipated.

Perpetrators

A profile of perpetrators is also difficult to establish, being in many cases determined by setting. In agencies with a varied client base, however, such as social services departments, Rowett for example found that 38 per cent of assailants had had one or more admissions to psychiatric care and 45 per cent had a previous criminal offence, of which 28 per cent were for a crime of violence. He also found that while institutional workers were more likely to be attacked by male clients, field workers were more likely to be attacked by female clients (Rowett 1986). None of this is particularly surprising except that fashionable attitudes have tended to cloud perception and contributed to risk. Campaigns to destigmatise mental illness have properly made the case that the vast majority of those labelled mentally ill present no threat to anyone, while feminist writers have equally properly sought to draw attention to the violence perpetrated by men against women in a patriarchal society. This should not, however, blind us to the fact that a small proportion of those labelled mentally ill do present a threat, sometimes a severe one, and that while the bulk of recorded violence is male perpetrated (a significant proportion against other males), women are also capable of all forms of violence including murder. Well-meaning propaganda is no substitute for clear thinking and professional judgement and does a disservice to worker and potential perpetrator alike.

A range of explanations has been advanced to explain perpetrator violence; among them are: psychological – innate aggression improperly socialised due to dysfunctional upbringing; social learning – some families and cultures reward violence and bullying, further reinforced (though not necessarily caused) by other factors, notably the media which glamorises not just violence but disinhibitors such as drugs and alcohol; sociological – low social status, disqualification from citizenship in education, housing, employment leading to alienation and asocial behaviour. In some cases there may be a complex interaction of all three. Triggers for the perpetrator may be frustration, refusal to meet perceived need, physical or emotional pain, humiliation, fear, confusion, desperation, exercise of power and transference (described above).

Given that such theories accord with the research findings on the settings and activities where violence occurs, it will be apparent that the policies of the previous Conservative government, designed to widen the gap between rich and poor, powerful and powerless, steadily exacerbated the situation and contributed to a steady deterioration in the conditions in which social workers try to function. Traditionally placed in the difficult position of straddling the divide between the powerful and the disadvantaged, social workers have found themselves attempting to bridge a constantly widening gap with dwindling resources which attracting fierce criticism from both sides – from clients for policies over which they had no control, and from a government which, doubtless perceiving them as over-identified with marginal and 'undeserving' groups, continued its attacks on the profession's existence right up until the election campaign of Spring 1997, eloquently supported by frequent vilification in the press. This public scapegoating may in itself have contributed to a climate where abusing social workers was felt to be permissible. (It is too early to say what difference the arrival of a Labour government will make: while some change is already apparent, a major shift in policy and certainly in resource allocation is unlikely and in any case would take some while to bear fruit.)

Social workers do, however, have more control over some aspects of their work which have been shown to contribute to danger. The following are all to be avoided:

- Failure to be clear about role so that the client falsely perceives the worker as a friend and is therefore unprepared for the exercise of authority

- Failure to be clear and to provide boundaries from the outset about expectations of client and worker behaviour

- Patronising or distancing behaviour, false cheerfulness as a defence against client chaos and distress

- Inconsistency in policy or behaviour

- Undue officiousness, taking refuge in overplaying the professional.

This leads on to a further consideration of ways in which social workers are shown by research to have endangered themselves. Many studies show that workers are involved in repeat incidents which suggests that lessons have not been learned. Workers' own accounts of incidents show that all too frequently they went into situations aware that there was a risk, in many cases in a state of acute anxiety, and yet neither alerted colleagues nor felt able to call off the interview. To some extent this reflects poor management, since a positive culture renders such behaviour less likely. Most workers, however, female, male, black, white, gay, straight, newly qualified or experienced, all feel for different reasons that they cannot be seen not to cope and an exploitative agency culture simply reinforces the pressure. Furthermore, constant exposure to challenging behaviour, long-term stress and sheer fatigue blunt workers' perceptions, skew their judgement and slow their reactions. Good management, especially good quality worker-centred supervision, is essential if this slippage is not to occur.

This links with the broader and more fundamental question of self-care for which social workers themselves have to take responsibility as a complement to and not a substitute for management responsibility. Social workers have not traditionally been known for asserting themselves either as a profession or as individual workers. A number of hypotheses have been put forward. The experiences which motivate entry to the profession, often painful, may leave social workers with a level of self-esteem not very different from that of their clients; the predominance of women, especially at ground level, whose gender socialisation may have been to put care for others before their own; the social class profile of workers which may loosely be described as 'lower middle class': all these doubtless play a part. This is a complex matter which warrants a volume in itself. The point at issue here is that workers need to reflect on the wider issue as well as the specific, since it makes no sense to expect anyone, manager, worker or student, to take care with respect to violence if their general attitude to self-care is poor or even destructive.

Government response

If social workers were slow to take action for their own safety, the public and governmental response was even slower. It was only as a result of a great deal of pressure, in one case after persistent lobbying by the father of murdered social worker Isabel Schwarz, that two government reports were produced. Lord Skelmersdale in *Violence to Staff: Report of the DHSS Advisory Committee on Violence to Staff* (Department of Health and Social Security 1988) and John Spokes QC in the *Report of the Committee of Inquiry into the Care and Aftercare of Miss Sharon Campbell* (Department of Health and Social Security 1988) both made a number of constructive recommendations. Among the most important of these were that buildings should be safety audited and made secure; that public access to staff working areas should be carefully controlled; that emergency alarms be installed, maintained and staff trained in appropriate response; that the use of personal alarms be considered; that workers should never be alone in a building especially out of normal hours; that good communication between workers is essential to safe working especially in multi-disciplinary contexts or where clients are making threats or have a history of aggressive behaviour. The moving report on Isabel Schwarz, only two years qualified, illustrates a number of other points: threats should always be taken seriously – the client, Ms Sharon Campbell, had repeatedly threatened her and had assaulted her once before; good supervision is essential – due to changes in supervisor, Ms Schwarz did not share at work the fears she expressed to family and friends; misapplied attempts at anti-discriminatory practice can be damaging to client and worker. Prior to the murder, Ms Campbell, who was black, had been behaving violently to others in her hostel and in the community; it may be that she was not readmitted to hospital when hindsight suggests she clearly needed to be, in an attempt to respond to information about the over-representation of black residents in mental health institutions.

Unfortunately much of the impact of these reports was lost since it was made clear that no extra resources would be forthcoming for their implementation. In the same way, the *Guidelines and Recommendations to Employers on Violence Against Employees* (Association of Directors of Social Services 1987) and *Management Services Paper No. 13* (Association of Chiefs of Probation

1988) gave a clear, helpful and thorough message to staff, but had a limited effect as no timescale was given for their enactment.

Social services and probation response

My own review of practice in social services and probation departments (Norris with Kedward 1990) showed a wide range of response from a full policy on prevention, training and post-incident care to the non-existent. It was only possible to say with certainty that approximately a third of each service was making adequate provision. Since as far as I am aware this is the last national survey, it is impossible to know what the present situation is. From personal and professional contacts it looks as though some authorities have improved on their performance at that time while others have maintained a high standard. For others, however, the combination of accommodating new legislation – the Children Act 1989, Community Care Act 1990, and a stream of criminal justice legislation – with cuts in resources has seriously hampered progress or, worse, caused ground to be lost. It is probably worth repeating the framework which we set out at the time as the required standard for good practice, along with a plea for a firm deadline for its implementation. The fact that during the 1990s, a number of employees have successfully sued their employing authorities after incidents of violence for not meeting the standards below, on the grounds that many employers do meet their obligations, has provided a powerful impetus for change.

Responsible employers should (and practice teachers should expect them to):

- monitor violent incidents and threats
- work towards use of agreed definitions and methodology
- address issues of disability, gender, race and sexuality
- designate a person or persons in senior management to lead and co-ordinate policy
- establish the training needs of all staff groups, mount and maintain a systematic training programme for meeting them
- provide victims of violence with adequate counselling, legal and financial help
- produce guidelines in a clear and readable style which cover definition, frequency, prevention, risk situations and clients, building

safety, good working practices, post-violence help and debriefing, union representation and employer responsibility.

The appointment of a member of senior management to lead policy is pivotal since all the best intentions will come to nothing without an unequivocal lead from the top. Even when there is no formal appointment, practice teachers might find it useful to discover whether any senior manager has an interest in the subject, since a committed manager can achieve a great deal. Training is also a key issue. Cash-strapped employers are unlikely to be able to offer the ideal; but training, especially for those in high-risk positions, cannot simply be abandoned, as has happened in some cases, and should be available to practice teachers who can act as a resource even if students themselves cannot participate. Debates continue about the relative merits of different restraint methods or 'low' or 'high' arousal responses, and practice teachers will need to make their own judgements in respect of their own agency. There is general agreement that 'martial arts' type training is counter-productive and may encourage over-confidence in workers, but that 'breakaway techniques', properly taught and maintained, are useful though even they are not guaranteed success.

The student placement

Before moving on to a discussion of the practice teacher's handling of the placement, it is worth considering the levels of violence affecting students themselves. If it was at one time unthinkable that violence was really an issue for social workers, then it was perceived as even less so for students whose protected workload was thought to shield them from risk. To a large extent this is likely to have been the case although it is also probable that in common with others, students always had to contend with more than was known. The decrease in the preventive arena, however, and the corresponding shift towards a high proportion of difficult and demanding work have meant that today's student is less protected and shares many of the same risks as experienced workers.

There has been no national research as far as I am aware, but a brief summary of findings from my own monitoring of the Master in Social Work and Diploma in Higher Education programmes at the University of Sussex since 1989 may provide some pointers. Both are two-year programmes with between 20 and 24 students in each cohort, amounting to 85 to 90 placements each academic year. While many students will complete two placements and have nothing to report from either, the overall picture bears considerable resemblance to the overall research. On average, four per year cohort or 16 across the two programmes report serious incidents. There is no space here to enter into the vexed question of definition; it is clear from student reporting, however, that dealing with difficult and upset clients is routine, so that 'serious' means incidents which went beyond the usual bounds and where they felt they were no longer in control. At least two students per year are involved in very serious incidents. Examples from recent years include: a student punched and kicked by a family who pursued her down the street after she delivered a letter asking them to attend a case conference about their children; a student in a day centre pinned in a room by a client with previous convictions for violent assault shouting obscenities and threatening to kill her until rescued by a vigilant colleague; a student and practice teacher barricaded in the office of a substance abuse recovery project while a knife-wielding client, recently barred for infringeing the house rules, broke into the house to get to them; a student attacked along with the senior colleague she was accompanying on a home visit to discuss child care concerns. Students also get caught up in conditions prevailing in the agency, for example being in an office when a client previously imprisoned for targeting and assaulting a worker there was released and returned to stalk the neighbourhood. While it is clear from student reporting that considerable progress has been made, especially in post-incident follow-up, it should be equally clear from the above that student safety should be taken very seriously, since the sanitised account on the printed page bears little relation to the shocking and distressing nature of the real thing. While accepting that some incidents are totally unpredictable and therefore that we cannot eradicate violence, the focus should be very firmly on prevention.

One further nettle needs to be grasped with regard to student safety. The bulk of this article concerns risk from clients. While practice teachers may feel that student behaviour may at times leave much to be desired, students can at times feel more threatened by their practice teachers, team or indeed tutors than by their clients. While the vast majority of students report positively on their experiences of both practice teacher and team, and others have criticisms which are nonetheless contained within professional boundaries, a small minority experience what they see as unjustifiable exercise of power, usually encapsulated in the assessment process and final report. Students have also complained of sexual harassment, and homophobic and racist behaviour direct and indirect, perpetrated deliberately or at other times through ignorance. Attempting to disentangle such situations can prove exceptionally complex and there is insufficient space here to do the matter justice. The following points, born out of grappling with such issues, may prove helpful. Those of us in positions of power need constantly to remind ourselves just how powerful we seem to those whose future is in our hands. Our behaviour may be received in a completely different way from our intentions so that we need first to create conditions for honest dialogue and then to check carefully whether we come over as we intend. We need to take responsibility first for our own behaviour but then for team and agency so that students are not exposed to inappropriate behaviour from others. While problems are best dealt with between those concerned, students should know that where this is too difficult, they have access to others such as tutors, the programme director, independent support group etc., so that they are not left alone.

Placement preparation

As the preceding section shows, there now exists a considerable amount of information to help practice teachers plan for the safe working of their student, themselves and their team. Experience suggests that the best placements are those where the whole team is fully involved and shares responsibility for the student: keeping managers and colleagues briefed and consulting them where appropriate is part of good placement conduct in any case, but essential with regard to safety where collective working is crucial. Prior to the student's arrival an audit can be made of the key areas, as a result of which the practice teacher should be clear as to whether agency practice is satisfactory and where change needs to be made. The key areas are:

- Agency location, building safety, systems and maintenance
- Agency role, function, level of statutory requirement
- Client group
- Agency policy, practice and culture with regard to violence at wider and immediate team level.

Where all these factors are properly dealt with, this signals a most positive environment in which to work and undertake a student placement and greatly reduces the burden of responsibility on the practice teacher. Where all is not well, however, the practice teacher needs to enlist the support of the team to make changes. This can be a painstakingly slow process with lack of resources, entrenched attitudes, and pressure of urgent work contributing to put obstacles in the way. The imminent arrival of a student can prove a catalyst, however, and tutors might usefully be recruited for support, since they are not part of the agency and may be able to put points forward without suffering the repercussions from management which might affect workers.

As with all aspects of practice teaching, preparation will involve the practice teacher reflecting on their own attitudes and practice since it is obvious to all involved in training that modelling is an infinitely more powerful learning tool than preaching, and any gap between behaviour and rhetoric is glaringly obvious to the least perceptive student. Starting with attitudes is an important precursor to helping the student do likewise; they will clearly be heavily affected by personal experience and family norms, as well as gender, race, class, culture and previous work experience. Depending on circumstance, this reflection may be self-confirming or reveal that work needs to be done; some of it may well be painful. It is also linked to wider issues of self-esteem touched on earlier. The important point is that the practice teacher's issues should not be worked out through or visited on the student, nor should they prevent the student's issues being cleanly addressed.

When the student first visits the placement, agency norms and policy will form part of the initial discussion to establish that safety is an integral part of mainstream work. Students should be given any written material as early as possible and clear undertakings should be included in the contract agreed between student, practice teacher and tutor early in the placement. If there is no formal section on violence in the college contract *pro-forma*, a form of words will need to be agreed *ad hoc*, but teaching institutions should be strongly urged to include it formally. Some discussion of students' previous experience of challenging behaviour is helpfully placed at the start of placement along with other relationship-building issues such as gender, age, sexual orientation, power and so on, all of which will be interlinked. The practice teacher will need to bear in mind how they personally affect this discussion: a young female student may find it hard to discuss violence with a male practice teacher if she is a survivor of male abuse, familial or otherwise; black students may hesitate to share information with a white practice teacher; homophobic experiences are impossible to disclose if one is uncertain about the values of the person in power. Very personal details are unlikely to emerge for a while, if ever, but some open and honest discussion, undertaken in a non-inquisitorial manner, is essential at the start to establish a sound working basis.

Thought should also be given to the special circumstances of the student. For example, many students do not have cars, so how does this affect their safety in terms of access to the office, home visits, or journeys after dark; does the student have access to the team's mobile phone, etc? As regards the agency, students need to be told not just about the standard risks, but about any special circumstances such as a vindictive client loitering in the car park, without of course being unduly alarmist. Witholding information in an attempt not to worry the student will not only put them at risk, but will also certainly backfire, since the information will 'leak' in any case in potentially unhelpful ways. Establishing clear norms and open discussion in this way at the start not only creates a fruitful working context for the rest of placement but models the risk-reducing behaviour required of workers and students with new clients.

Initial discussion should also establish the student's skill level in handling challenging behaviour and what gaps need to be filled in respect of the particular agency. The practice teacher will then plan how best to respond in concert with the student's other learning needs. Where there is agency training, the student should obviously be included where possible. If not, the practice teacher will do the training themselves using the resources available such as appropriate texts, the practice curriculum, agency guidelines, training department videos, and so on. *Handling Aggression and Violence at Work* (Leadbetter and Trewartha 1996) is an excellent training manual designed by two former social workers for use by practitioners, and full of accessible, practical material. Other agencies who regularly undertake their own training may be willing to have the student join in. Some training may be interprofessional: 'breakaway techniques' are useful to teachers, health care workers and others, and may be provided outside the social work sphere. The student's arrival may also provide an opportunity for the team to devote a meeting or half-day to refreshing their own practice, since, like all learning, it needs regular reinforcement if it is not to fade.

Once these foundations are in place, practice teacher and student will be able to discuss specific situations and pieces of work as they arise. Where placements involve daily contact with challenging behaviour, the induction process will familiarise students with the team's ways of handling this at the earliest possible opportunity. Since consistency of staff behaviour is vital if everyone is not to be put at risk, the practice teacher will need to be vigilant in ensuring this happens and in allowing the student time to discuss any issues which may arise, stemming either from concerns about values – some strict boundary-setting regimes can seem harsh at first glance – or from lack of confidence or skill. Confrontation of angry clients is best done with the support of colleagues in the early stages, with a target date set for when the student will be expected to cope on their own.

In agencies where the work is done with a range of clients, seen either at home or in the office, the safety aspect forms part of the process from assessment stage, through intervention, long or short, to outcome and evaluation. A comprehensive list of 'do's and don'ts' is appended at the end of the chapter, but the following framework may also prove useful:

- Given the information available on the case what risk potential is there and for what reason?

- Given the above, should the interview be conducted at home or at the office, alone or with a colleague, and what back-up arrangements need to be made?

- What are the most likely signs of rising tension or potential trouble in each case? (These may vary widely, for example unusual calm bodes ill in some cases, in others unusual agitation or excitement.)

- What possible directions might the interview take and what are the best ways of defusing escalating aggression in each? (Role play is especially useful here since the best plans are likely to fly out of the student's head in a tense moment unless solidly established.)

- If attempts to keep the situation under control fail, or violence erupts unexpectedly, what action should the student take?

- If the student has had to deal with a particularly difficult interview, or, worse, been subject to verbal or physical abuse, or any other circumstance has arisen which cannot wait for the routine supervision session, what plans are in place for debriefing and what arrangements have been made if the practice teacher is not available?

My own view on the penultimate point is that any student or worker who feels themselves seriously at risk during an interview should leave as calmly as possible but at the earliest possible opportunity, and should never be made to feel that it will count against them in assessment terms if they leave a situation where they were in danger. On the contrary, students who engage in needless heroics are those about whom we should have concerns. At the other end of the spectrum there will be students who, in the professional judgement of the practice teacher, are unduly anxious and not sufficiently competent in managing reasonable risk: this will have to be dealt with along with any other areas of concern about the student's work.

Post-incident support and action

Once an incident has occurred, verbal or physical, which the student has experienced as violent or intimidating, practice teacher and team should be clear about how to handle the situation. In the first place the student is likely to go through a variant of the stages of post-traumatic shock syndrome: first, high arousal accompanied by irritability, sleeplessness, and startle response; second, avoidance, characterised by numbness and avoidance of reminders of the event; and finally re-experiencing, characterised by flashbacks. As with grief and other crises, individuals vary as to whether they pass classically through the stages and how long each stage lasts. Initially the student is likely to want to talk about what happened; practice teacher and manager should formally hear the account but it is therapeutic if other team members express a willingness to listen if the student wants, and show support. Practice teacher and manager will also help the student with necessary formalities such as filling in an incident form and will tell them what to expect in terms of time off, entitlement to counselling, and what help they may expect if they wish to bring charges against an assailant. Whether charges are brought or not, decisions must also be taken quickly on the agency response to the client and in particular whether there is to be further work with them (in statutory cases or institutional settings there may be no choice), and if so under what circumstances. In general, students or workers should not have to continue working with clients who have abused or assaulted them, though there may be particular reasons why this principle should not be adhered to. It is essential that all this is dealt with as soon as possible and made clear to the student, or the ensuing anxiety will hamper recovery.

While students are often best able to make their own decisions about their needs, practice teachers may sometimes need to exercise professional judgement and 'order' a student to take some time off; while operating 'business as usual' may be the best way for some, others may be too shocked to be able to carry on or to see that they are not fit to function. The student's college and personal tutor should be informed as soon as possible and a co-ordinated programme drawn up for short and long-term support.

While proper support at the time and subsequently should enable the student to work through to a proper resolution of the event, some matters have to be dealt with when the initial trauma is still fresh. The vexed question of whether or not to prosecute has to be faced immediately if the chance is not to be lost through lack of evidence and failure to follow procedure. The attitudes of agencies and the police vary from bringing charges wherever possible to never bringing any and from active support to downright obstruction. This is a complicated matter and opinions vary; my own view is that prosecution should always be seriously considered as a signal that assault on workers properly carrying out their duties is totally unacceptable. Where a student wishes to prosecute and is faced with resistance from agency and police, they should be free to consult their union representative and should not be made to feel that they are jeopardising their assessment outcome by so doing.

Considerations about the student's handling of the situation are ideally best left until some equilibrium has been restored but may sometimes be raised early on by the student. It is crucial here that the context of the discussion is good practice – that is, was the student's practice of good standard, and how might it have been improved, and not how did the student's behaviour cause the client/s to hit them. The fundamental point here is that while it may be understandable for a client to be angry or upset, it is never permissible for a client to abuse or strike a worker properly carrying out their professional task (I say 'properly' since of course abusing or striking a client would not be proper and, while not justifying violence, would put a different complexion on matters). Great care should be taken not to allow a student to turn insights into how they might have managed things better into self-blame. This is a very fine line and needs delicate handling.

In some cases the practice teacher may have been the victim of the same incident as the student and therefore be in need of their own post-incident support. This eventuality should be planned for in advance, the usual responsible person being the manager, but as always it is helpful if the team can share the task, as busy managers are unlikely to have sufficient time to support two traumatised staff members especially over a period of time. One very important point here is that while practice teachers' needs should be addressed for their own sake, experience shows that students become distressed and guilty if they feel colleagues' needs are being neglected, and they are consequently unable to make the best use of their own help.

Once the early stages have been negotiated the longer-term response will be governed by a multiplicity of factors: the seriousness of the event; the student's previous experience of violence personal and professional; the student's level of preparedness, training and skill; the role played by gender, sexuality, race, disability and age and their resonance for the student; the level of support offered to the student; subsequent life events or work experiences (events with perceived similarities may trigger renewed trauma). Practice teachers will need to take responsibility for checking the student's progress so that the opportunity is always there for discussion and it is not left to the student to raise the topic. While remaining sensitive to student wishes about whether to broach the subject or not, they may judge that silence is dysfunctional, in which case the matter will need to be constructively confronted.

The end of placement will signal a review of the student's experience of and ability to handle threatening and violent behaviour as part of the overall assessment process. As is normal practice, an account should be given in the final report of the student's starting point, placement progress and finishing point, with a clear statement of strengths and weaknesses, and future learning needs for those going to a second placement, or training and support needs for qualifying students. This is particularly important where the student has issues to address or has survived traumatic incidents. The account should be an agreed version following full discussion with the student.

Summary

Handling challenging and violent behaviour is part of the social work task. To some extent this simply reflects a pre-existing situation which was previously unacknowledged, but it is also likely that there is a real increase in such behaviour reflected also in the experience of other professions and wider society. In some respects, however, it is a consequence of the social work task itself which involves the exercise of authority, the gatekeeping of resources, and interaction with structurally disadvantaged people experiencing pain and distress both physical and emotional, all known precipitators of aggressive behaviour.

While much remains to be done, a considerable body of information and clear guidelines now exist on building safety, risk factors, preventive measures, training, good practice and post-incident support on which practice teachers can draw when planning for the arrival of their student and which should inform their work throughout the whole of the placement. The integration of this aspect of the work as part of the mainstream will be reflected in the end of placement report, fully agreed with the student. The best results will be achieved where team and agency share responsibility for creating and maintaining safe working conditions which are part of a positive culture of staff support.

Appendix: Violence Against Social Workers: Some Do's and Don'ts

Do:

- take safety issues into consideration as part of your approach to all your work
- make sure you know what agency policy is and what your entitlements are in respect of training, support and post-incident help
- make sure that you know that the building/s you work in are safe, that you know where the emergency buttons are etc.
- point out the need for safe buildings, proper guidelines and an adequate policy where there is none
- listen to your instincts: if you feel there is cause for concern, take it seriously and discuss it with colleagues
- proceed with caution when you have to see clients on whom there is little information: this is a known source of danger
- give clear signals from the outset and make it clear that you will not tolerate abuse
- make sure you are always near the door when you have any concern about a client
- remove yourself from the scene SOONER rather than later when attempts to defuse a situation are clearly not working.

Don't:

- assume that violence or the threat of it is unlikely to happen to you: it is now part of the job and you need to plan for it
- allow your particular circumstances (being female, male, black, gay, newly qualified, a student, very experienced etc.) make you feel you have to be seen to cope whatever the odds
- ever escort a client in a car or carry out a home visit alone unless you have fully considered the safety angle and feel 100 per cent sure it is safe to do so
- ever work in a building on your own when everyone else has gone home

- forget that many violent attacks are committed by clients who have known their workers for six months or more

- make the assumption that you have unique gifts so that clients with a history of violent behaviour, especially to workers, will behave differently with you

- get blasé, because you deal with difficult behaviour all day long so that you fail to spot it when someone is really dangerous

- assume that certain types of client will not be dangerous, such as women, young people, old people etc. – everyone is capable of violence in certain circumstances.

TAKE SAFETY SERIOUSLY – YOU MAY WISH TO ADD TO THE LIST...

References

Association of Chiefs of Probation (1988) *Management Services Manual.* Paper 13. London: ACP.

Association of Directors of Social Services (1987) *Guidelines and Recommendations to Employers on Violence Against Employees.* London: ADSS.

Brown, R., Bute, S.F. and Ford, P. (1986) *Social Workers at Risk: The Prevention and Management of Violence.* London: Macmillan.

Bute, S.F. (1979a) 'An indictment upon us for failing to learn.' *Social Work Today 10, 23, 11.*

Bute, S.F. (1979b) 'The threat of violence in close encounters with clients.' *Social Work Today 11, 14, 13–15.*

Bute, S.F. (1979c) 'Guidelines for coping with violence by clients.' *Social Work Today 11, 15, 13–15.*

Department of Health and Social Security (1988) *Report of the Committee of Inquiry into the Care and Aftercare of Miss Sharon Campbell.* London: HMSO.

Department of Health and Social Security (1988) *Violence to Staff: Report of the DHSS Advisory Committee on Violence to Staff.* London: HMSO.

Leadbetter, D. and Trewartha, R. (1996) *Handling Aggression and Violence at Work: A Training Manual.* Lyme Regis: Russell House Publishing.

Norris, D. with Kedward, C. (1990) *Violence Against Social Workers: The Implications for Practice.* London: Jessica Kingsley Publishers.

Rowett, C. (1986) *Violence in Social Work.* Cambridge: University of Cambridge Institute of Criminology.

Wykes, T. (ed) (1994) *Violence and Health Care Professionals.* London: Chapman and Hall.

Further reading

Crane, D. (1986) *Violence on Social Workers.* Norwich: University of East Anglia Social Work Monographs.

Strathclyde Regional Council Social Work Department (1986) *Violence to Staff.* Strathclyde: SRCSWD.

Surrey County Department (1987) *Safe and Secure in Surrey.* Surrey Social Services Council.

University of Southampton Department of Social Work Studies (1989) *Social Work in Crisis: A Study of Conditions in Six Local Authorities.* London: NALGO.

CHAPTER 15

Inside the Long-Arm Model
of Practice Teaching

The Experiences of Students, Practice Teachers
and On-Site Supervisors

Hilary Lawson

The long-arm model of practice teaching is enjoying increasing popularity as a model of practice teaching that 'reaches the parts that other models can't reach'. Its potential has been recognised in both statutory and voluntary organisations as a means whereby students can be taken on in those settings where skilled workers have the necessary social work expertise but neither the time nor specific practice teaching training to take sole responsibility for student placements. In this chapter I consider the advantages of the model for social work education but also focus more specifically on how it is experienced by those who have been a part of it: the 'user view'. I will draw on concepts more usually applied to family work to analyse the interpersonal dynamics and processes at play within the model.

The view from the outside

The long-arm model is where an identified supervisor based in the same location as the student has responsibility for the student's day-to-day practice but another, qualified, practice teacher links in with both the student and supervisor and has a wider managerial, teaching, and assessment role. As the role, tasks, and organisational settings of social work have changed, so has the need for a wide variety of placements and the long-arm model offers the opportunity to create innovative placements which reflect this diversity.

Certainly CCETSW, in its *Guidance on the 'Long Arm' Model of Practice Teaching* (1996) is clear that the model has advantages for all participants: the student, the supervisor and the practice teacher. In that it enables organisations to offer placements where without the model they could not, the model is also seen to be advantageous for organisations, particularly voluntary organisations, where the growth of long-arm placements has been the most rapid (Prevatt Goldstein and Harris 1996).

For the student, the advantages of the model are claimed to be the dual sources of experience and knowledge from which they can draw. For the long-arm practice teacher the model is seen as a chance for career enhancement, affording the opportunity for one practice teacher to supervise several placements at any one time, building up a wealth of knowledge and expertise. The advantages for the on-site supervisor are that it enables them to experience having a student without the full responsibility of teaching and assessment. Many, having had a taster, go on to undertake the practice teacher training at a later date. In some situations the supervisor is already a qualified practice teacher who hasn't sufficient time or relevant current experience to feel confident in taking on the main practice teaching role at the time a placement is required. From my own experience of teaching on social work programmes, I would say that the advantages to the tutor are in the continuity and quality assurance the long-arm model affords. Placements are increasingly difficult to find and each year new, untried and untested placements are offered. Where these are linked in with a long-arm practice teacher the latter's experience and knowledge of the requirements of placements provides an essential anchoring point in otherwise uncharted territories.

So, generally, from the outside in, the model would seem to offer many advantages. But how is being a part of this long-arm model of practice teaching really experienced? Having taught students and practice teachers on their qualifying programmes I had gained some insight into both the rewards and frustrations the model affords the three participants, and believed that this 'inside view' warranted further exploration. I have been consistently struck by the way both students and practice teachers frequently use words and phrases when describing their practice teaching relationship that are more generally used in connection with family relationships. Whereas, as I explain below, writers such as Kadushin have drawn convincing links between the two different types of relationships, I was intrigued to know how power relations and family dynamics might get played out in this triangular practice teaching relationship. To this end I conducted a small research project inviting some participants of the model to comment on their experiences of it. The following discussion is largely based on the views of the ten supervisors, nine students and four long-arm practice teachers who responded to my questionnaire. It is supplemented by more anecdotal evidence drawn from my experience of teaching social work students and practice teachers over the last five years.

Gaining credibility

In a paper written by Foulds *et al.* in 1991 it is argued that 'the model of long arm supervision was originally developed as an expedient and was seen as second best to the traditional, exclusive diadic practice teacher–student model' (1991, p.67). Some long-arm practice teachers have approached new placements with trepidation believing that their students, too, will have doubts and feelings of disappointment that they have been allocated a some-what 'cobbled together' second-rate placement. In fact the students in my survey reported very different reactions to the news they were to have a long-arm placement. The majority felt either pleasure that they were to have two people involved in their learning, or a neutrality, and only two of the nine described some disappointment. So it would seem that, as the model has developed and become more widely used within social work education, it has lost some of the stigma associated with its early days of being a way of 'getting round' CCETSW's new, more stringent regulations and is emerging as a 'different but equal' placement model. That 'long arm supervision has come out of the closet' (Foulds *et al.* 1991) has meant that the long-arm prac-tice teacher has felt more valued in the role and more able to inspire confidence in the student and supervisor.

Clarity of roles and responsibilities

As the long-arm model has matured, open communication between the prac-tice teacher, supervisor and student, and clarity of their respective roles and responsibilities have been increasingly recognised as the key to its working effectively. Most long-arm placements do now manage to achieve this cli-mate of open communication and clear delineation of roles and this is the result of a time-consuming but important series of meetings. Several respon-dents of my survey described an initial meeting between the student and supervisor (often pre-placement) followed by a three-way meeting including the practice teacher in the early weeks of the placement, and a four-way meeting also with the tutor before the roles and responsibilities were finally clarified and enshrined in the practice placement agreement. Drawing up the agreement in a series of sessions allows the participants to focus on both the content and the process of it, an important time of jockeying for position, making demands and clarifying responsibilities. There is some advantage in the agreement only being finalised some weeks into the placement to give time to this process, and so that issues that had not been anticipated have arisen and can be incorporated. Some long-arm practice teachers also reported they met with the supervisor pre-placement in order to arrive at some consensus of boundaries before the student arrived.

Several students commented on the importance of the supervisor and long-arm practice teacher having worked together before as this eased the clarification process. For example 'They had worked together like this previously and this gave me confidence it would be managed well'. Long-arm practice teachers were concerned that they ensured they attended to the needs and expectations of the on-site supervisor as well as the student. Supervisors varied in the extent they wanted to be involved in different aspects of the role, for example, reading written work and direct observation. The division of labour needs to be negotiated sensitively and with clarity.

Although each situation will vary depending on the expertise of the on-site supervisor, CCETSW (1996, p.4) has suggested guidelines for the delineation of areas of responsibility. The practice teacher will always have overall responsibility for the management of the placement and the linkage with the student's qualifying course. They have responsibility for ensuring the direct observation of the student's practice takes place, writing the student's placement report after seeking contributions from students and supervisors, and, where necessary, attending the examination board. The supervisor, through their own line management system, will oversee the day-to-day management of the student's time and work and identify suitable work for the student in consultation with the practice teacher. Although both supervisor and practice teacher are to have some responsibility for teaching and assessment, CCETSW makes it clear the practice teacher has overall responsibility for what might be termed meta-learning, facilitating the integration of theory and practice, developing anti-discriminatory practice and drawing out the values in social work.

Supervision sessions

All students are entitled to a minimum of 1.5 hour's formal supervision a week. CCETSW only stipulates that supervision by the practice teacher should be regular and preferably on-site, and that the supervisor is to provide 'day-to-day supervision and advice'. This is obviously an area where there is room for negotiation about how much formal supervision each offers. The most frequent pattern cited in my research was that the student would be supervised by the supervisor for about an hour each week, plus two hours with the long arm every fortnight, and a three-way meeting of about an hour and a half every month. This did vary according to individual circumstances, but no one complained of a lack of supervision! Rather, there is a tendency for the student to be over-supervised and both students and on-site supervisors complained of 'going over the same ground' in supervision with the supervisor and with the practice teacher. One supervisor wrote: 'It was tiresome having to keep the long arm practice teacher up to date with case developments'.

But overall this duplication did not feature in the respondents' comments as frequently as I had anticipated and again it points to the maturity of the model. The complaints I had heard from social work students three or four years ago are no longer being voiced as practice teachers and supervisors become more adept at clarifying their respective areas of work.

Supervision skills

Supervision sessions not only differed in the content, but also in the skills employed by the two supervisors. One aspect of the model that has perhaps been rather overlooked is that although the practice teacher has had training in supervision skills, the on-site supervisor may not have, yet they, too, need to be skilled to be effective in their work with the student. Helpful supervisor skills noted in my survey were the ability to give procedural information with clarity and to tease out salient case details and help the student plan client or case intervention. The skills of the practice teacher found most helpful were the probing, challenging skills which facilitated more generalised reflection on the work and social work values. Batchelor and Boutland (1996) argue persuasively that a practice teacher at arm's length from the day-to-day work is well positioned to enable the student to reflect on their actions and consider ethical dilemmas, 'potentially enhancing the process of reflection in supervision' (1996, p.105). This was echoed in my research. For example one student respondent commented that it was 'helpful to have (an) external long arm practice teacher to reflect at a distance about the placement experience'.

There are some dangers in a too rigid delineation of tasks and perspectives which I outline below. The majority of my respondents, however, felt that having two supervisors with differing skills, knowledge and experience provided a rich resource from which the student could benefit. Batchelor and Boutland, too, noted that the fact that students encountered different styles of working 'was generally experienced as a help rather than a hindrance' (1996, p.107).

The discussion relating to the delineation of roles and responsibilities is one that all participants of the long-arm model may now expect at the beginning of the placement. What is not usually made explicit, however, is reference to the more subtle processes that will affect the working relationship.

So what's it really like? The trouble with triangles

At the heart of the long-arm placement is a triangular relationship between the student, the supervisor and the practice teacher. What we know from our work with families is that triangular relationships suggest alliances, coalitions (Burnham 1986), inclusion/exclusion, distance regulation (Byng-Hall 1980). What we know from our own experiences of a baby joining an existing twosome, a sibling group of three or a group of three schoolfriends continually 'falling in and out with each other' is that threesomes can at times be uncomfortable. That 'two's company, three's a crowd' is part of our inherited wisdom. Janet Mattinson, in a paper entitled 'The Deadly Equal Triangle' puts forward some ideas drawn from psychoanalytic theory to offer an explanation of why triangular relationships can be so complex. The problem inherent in this kind of relationship, she argues, is oedipal. Most humans have had an initial experience of a strong pair bonding between mother and child and, although each person's experience of moving from a twosome to the need to share that person with others will be different, Mattinson believes that 'no-one…so completely solves oedipal problems the first time around that life is entirely carefree from then on when encountering threesome situations' (1997, p.5).

Mattinson neatly conveys the kinds of processes that occur within any interaction between threes, whether it is a threesome of long-arm practice teacher, on-site supervisor and student in a supervision session or three friends having a drink together in the pub:

> The encompassing of a third person in a relationship demands a flexibility of movement between the three, one party allowing temporary pairing of the other two – all parties allowing the other two to have something special between them – and a freedom for one party to allow

himself (*sic*) to be in or out of the various transactions at any one time. (1997, p.6)

Each of the participants may be excluded by the others or may exclude themselves. Mattinson argues that the corner of a supervisory triangle most likely to be excluded is that which is causing most anxiety to the others. The practice teacher, with the main responsibility for assessment, may feel like a sitting duck in this respect! However, this may not always be the case. A difficult or failing student may be causing both supervisor and practice teacher such anxiety they form a coalition which the student experiences as being 'ganged up against'. An example of the supervisor being excluded may be where in a placement experiencing pressures of heavy workloads and/or change the supervisor may be the one transmitting anxiety into the triangle, and the practice teacher, away from the setting, is able to provide a welcome haven of calm. Participants may exclude themselves, for example the practice teacher who does not feel comfortable with their unfamiliarity of the setting in which the student is located may unconsciously discount themselves from the relationship.

The practice teacher may also, for example, feel excluded by the closer day-to-day working relationship established between the supervisor and the student. Work with social groups has highlighted the preoccupation individuals display with notions of exclusion and inclusion. The triangular relationship brings this tension into sharp focus. A supervisor respondent wrote that throughout the placement he felt 'marginalised and de-valued'. Another supervisor's words highlight the discomfort of a third presence in what seemed a more manageable dyad: 'The relationship between the three (of us) was basically good, however I felt the long arm practice teacher quite intrusive, although I do appreciate she was very tactful and careful'. One astute student acknowledged she deliberately exploited the potential for competition and rivalry between her practice teacher and supervisor and this ensured both were 'kept on their toes'.

Power and families

In response to a question about where power was perceived to lie within the long-arm model, most student respondents were able to differentiate between the power that was vested in the role of the supervisor and practice teacher and that which was as a result of the particular qualities of the individuals. Eight of the nine students thought their long-arm practice teacher had the most formal power in the relationship and this was clearly linked to the practice teacher's closer ties to the university/college, jointly marking assignments in some situations, and writing the final report. Mattinson's analogy between triangular relationships and primary familial relationships has some relevance here because of the way in which both students and practice teachers used words and phrases that suggest parent–child relationships. For example, students acknowledged the power of the practice teacher and also, in several cases, reported feeling closer to the on-site supervisor. The analogy of being the child of two parents, one of whom was more distant but who ultimately carried more formal power and the other being the one with whom one spent most of the day and with whom one developed a more comfortable familiarity, was drawn by more than one student.

A student's reference to feeling quite powerful in the threesome as she could 'control how much information each had about my workload' seemed to reflect the scenario of the child playing one parent off against the other! One student wrote 'I sometimes felt that they held the power and I had to revert to childish [behaviour]...to get my needs met'. This same student also commented 'Sometimes they had different views of what was important...I felt like pig-in-the-middle'. Another student, when invited to reflect on the experience of being in a long arm placement instinctively drew a parallel with the embrace of a supportive family: 'At one stage I remember feeling like the child in a parental situation. It felt like both parents were responsible'.

Just as in families, there is of course the potential for the 'adults' in the relationship to abuse their power. A student emerging from a particularly difficult placement recently told me he felt his practice teacher to be a critical parent and that 'whatever I did was wrong, just like I was a child again. I decided to keep my head down and just get to the end of it'. Students in another study complained that their practice teachers were 'constrictive and restrictive, with continual checking up of student behaviour and displaying an inability to allow sufficient independence and autonomy' (Collins *et al.* 1992, p.22 on Hawthorne, Roenblatt and Mayer 1975).

The role of the practice teacher does indeed invite some parallels with the parenting of a child, and the need to manage the tension between protection and separation. Kadushin, in an article on the supervisee's need to develop strategies to defend against anxiety, also describes how the supervisor–supervisee relationship can re-kindle feelings about the parent–child relationship: 'The supervisor is in a position of authority and the supervisee is, in some measure, dependent on him... The situation is therefore one that threatens the reactivation...of residual difficulties in the parent–child relationship' (1979, p.184). The dependence of the student on the practice teacher for the success of the placement, and ultimately for their social work qualification, sets the scene for this 'reactivation' of the parent–child relationship. The fundamental nature of the learning that needs to take place – learning that involves both the acquisition of skills and also the re-evaluation of values, 'a change in behaviour and, perhaps, personality' (*ibid.*) – forges connections with previous early learning experiences. Kadushin also describes some students feeling a sense of betrayal if the new work calls for values very different from the ones instilled in them by parental figures. This may be something like the need to be open and work with feelings which may run counter to the student's familial values. Anti-oppressive practice also exposes students to values that may be at variance with those derived from the family and students may experience much anxiety as they find their fundamental value base being scrutinised, found wanting, and knocked into shape.

Hughes and Pengelly (1995) argue that attitudes to authority figures, including teachers and supervisors, are not just influenced by early family life but also previous or current difficulties with management being experienced in the workplace. Students who have worked in settings where there have been difficulties with management may be bringing attitudes not only formed in early childhood, but which have recently been 'topped up' by work experiences.

Concepts drawn from psychoanalytic theory

A concept drawn from psychoanalytic theory much used in helping social workers think through emotional reactions displayed by individuals under stress and which may have relevance to the practice teaching relationship is the Kleinian concept of splitting. A difficulty in accommodating a range of conflicting emotions causes certain of those emotions to be split off and redistributed. The student may find managing the tension of being scrutinised by two authority figures can only be achieved by such splitting into, for example, the supervisor in the role of 'bad, task-oriented parent' and the practice teacher, freed from the more bureaucratic aspects of the work, the 'good nurturing parent'. It is likely that elements of splitting may be a feature of the way the student relates to the two 'authority figures' and through the process of projective identification the practice teacher or supervisor finds themselves playing the role. Interestingly, Mattinson has noted that an 'operative fantasy' of some individuals who have had difficult childhoods, and that, as we know from research, includes many social workers (*see* Barter 1997 for summary), is that there can only be one good parent.

When the responsibilities of the practice teacher and supervisor are delineated in those early days of the placement it is important that decisions are not made which might have the unintended effect of splitting or polarising different aspects of the work. Tensions and contradictions lie at the heart of much of social work and the practitioner needs skill to integrate them. The needs–resource tension should not become polarised by the supervisor being forced into pragmatic resource-led solutions while the practice teacher can enjoy a one-removed indulgence in an all-encompassing multi-needs-led care package. One respondent in my research wrote 'the long arm practice teacher placed greater emphasis on social work values, the on-site supervisor on organisational values, for example the practice teacher would urge me to offer space to talk about loss and grief while the supervisor would be suggesting I closed the case and moved on to the next assessment. At times I felt caught between the two sets of values'. A statement such as this, if expressed within supervision, gives an important opportunity to work with the student to reflect on how the seemingly conflicting perspectives may be managed.

Similarly, the care/control dichotomy many new social worker students struggle with should not be replicated in the practice teacher/supervisor dyad. Both practice teacher and supervisor need to model an integration of managing feelings *and* procedures, of attending to process *and* content. Hawkins and Shohet (1989) have coined the phrase 'helicopter ability' to describe the skills of the supervisor in attending to the total context of the work the supervisee is bringing to supervision. A supervision session should be able to focus on the minutiae of interpersonal interaction as well as the wider organisational setting. Because of the importance of ensuring supervision does not disaggregate the different roles and functions of social work, it follows that *both* practice teacher and supervisor will need to be equipped with practice teaching skills which facilitate exploration of apparent tensions and dichotomies.

Concepts drawn from Transactional Analysis

In their work training supervisors, Hughes and Pengelly noted that the concept which had particular resonance for the supervisors was that of Karpman's drama triangle. The concept is often already familiar to social workers because of its use in analysing child abuse situations. It is based on three roles, the Victim, Persecutor and Rescuer, and it is suggested each individual has a 'favourite' role but that each is able to move effortlessly in and out of them when the drama triangle is initiated. Hughes and Pengelly believe social workers tend to the rescue role as their preferred role and state 'in our courses we have often been amazed at supervisors' apparently endless patience with difficult supervisees, which may eventually be revealed as a fear of being (or being experienced as) persecuting' (1997, p.104). They then continue to describe how some supervisors 'deal with the issue of hate or aggression by abandoning mediating care as merely "rescue", taking instead a persecuting stance under the guise of "being straight", determined that the supervisee is "not going to make a victim out of me"' (*ibid.*). In the triangular relationship of the practice teacher, student and supervisor, the allocating of roles of Persecutor, Rescuer and Victim may also have some relevance. The practice teacher being overly nurturing to overcome anger with a failing student, or masking insecurity with a controlling authoritarianism are two familiar scenarios which could be analysed using the above framework.

A long-arm practice teacher wrote of her use of the model in identifying some of the feelings which could be experienced by each of the participants in the long-arm placement as they take up positions at each of the three points of the triangle at various stages during the placement (Madden 1995). Although the use of Transactional Analysis in practice teaching is explored elsewhere in this book, I reproduce some of her 'role-thinking' here because of the way it replicates some of the feelings the participants of my research articulated. As Victim, the supervisor's role-thinking may be 'No one told me it would be as hard as this' or 'I'm doing all the work and getting none of the credit'. The practice teacher's Victim role-thinking may be 'They spend so much time together. I feel like an outsider'. For the student it may be, 'What are they saying behind my back?'. An example of the practice teacher in persecutory role is 'What a nasty little team, glad I only visit' and the student in Rescue not wanting to confront difficult issues may be thinking 'They must know what they're doing, better not ask'. I suspect these phrases 'ring bells' for many participants of the long-arm model, and could easily be supplemented with plenty more.

Assessment

In all models of practice teaching it is probably the assessment element which raises most anxiety both for the student and the practice teacher. Assessment involves the practice teacher owning the power and authority in the role, and ensuring sound judgements are made based on sufficient and wide-ranging evidence. I was interested to know how the gathering of evidence and compilation of the final report was achieved within the long-arm model, and whether all parties genuinely felt they had a good enough sense of the student's work to make sound judgements of it. In particular I had wondered how easy it would be for the long-arm practice teacher to make informed judgements about different aspects of the student's work from their one-removed position.

From my research and discussions with practice teachers it emerged that this was clearly an area that both supervisors and long-arm practice teachers had given much thought to and seemed to represent another area in which the model has developed from its earlier days. The long-arm practice teacher relied to a large extent on the student's written material to gain evidence. It was felt that this, supplemented by direct observation of the student's practice and eliciting feedback from users and colleagues as well as the supervisor was generally sufficient to gain an accurate picture of the student's competence. However it was reported that the process was time-consuming because evidence could not be gleaned through the normal course of day-to-day work as in a singleton (one practice teacher to one student) model and there were often practical constraints such as time and distance which meant observations were sometimes hard to arrange. Also, although direct observation gave very good evaluative information, using it as the sole method of evaluation could be problematic. Some students' reluctance to be observed meant opportunities were few, and when they did occur anxiety marred the student's performance.

As in all practice teaching models, it is essential that a programme of learning with a clear indication of how and when the learning is to be assessed is planned at the beginning of the placement. Shardlow and Doel's argument that observation and other forms of assessment such as process recordings, case summaries and audio/visual material should be used in a strategic, targeted way is very pertinent here. In a paper entitled 'Examination by Triangulation' (1993) they claim that utilising three principles, selection (ensuring a fit between the skill to be assessed and the method of assessment), correspondence (assessing the skill from different sources of evidence to see if judgements correspond) and sampling (assessing the skill at different points of the placement) should ensure assessment is effective.

What emerged from my research was that both the practice teacher and the supervisor felt they had developed a good understanding of the student's work but that they were each better acquainted with different aspects of it.

The long-arm practice teacher, due to their one-removed position, was able to facilitate, and make judgements about, the student's ability to reflect on their learning and also to transfer learning from the specific to the general and from one situation to another (Batchelor and Boutland 1996). One respondent practice teacher who felt her judgement was enhanced by her more distant perspective wrote 'it has been difficult for the on-site supervisor to be sufficiently objective, looking only at the student's ability with the particular client group'. The supervisors, on the other hand, were able to make comments on the student's day-to-day work and their abilities to work as part of a team. However, several respondents made the point that it should not be assumed that the on-site supervisor always has greater access to the student's work. Where a student is seated away from their supervisor, or the supervisor is often away from the office, there may be little contact time apart from snatched case discussion and monitoring.

While most supervisors and practice teachers thought that they were both equally equipped to make judgements about the student, half of the students had a different view and felt it was the on-site supervisor who knew them and their work best. Each situation is of course different, however. While one student felt it was the long-arm practice teacher who knew him best because of the in-depth discussions they had, another commented that because it was the long-arm practice teacher who had primary responsibility for assessment she felt freer to be honest with her supervisor and consequently it was the supervisor who knew her and her work best.

Writing the final report

Of those students who stated unequivocally that their on-site supervisor knew them and their work better than the long-arm practice teacher, all felt that this sat uncomfortably with the fact that it was the long-arm practice teacher who wrote the final report. For example one student wrote 'The on-site supervisor definitely had a better insight into the work I was doing [but] had no part in the final report'. Others expressed the view that it was a question of emphasis: 'the long arm practice teacher had much the bigger influence on the report'.

Given that the practice teacher and supervisor come to know different aspects of the student's work, the report should represent a clear holistic understanding of the student's functioning in all aspects of the role. The trick is, of course, finding a way of conveying both perspectives in the compilation of the report. The evidence from my research was that this was an area where some more thinking needs to take place. The two (of nine) on-site supervisors who felt they had contributed a 'great deal' to the final report had actually written their own report addressing the main competences but in a more succinct form than the report written by the long arm, and given it to the long arm for appending to the report. In the main, those that felt they contributed little to the report were those whose views were only given verbally to the long-arm practice teacher. Others had made notes for the long arm to rework and include in the final report.

The long-arm practice teacher needs to attend to the process of drawing up the final report and a discussion of how the supervisor wants to contribute should be made explicit at the contract stage. The practice of giving a draft to the student to comment on before the report is finalised should be extended to include the supervisor. Some better planning and consultation around this crucial element of the placement may prevent some of the ill feeling that was apparent from some supervisors' replies: 'If I were to take on another student I would certainly ask to see [the report]to ensure my comments and observations were represented accurately'. 'I had no opportunity to see the final report which was prepared by the long arm practice teacher. I feel this should have been shared with me.' 'After all the work I put in, it then seemed odd that some-one else was writing the assessment report.'

A model for the future? The changing context of social work

In recent discourse on social work organisation there is frequent reference to re-structuring, change and turbulence (for example Bamford 1990; Pietroni 1995) and this is certainly the context in which many social work students undertake placements. Whether the 'turbulent environment' (Hughes and Pengelly 1997) has detracted from the enjoyment and learning afforded by the placement or contributed to it (see Cox, Chapter 10) often seems to depend on the skill of both the practice teacher and the team to manage the tensions and insecurity changes often bring with them. An interesting finding from my research is that the long-arm model of practice teaching is able to provide an effective buffer against some of the more damaging effects of change. Several students commented on the importance of the long-arm practice teacher being there to provide continuity and safety when an on-site supervisor was absent either through illness, leave or having been re-located to another post during the placement. Frequent movement of staff and stress-related sickness in times of organisational change can leave a student high and dry. It is disruptive and anxiety-provoking for students. The long-arm model provides a safety net for those students who suddenly find their supervisor unavailable.

Using a long-arm model of practice teaching may also be an important way of ensuring race, gender, sexuality and other attributes are taken into consideration. A third person involved in the practice teaching relationship opens up possibilities of matching the student's race or gender, for example, so that the student feels supported and has a reference point. Early attention to socially structured difference will facilitate a discussion within practice teaching sessions of crucial issues of power relations and personal aspects of difference. But while it is important a student has the opportunity of a supervisor or practice teacher who may share common experiences of discrimination, it introduces another potential of collusion and exclusion that will affect the triangular dynamic. Participants must be open to acknowledging and exploring this.

Advantages and disadvantages of long-arm models of practice teaching

The small-scale research that I conducted pointed to both advantages and disadvantages of the model. As in all things, the application of the model depends on the organisations within which it is sited, and the participants of whom it is comprised. Whereas long-arm practice teachers generally apply for the post and have had experience and training in practice teaching, on-site supervisors have varying degrees of understanding of, and enthusiasm for, the task of supervising. The time-consuming nature of the task takes some unawares. This may result in the reluctant supervisor who is only marginally less distant than the long-arm practice teacher. The team and wider organisational structures and culture affect the learning that can be achieved as in all practice placements. Another variable is of course the student. Confident students can thrive in the attention and scrutiny of two supervisors rather than one. A confident student is quick to understand the difference in role and what material to take to which supervision session and can play an important part in helping both the supervisor and the practice teacher gather evidence. A less confident or less able student may find the model overwhelming or confusing. The educational context also has a bearing on the success or otherwise of the mode and the tutor may be able to play an important part in supporting the practice teacher and placement.

All three participants expended a huge amount of energy in the early weeks of the placement getting to know each other and where the experience and expertise of each lay. This was an anxiety-provoking time for the student, in particular where the success of the placement depended on these relationships, and also for the practice teacher endeavouring to make relationships at a distance. But time invested at the beginning of the placement was generally felt to be time well spent.

The student's view

When the different theoretical and ideological perspectives, experiences and skills the supervisor and long-arm practice teacher bring to the learning relationship complement each other, the model provides a rich source from which the student can draw, and a flexibility which allows a student to use the two parties differentially to meet learning needs. For the student, this was the most quoted advantage of the model. Important, too, was the continuity the 'extra person' provided if there was some disruption in the placement. The presence of a third person in the supervisory relationship was also seen as a welcome dilution of what can be an intense dyadic relationship. Several students commented that it relieved the anxiety many students experience before embarking on their placement that they won't 'get on' with their practice teacher. However skilled a practice teacher may be, the personality of both student and practice teacher does, undoubtedly, affect the nature and experience of the teaching relationship and many students were aware of the advantages of having a choice of two.

Conversely, some students found two supervisors overpowering, particularly if the student was struggling. The most voiced disadvantages of the model for the student were feeling over-supervised, and the supervision sessions at times being repetitive. Some comments were made about the high number of meetings at the beginning of the placement which were necessary to ensure communication was effective but which were time-consuming. Four-way meetings involving the tutor can feel overwhelming for the student. Although having two different sources of information was generally viewed as helpful, it also had its pitfalls where, for example, the views of the supervisor and the practice teacher conflicted which left some students feeling confused. One student in my research also admitted that having two people involved meant some aspects of her work were easily hidden, a situation she ruthlessly exploited!

The on-site supervisor's view

In many ways it was this group who had the most ambivalent views about the role. Some saw it as a welcome opportunity to engage in working with a student without the full responsibility of teaching and assessment. More than one commented that they were pleased not to have to concentrate on integrating theory in discussions on practice. Others used it as an opportunity to decide whether to embark on the practice teaching training. They enjoyed being able to derive support and learning from the more experienced practice teacher particularly where a student was giving cause for concern or where there were difficulties in the placement.

But others felt undermined by the more experienced long-arm practice teacher and conscious of a power imbalance. One supervisor reported that he felt his supervision decisions were being questioned. Some found there were difficulties in working with only a fragmentary picture of the student: 'In retrospect I feel I would have appreciated having more of an overview of the other work the student was completing during her time with me, for example university related work'. Supervisors also found the role time-consuming and some experienced a growing resentment that the task was more onerous than they had at first imagined, but that the status was attached to the practice teacher. A supervisor respondent wrote: 'you are always aware that the long arm exists because you haven't got a qualification, despite masses of experience'. 'Always the bridesmaid but never the bride.'

The practice teacher's view

The practice teacher is in the pivotal position of the relationship linking in with the placement and the educational establishment. This role can be rather isolating, caught between the college or university and the work setting but not belonging to either. Being more closely aligned to the authority/assessment corner of the practice teaching triangle, the practice teacher might find him or herself suffering the same contradictory fate as that described by Hughes and Pengelly 'on the one hand...idealised as a wonderful, protected ivory tower, in which members find relief from the demands of a non-understanding work-place; on the other,...angrily criticised as useless because so removed from the realities of everyday work' (1995, p.154).

The practice teacher can also be the focus of some resentment from the supervisor, particularly if the team setting is difficult, or if the supervisor would have rather managed the placement alone but was prevented from doing so either because of a management decision or the lack of the 'right sort' of qualifications. Some supervisors enter the relationship reluctantly, having been 'press-ganged' by a higher authority. It is the practice teacher who has to be skilful in ensuring these issues are heard and that the needs of both student and supervisor are met so that the three participants work together effectively. My research pointed to a certain element of 'informal caring' in the role of the practice teacher. One long-arm practice teacher likened it to 'Grandmother keeping an eye on the new mother and baby'.

From the inside, then, long-arm practice teaching can be experienced as a supportive context in which a student has two other adults attending to their needs, or a place where one adult feels resentful having to balance others' needs without getting their own met, or where a student exploits the rivalry or lack of communication between the two others. A bit like families, really.

Conclusions

The long-arm model of practice teaching has matured since its infancy in the late 1980s and it has proved to be well suited to the new demands of social work education, opening up learning opportunities and creating placements which develop partnerships within and between agencies. The model requires, and teaches, essential skills of communication, negotiation and mediation that are at the heart of effective social work in the current changing and interdisciplinary social work context.

Most long-arm placements now manage to ensure the clarity of roles and responsibilities of their participants which is essential for their effective functioning. However, more discussion needs to take place in the initial learning agreement phase on how different participants' evidence is contributed to the compilation of the final student report.

Long-arm models may involve just one on-site supervisor, or the practice teacher may be co-ordinating several practice-settings in the one 'network' placement (Boutland and Baldwin 1991; Batchelor and Boutland 1996). Long-arm practice teaching moves away from the more self-contained one-to-one relationship of singleton practice teaching and can involve a greater number of people in student learning. In this way practice teaching takes a more centralised position within practice and moves away from the margins.

It also offers opportunities for professional development and becomes more firmly embedded in a career structure. But, although many supervisors go on to train as practice teachers, the skills they need to have in their own right in the long-arm model should not be under-estimated. I have argued that, although the practice teacher and supervisor have different areas of responsibility within the relationship, it is important that this is seen as a difference in emphasis rather than mutually exclusive areas of work to avoid the replication of potential polarisation and tensions which lie at the heart of social work. This, then, assumes that both practice teacher and supervisor are operating with a high level of skill. Agencies should ensure that staff appointed to be supervisors are equipped for the task and have access to as much relevant training as possible.

CCETSW has suggested that the long-arm practice teacher may 'closely supervise and support the unqualified on-site supervisor' (1996, p.2) but I would argue against this blurring of needs within the practice teaching relationship. I have alluded already to the practice teacher's awareness of the importance of 'tuning in' to the motives and attitudes of the supervisor and an element of informal caring in the role. The practice teacher role should not be expected to incorporate even more responsibility for the learning needs of the supervisor. Indeed, what should be built into the model is support for the practice teacher: the question of who supports the practice teacher should be addressed at the time the placement is established.

Practice teaching programmes themselves have been slow to address directly the needs of the long-arm practice teacher. What has emerged from my work is that in addition to supervision and practice teaching skills already well documented in the practice teaching literature, there is another body of knowledge and skills needed by those working in a long-arm model: the understanding of, and ability to work with, the processes and dynamics peculiar to three-way relationships. All those involved in practice teaching become entangled with supervisory triangles. This may be the long-arm model itself, or the supervisor working with the student and client, or the practice teacher in the triangle of the student and tutor. Mattinson wrote, (not of the long-arm model of practice teaching, but the relevance is apparent): 'the main attribute of effective supervision over and above the possession of a certain amount of skill in the craft is an ability to know about threesome relationships' (1997, p.12). My research has also highlighted that thinking about the parallels and making connections between what we know about families and what goes on in practice teaching relationships will contribute to the understanding and effectiveness of both sets of those most crucial of relationships.

References

Bamford, T. (1990) *The Future of Social Work*. London: Macmillan.

Barter, S. (1997) 'Social work students with personal experience of sexual abuse: implications for Diploma in Social Work programme providers.' In *Social Work Education 16*, 2, 113–132.

Batchelor, J. and Boutland, K. (1996) '"Patterns that connect": opportunities for reflective practice in network placements.' In N. Gould and I. Taylor (ed) *Reflective Learning for Social Work.* Aldershot: Arena.

Boutland, K. and Baldwin, M. (1991) *Only Connect.* Bath: Bath University Practice Learning Centre.

Burnham, J. (1986) *Family Therapy.* London: Tavistock.

Byng-Hall, J. (1980) 'Symptom bearer as marital distance regulator.' In *Family Process 19*, 355–365.

CCETSW (1996) *Guidance on the 'Long Arm' Model of Practice Teaching.* London: CCETSW.

Collins, S., Ottley, G. and McMurran, M. (1992) 'Student and practice teacher perceptions of the enabling role in practice teaching.' *Social Work Education 11*, 2, 20–40.

Foulds, J., Sanders, A. and Williams, J. (1991) 'Coordinating learning: the future of practice teaching.' *Social Work Education 10*, 2, 60–68.

Hawkins, P. and Shohet, R. (1989) *Supervision in the Helping Professions.* Milton Keynes: Open University Press.

Hughes, L. and Pengelly, P. (1995) 'Who cares if the room is cold? Practicalities, projections and the trainer's authority.' In M. Yelloly and M. Henkel *Learning and Teaching in Social Work: Towards Reflective Practice.* London: Jessica Kingsley Publishers.

Hughes, L. and Pengelly, P. (1997) *Staff Supervision in a Turbulent Environment.* London: Jessica Kingsley Publisher.

Kadushin, A. (1979) 'Games people play in supervision.' In C.E. Hunson (ed) *Social Work Supervision: Classic Statements and Critical Issues.* New York: Free Press.

Klein, M. (1946) 'Notes on some schizoid mechanisms.' *International Journal of Psycho-Analysis 27*, 99–110.

Madden, T. (1995) *The Experience of Long Arm Practice Teaching in Terms of Empowerment and Openness.* Unpublished.

Mattinson, J. (1997) *The Deadly Equal Triangle.* London: Tavistock Institute of Medical Psychology.

Pietroni, M. (1995) 'The nature and aims of professional education for social workers: a postmodern perspective.' In M. Yelloly and M. Henkel (eds) *Learning and Teaching in Social Work.* London: Jessica Kingsley Publishers.

Prevatt Goldstein, B. and Harris, V. (1996) 'Innovations in practice teaching.' In S. Jackson and M. Preston-Shoot *Educating Social Workers in a Changing Policy Context.* London: Whiting and Birch.

Shardlow, S. and Doel, M. (1993) 'Examination by triangulation: a model for practice teaching.' *Social Work Education 12*, 3, 67–79.

Further reading

Bell, L. (1991) 'The lore of the long arm.' In *National Organisation of Practice Teachers Newsletter* August.

Johnson, S. and Shabbaiz, A. (1990) *Integrated Practice Placements: A Model for Development in Practice* Vol.3, 240–224.

Mattinson, J. (1992) *The Reflection Process in Casework Supervision.* London: Tavistock Institute of Medical Psychology.

Sawdon, C. and Sawdon, D. (1995) 'The supervision partnership: a whole greater than the sum of its parts.' In J. Pritchard *Good Practice in Supervision.* London: Jessica Kingsley Publishers.

Stewart, R.H., Peters, T.C., Marsh, S. and Peters, M.J. (1975) 'An object relations approach to psychotherapy with marital couples, families, and children.' *Family Process 14*, 161–178.

CHAPTER 16

Changing Times
for the Practice Teacher

The Conflict of Priorities
for Social Work Education

Hugh England

The sense of crisis which hangs over British social work education comes at a time when tutors and practice teachers might have expected to feel more secure. Since the development of 'generic' programmes in the 1960s, social work education has made great strides: in those three decades it has developed a substantial base in British higher education, its scholarship has been pivotal in the development of a sophisticated body of social work theory and research, competence in practice – partly as a result of that development – is defined as the object of professional education, and practice teacher courses leading to accreditation nominally secure the quality of practice teaching. Given these gains, it might seem odd that so many in social work education seem to doubt the security of the achievement.

But the threats to social work education are substantial. Qualifying programmes may not survive because they cannot provide the required practice placements – practice agencies under financial constraint cannot give priority to professional training matters. The turmoil in higher education means that university social work departments cannot readily meet the contradictory and undermining demands of different paymasters. Most importantly, a shift in the intellectual and professional climate causes tenets which are central to social work to be questioned; the emphasis on 'competences' and on new specialisms weakens social work's always tenuous understanding of its practice and limits the scope for achievement and effectiveness. All of these changes bear directly on the future of the practice teacher.

Priority for practice: the achievement of social work education

Social work education may not quite have reached maturity, but it has grown up. Social work in the universities is no longer the poor and not-very-academic relation of social policy or sociology. It is established across the country. That development lay originally in the availability of ear-marked funding for social work education. But it reflects now a great growth in social work's knowledge and scholarship; it both mirrors and furthers social work's own increased substance. In difficult times it may be hard to remember that these achievements offer ground for confidence. But the development of social work education has been a measure of the real progress of social work itself. The development of a generic social work was central to that progress. That recognition of the core elements of social work allowed a focus on practice which was at last realistic and practical: the way was cleared for a proper discussion of purpose, process and outcome, and the relevance of knowledge to these ends. In the 1970s and 1980s social work developed new theory – unitary models, task-centred models, client-centred frameworks (e.g. Pincus and Minahan 1973; Reid and Epstein 1972; Egan 1975) – which enabled it to characterise social work practice much more accurately. In those decades social work became more intelligible and accessible. It did so because of the development of generic social work.

There is now a contemporary wisdom that generic social work is dead. That is too simple a construction. It is right that social work should establish a different balance between its core and its more specific knowledge, but there are risks if that balance is wrong in either direction. It was the development of 'generic social work' which underpinned social work's subsequent growth. Social work is now informed by a rich body of research; its knowledge base is empirically and theoretically grounded. Much of this work is focused on the needs of particular groups, and this appears to lend weight to claims that social work is a specialist activity. But such claims tend to ignore the extent to which this specialist knowledge is based on the new grasp that social work has of its core processes and procedures. Social work has been able to extend its grasp only because it is now grounded on a more secure and common base. It will be an appalling irony if the development of the new specialisms puts at risk the foundation on which they actually rest – if the focus on the particular knowledge needed to work with particular problems leads social work to lose its grasp of the way that knowledge is applied. Such an outcome – which now seems very possible – would eventually require the re-discovery of social work.

'Generic social work' would have been better understood if it had been characterised as a framework which furthered the integration of theory with practice, a framework which made more possible the application of knowledge to practice in social work. That process of integration has always been something of a puzzle to social work. Yet the growing strength of social work education has been the growing prominence it has been able to give to practice, and it was the development of a generic social work which made possible that prominence. It has been achieved by developing frameworks which allow a clear and sensible focus on the social worker's thinking and behaviour – a practical emphasis upon the 'use of self'. A generation ago practice was not at the centre of professional education. For many years there was an assumption that students would somehow themselves make the links between possibly relevant theory and their practice. The social work curriculum was an interesting, eclectic, certainly creative, but not really coherent mix of elements; the real process of social work was too little emphasised, despite a rather confused but now too often derided focus on 'the relationship'. There was too little priority given to the integration or application of knowledge; an academic emphasis too often did indeed mean a focus which was insufficiently relevant. But, over a generation, that has changed; it has changed because a generic social work allowed a more explicit and coherent emphasis upon the person. Social work – the core of the *personal* social services – had always asserted the priority of 'respect for persons'; the development of social work education over recent decades has been the realisation – in the classroom and in the agency – of that priority. It is that change which has made possible the greater focus on practice and so increased social work's awareness of the practice teacher's role.

Recent years have seen profound changes in the general intellectual climate. Some have been hostile to social work. But some may have made the development of social work more possible. 'Theoretical' social work started life at a time when the social sciences sought to be *sciences*; there was too little sympathy for the imaginative, individualistic and phenomenological emphasis which is a necessary part of social work. So its emphasis upon 'the person' was often derided. Times have changed though; in a 'postmodern' world, when some see all knowledge as relative and subjective (Howe 1996), social work's concern with experience and perception is cast in a more mainstream mould. Social work no longer stands out as exceptional in such ways. It is this same new culture which – for complex reasons – also demands a greater 'relevance'; in this way too social work education is able to show it is now a part of the new mainstream. So in present times social work's necessary emphasis on 'the person' can be seen in a much more favourable light.

Social workers, and social work students, now draw on a much more appropriate and focused body of knowledge, with a specific emphasis on the integration of learning and its application to practice. This priority for practice is now, belatedly, confirmed in the regulations which govern qualifying social work programmes. This is an achievement. Yet social work still has an uncertain grasp of the place of the person and the personal in its work, and in troubled times uncertain achievements are too easily overlooked. Such a person-centred emphasis also has significant resource implications. An emphasis upon the person and the personal is expensive – it requires a framework for supervision, for the preparation of detailed reports, for the assessment not just of thinking and knowledge but of detailed behaviour. So at times of financial pressure this uncertain grasp is undermined particularly quickly. The achievement of a new prominence for practice has a great bearing on the role and place of the practice teacher, but so too does the climate in which this prominence is urged; emphasising greater cost at a time of stringency is problematic. It may not prove to have been the most strategically effective time for the achievement to have been achieved.

Social work education under stress

Social work education has become more coherent; it is potentially stronger. But learning to swim in calm waters may not prove sufficient when the current is more dangerous. Social work education now has better strokes, but progress and change in social work education – even in social work itself – could yet prove to have been 'too little, too late'. The threats are substantial; the need for clear direction is urgent. Practice agencies face major cuts in funding and are no longer easily able to give priority to professional training matters; intellectual and political changes mean that potentially advantageous specialisms and frameworks for 'competences' (as opposed to competence) are introduced in ways which do not strengthen but rather may eventually undermine social work; different regulatory bodies (the Central Council for Education and Training in Social Work – CCETSW – and the higher education funding councils) impose new requirements – for audit, research, programme management etc. – which lack co-ordination and sometimes conflict. Social work education – founded on a principle of optimism about the possibility of change – struggles with the widespread pessimism in the public services, duplicated in both social work and in education. However unfairly, it is no longer just idiosyncratic outsiders who ask 'can social work survive?' (for examples, compare Brewer and Lait 1980 with Clarke 1993) – or question the future of education for social work. The fate of the practice teacher is going to be determined by these issues.

The 'placement crisis' in particular bites deep into social work education. Agencies review their services and – such is the uncertainty about the character of good practice – some are not sure of the priority or even the plausibility of a professional social work service. They may anyway feel unable to fund practice placements from which they anticipate no immediate or adequate direct benefit. Programmes have now so long started practice periods without sufficient practice placements that in some areas it can seem familiar. Yet the situation actually threatens the viability of the structure itself: programmes restrict their intake to match more closely the numbers for which they can provide practice experiences, so the funding/staffing base (which is calculated with reference to student numbers) of the programme itself is threatened. So this dearth of practice placements may eventually render the whole structure unworkable. Some posts and programmes are already lost.

This problem has its roots in an enduring and irresponsible blurring of the financial basis of practice teaching. Social work has tolerated a system in which programmes lack contract or control over half the provision they undertake to provide. Students accepted onto programmes sometimes have themselves to help in the search for a suitable placement and practice teacher – in effect to find both their place of learning and their teacher-examiner. CCETSW's requirements (CCETSW 1995) that there should be 'programme provider groups' – consortia of agencies and higher education institutions responsible for programmes – appears to be in part an attempt to address this problem; it makes those who could provide some placements assume at least some responsibility for programmes. But it is no surprise that this has too often proved only a nominal responsibility; agencies have shown no appetite to share the real responsibility for programmes, nor – at a time when they can barely meet existing obligations – to commit themselves to the cost of long-term placement provision. So the framework comes actually to add to the burden: the rhetorical observation of requirements becomes just a mandatory but ritual bureaucracy. At least the problem has been made explicit though: who pays for placements? It is good too that CCETSW has at last secured

ds to tackle this problem, to try to stem the consequences of the long
ut it is bad that this change comes so late in the day that more drastic
s – perhaps even the suspension of placement requirements – may
be necessary. And bad too if CCETSW's plausible but too belated
strategy of raising the profile of practice and practice teaching in social work
education may then itself become an obstacle to the survival of social work
education; the need may *temporarily* be for drastic measures which suspend
altogether the requirement for supervised practice.

Cuts in placement funding are not the only financial threats. Social work
education exists within a complex framework. Changes in the funding of
higher education also have a profound effect: major changes in the staff–student
ratio, a much tighter accountability for tutor time, the new imperative to
join expensive competition for research resources: all these changes mean
that the time previously available for social work education is reduced. Yet
social work education is peculiarly heavy on time. These changes have
revealed another fudge: the high costs of social work education had previously
been concealed by tutors neglecting their research obligations. It is
good that this has been made explicit: the true costs of social work education
should be clear, and social work should ensure that it protects its scarce
research resources. Yet if 'the person' is to be the priority for social work education,
the costs of such priority must be met. And for tutors as well as
practice teachers the costs of such provision are high. So recent changes
threaten the core of social work education.

Nor are the threats to social work education just financial; in a period of
turmoil, new financial arrangements may actually be the vehicle for new
ways of thinking. Recent intellectual and cultural changes may have brought
social work some benefit, but they have cut two ways; they have damaged
social work as much as they have helped it. The apparent goal of a greater
efficiency and relevance embodied in the requirements for 'audit' and for collaborative
'programme provider' structures, the reshaping of curricula
around 'competence' frameworks – these reflect a major intellectual change.
These changes could have brought good; they could have brought to social
work a greater clarity and accountability which would have been welcome.
Social work needed such change. But they have brought instead a greater
emphasis on ritual and superficiality, and introduced into social work an
underlying dishonesty. Such an effect is not unique to social work, but in
social work it is peculiarly pernicious. It is inimical to the emphasis which
must be at the heart of social work if social work is to remain a moral venture.

For social work *is* a moral activity; it makes no sense if integrity, feeling and compassion are not its core. Yet the tendency of these recent developments – as an excellent collection of social work papers (Parton 1996) has recently made clear – has been to distort the truth and to establish the 'superficial' in its place. These processes undermine the priority of 'the person' in social work education, and so bear immediately upon the practice teacher's role. Social work is necessarily holistic; it has to be about understanding and behaviour. Yet contemporary assessment frameworks require student and practice teacher to conduct assessment against a template of competences which mitigate against any overall coherence. In consequence students increasingly approach their work in an 'instrumental' fashion – what particular activity will enable them to notch up a specific competence? – and practice teachers are required by the frameworks to write reports in which the relevance and value of the information they contain is increasingly limited. In the name of a nominal 'excellence' it has in fact become harder to achieve quality.

Perhaps social work was inevitably going to be victim of such measures. Over the years it has failed to get its house into sufficient order; whilst it has struggled with its idiosyncratic character, it has moved too little and too late in the directions which would have brought adequate clarity. It has left itself vulnerable (England 1998). But there is something violent in the inappropriate application of such frameworks to social work. Social work must have a particularly delicate approach to 'truth': it has to establish not just an 'objective' vision, but also the different realities for all those involved and the interrelated significance of those realities. There is an emotional and intellectual exactness in such striving. So social work sits particularly ill with frameworks which tend to distort the reality they purport to describe – educational programmes which discourage understanding, frameworks for assessment which boast grandly but allow too little to be assessed, mandatory programme 'provider' groups which cannot actually provide. It is nowhere right that such undermining rhetoric should be set in the doublespeak of 'excellence' but in social work it is particularly wrong; social work – although this is hardly the language which is usually used to describe it – exists to seek for understanding and for truth. So recent changes in social work education do more than threaten its resources; they threaten its professional rationale. They challenge the root of its commitment to professional practice. They therefore intrude directly on the place and plausibility of the practice teacher.

e of the practice teacher

:tice teacher's role is now much more established; there is a real rec-
of the nature of the task and of the importance of the work. This has
ibstantial shift. Yet the place of the practice teacher, for so long something of an anomaly, remains ambiguous; the importance of the role is still
relatively under-played. It is not always clear how much things have changed
today. The practice placement makes up half the qualifying programme. Yet
the practice teacher has often been given no workload relief or other agency
recognition for the work. The long blurring of the lines of responsibility for
providing and funding practice teaching has meant too often that the work
was done by 'volunteers', by social workers who chose just to add the task to
their duties – often those who were themselves recent and still enthusiastic
recruits. One necessary consequence has been an endless change of person-
nel; people take on an additional, and an increasingly onerous, role for only a
finite time – and that time reduces as other pressures increase. This massive,
quasi-official turnover has been a great cost to social work education: a routine haemorrhage of experience, a major burden to programme tutors who
must endlessly recruit and induct new practice teacher colleagues. It has been
one measure of the perceived insignificance of practice in social work; it has
not – or so it seems – mattered if the supervision of beginners was delegated
and relegated to those who were themselves only recently arrived and who
would soon move on. It was also a cost to the practice teachers who took on a
serious and time-consuming responsibility with so little apparent reward.

But it is a question of *apparent* reward. The system in the past was clearly
flawed and costly. Yet the system somehow worked for more than a generation. Why did it do so? One answer – the simpler one – is that taking on the
role of practice teacher seems often to have been related to career progress; an
effective practice teacher gained subsequent promotion in the employing
organisation. This has usually been one explanation of the high turnover in
practice teachers. This progression has its own significance. It highlights the
limited scope that exists in social work for reflection on professional practice
and assessment; practice teaching offers one of the few opportunities for
such reflection. It seems likely that fulfilling the role of practice teacher will
have played a part in subsequent selection for management tasks. So social
work *has* valued the role, but it has done so only obliquely; it has been a
largely unacknowledged staff development gain from participation in social
work education. It is also an implicit acknowledgement of the dearth in
social work of other chances to focus on practice and experience.

This lack of suitable opportunity for professional reflection is crucial in any understanding of the practice teacher's role. Not all practice teachers go on to seek such promotion. It is a commonplace that practice teachers take on the task because they 'like' it or that they find it 'interesting'. It seems to have its own intrinsic reward, despite the costs. It meets the need to share important experiences and commitments with others: practice teaching has offered thoughtful social workers one of their only opportunities to acknowledge their enthusiasm and personal involvement with their profession. In an occupation which often seems to scorn thoughtfulness and learning, practice teaching offers one of the few real opportunities for social workers to be 'reflective practitioners' (Schön 1983). Seen in this light, some are bound then to develop the policy and management implications of their reflection; it would be a loss for social work if they did not do so. But it is not surprising either if some strive to maintain the practice teacher role. If social work is a 'professional' activity, it must find ways to affirm the reflective *practitioner*, the practice teacher role may be the only way in which such detailed reflection can be achieved in social work. It is that need – to be able to reflect – which has motivated practice teachers and so allowed a shaky structure for professional education to survive so long.

On the face of it things now look different. CCETSW has in place a strategy for social work education which gives real substance to the prominence of practice. It is not just that there is recognition of the funding crisis in placement provision; the role of the practice teacher is given enormously greater prominence. There is a national practice teachers' award and a framework for the approval of practice learning agencies; there is potentially a requirement that all practice teachers of students on qualifying programmes must be qualified practice teachers; practice agencies formally share the responsibility for programmes through their membership of the 'programme provider groups'; regulations insist that the professional curriculum and its assessment must give proper place to practice and to the practice teacher. Institutionally, practice teaching has never had a higher profile. Why then is there a widespread feeling that the future for practice teaching remains uncertain – even in crisis?

Practice teaching does indeed now have much greater substance. In some ways – it is true – practice teachers have never had it so good; there has been real change. The development of qualifying courses for practice teachers has meant the development of a much clearer knowledge base for practice teachers. It has contributed to a much clearer definition of the process of practice teaching. It is explicit now that practice teachers must teach, that they must know about adult learning, that they must make complex assessments of professional competence and that they must be articulate about those assessments. All of this is reflected tangibly in a new infrastructure for the practice teacher: courses, accreditation, organisations, literature. This new definition offers a genuinely positive affirmation of the practice teacher. So practice teaching might now be thought to have come of age. The crisis is real though. 'Too little, too late' may mean that an effective prominence for practice and the practice teacher could still be lost. Despite this new institutional infrastructure, social work education is under stress *because* of practice placements, because of the shortage of practice placements. Some might say it is under threat – in some ways – because of the infrastructure.

Some of the causes of this shortfall in the number of practice placements are not new. Even today it seems that practice teaching is still a stepping stone to promotion. This may still be for the wider good of social work. But at a time when 'audit' makes for greater transparency, social work may soon be faced with a more explicit choice about whether to continue to fund professional development in so indirect a fashion. At a time when the future of social work is itself under question, agencies are effectively making choices about the priority they give to professional training. In this context 'too little, too late' may mean that CCETSW's new framework and requirements for practice teaching – however much they may in themselves be along the right lines – may prove a last straw on the camel's back. Those requirements make the practice teaching task daunting and newly stringent just at a time when the priority for many organisations – and the staff within them – is to find new ways of cutting corners. It is good that practice teachers must write more substantial reports (if the specification for their content is appropriate), but if such an imperative is issued at the wrong time – at a time when many doubt if they can meet existing demands – it may confirm rather than challenge doubt about the priority for a 'professional' practice. Some believe that this is already happening – that practice teachers and their agencies, when they become aware that regulations require practice teachers to mark essay assignments and to teach more theory, are reluctant to continue with the work. So it may transpire then that a strategy to enhance the place of practice has been implemented in a way which has been counter-productive, which places too large a burden on the practice teacher. Indeed the strategy may prove to have been doubly counter-productive; if the continuing placement shortage makes it necessary to consider altogether different approaches to preparation for practice, CCETSW's declared commitment to the present framework may inhibit its consideration of plausible alternatives.

The practice teacher and the future of social work

This has been a mixed assessment. A consideration of the role and position of the practice teacher proves to be one measure of social work itself. Social work and social work education have made great strides; they are in many ways stronger now and in better shape than in a generation past. This is a positive legacy of the Seebohm reforms, of the development of a generic social work. But things are not *so* much better that social work will necessarily survive the current strains; social work is not so safe that it will necessarily ride out the storm. The fate of the practice teacher remains a key indicator. Social work needs reflective practitioners more than ever before. Practice teachers both mirror and shape the changes in social work. Their position is a measure of the worth of practice in social work, their work and their reflections a unique channel for social work to describe and understand its practice. So the role and work of the practice teacher is a crucial yardstick. It is also an expression of social work's ambiguity about its practice.

Social work continues to labour over this ambiguity, over whether there is really *any* properly professional practice in social work. It centres around the importance of 'the personal' in the personal social services, around the integration of theory with practice and evaluating the success of that integration: in short, still around the social worker's 'use of self'. These processes are at the core of professional social work; they are also the territory of the practice teacher, the mentor of individual student behaviour and performance. If these issues of professional competence are ever to be clear in social work, that clarity will be evident early in the work of the practice teacher. The character of genuine professional competence in social work will be visible in – and shaped by – the actions and the role of the practice teacher. So what should the practice teacher do to realise these ends? And how will practice teaching in the future be organised to achieve that clarity?

The objectives of the practice teacher cannot change. They must in future continue to be the sensitive articulation and evaluation of imagination, experience and behaviour. These terms – though they are not the ones usually used to define it – are the integrating expressions of practice. There will be no social work if these objectives are not kept in view. More specifically and immediately practice teachers should focus on three areas. One is the accommodation of 'specialism' in social work. Practice teachers must ensure that a proper focus is maintained on the common core of social work at a time which will increasingly emphasise specialism. A growing specialist knowledge will be to social work's advantage, but social work has only achieved new strengths – and it *has* achieved new strengths – because of its recent grounding in a generic social work. It will be the practice teacher who will be charged particularly with the transmission and maintenance of the core, generic skills of social work – and with making clear that without these skills no specialist knowledge will make sense. It is these core processes which realise – which make real – social work's claim to respect the person. Given the pressures and politics surrounding specialism – so dramatically demonstrated in the recent decisions to extract probation training from the mainstream of social work education – it will be a difficult task to maintain this focus.

The two other areas to which practice teachers should give particular attention are both concerned with assessment. There are particular problems in making a proper assessment of student ability. One problem is the new frameworks for assessment; another could be solved by those same frameworks. New assessment schedules are being derived across the country from the CCETSW competence requirements which shape its regulatory framework for qualifying programmes. The common response to these schedules is to give the very specific information required – and too often to give no overall sense of student competence. The 'system' assumes that the specific parts add up to an adequate overall whole, yet they cannot do so. One curious outcome of a system intended to improve standards of practice and practice assessment is thus that it has become more difficult to write a good practice report. Practice teachers are at the centre of this stage; they must so write their reports that they ensure that a view of the wood is retained – without it the detail of particular trees serves no purpose.

But the same CCETSW framework also requires student material to be included in practice assessments. This can give programmes – and practice teachers – a lever which could much improve the overall standard of student assessment. Practice assessments of social work generally make too slight a use of detailed material prepared and submitted directly by the student, even though such material allows uniquely for the independent corroboration of the practice teacher's assessment. It thus offers a way of substantiating and dignifying the assessment process – of allowing social work to escape in some measure from the accusations of subjective and whimsical judgement. This could prove a credible avenue for a great strengthening of practice assessment, much more so than the always implausible 'second opinion practice teacher' – an earlier and now abandoned device to achieve those ends. The systematic use of such practice accounts would also bring into social work a new and qualitatively different culture of description and analysis; it would be a development which would bring benefit beyond its immediate educational context.

Any vision of future structures for practice teaching is wildly speculative. It could well be that the tutor and the practice teacher will not survive as we know them. One possibility in the present climate is that the role of the practice teacher may disappear. The problem of the shortage of placements may be solved by diluting the practice placement; practice learning could become a simulated part of the academic curriculum, reinforced by agency experience which is only minimally supervised. But the converse is also possible – the role of the practice teacher may be enhanced. Social work may be moved out of higher education altogether and placed in the agency; the practice teacher may become an agency-based teacher-tutor. Between these two possibilities there may be scope for new structures of professional teaching and learning – more akin to the teaching hospital – which blur the present divisions; the development of such structures would be a positive development. And the practice teacher's role may anyway be further enhanced by other developments in professional and vocational education: a different emphasis on pre-qualifying and post-qualifying awards gained largely within the agency. A measure of such provision is already in place; other changes might be realised fast in response to the growing pressure on resources.

References

Brewer, C. and Lait, J. (1980) *Can Social Work Survive?* London: Maurice Temple Smith.

CCETSW (1995) *Assuring Quality in the Diploma in Social Work: Rules and Requirements for the Dip SW.* London: CCETSW.

Clarke, J. (ed) (1993) *A Crisis in Care? Challenges to Social Work.* London: Sage.

Egan, G. (1975) *The Skilled Helper.* Monterey: Brooks-Cole.

England, H. (1998) *Social Work as Profession: The Naïve Aspiration.* Southampton: Centre for Evaluative and Developmental Research, Department of Social Work Studies, Southampton University.

Howe, D. (1996) 'Surface and depth in social work practice.' In N. Parton (ed) *Social Theory, Social Change and Social Work.* London: Routledge.

Parton, N. (ed) (1996) *Social Theory, Social Change and Social Work.* London: Routledge.

Pincus, A. and Minahan, A. (1973) *Social Work Practice: Model and Method.* Itasca, IL: Peacock.

Reid, W. and Epstein, L. (1972) *Task Centred Casework.* New York: Columbia University Press.

Schön, D.A. (1983) *The Reflective Practitioner.* London: Temple Smith.

The Contributors

Elaine Arnold trained as a teacher before qualifying in social work. She practised as a social worker both in Trinidad and Tobago, West Indies, and in England. She worked as a Student Unit Supervisor in a London borough before lecturing at Goldsmiths College and Sussex University, where she taught on the Practice Teacher programme. She has a keen interest in intercultural social work.

Carole Ballardie has been a Probation Officer for 18 years. For the past four years she has held a joint appointment between East Sussex Probation Service and the University of Sussex. She is actively involved within the National Association of Probation Officers in opposing the recent government's plans for probation training. She continues to train social work students for work in the criminal justice system.

Helen Cosis Brown is currently Head of Department of Health and Social Care at the University of Hertfordshire. She was a social worker and team leader for ten years in an inner London borough. She has continued to offer training in the field of fostering and adoption and has a number of publications relating to social work practice with lesbians and gay men including *Social Work and Sexuality: Working with Lesbians and Gay Men* (Macmillan, 1998).

Charlotte Clow works for Brighton Housing Trust, managing voluntary sector residential mental health projects. She has previous community mental health and counselling experience in London, where she qualified as a social worker in 1991. She has been a practice teacher since 1993 and is a consultant trainer on 'Endings'.

Tina Cox trained at the Polytechnic of North London during the time it was associated with the emergence of radical social work education. She has worked in Camden and Hackney and is currently a social worker in Brighton and Hove where she started as a generic worker and with each wave of change has been gradually 'specialised down' into a Children and Families worker. As well as practice teaching, she has a particular interest in mental health and the effects of loss and change.

Hugh England has worked as a probation officer in London and as a Lecturer in Social Work at Goldsmiths College in the University of London; he currently teaches social work at the University of Sussex.

Polly Hoad worked as a social worker and senior practitioner for East Sussex County Council for 14 years and, since 1994, has worked as a Guardian Ad Litem for the Kent and West Sussex Panels.

Jacqui Jenkins gained her CQSW from Nottingham in 1991. She was a generic social worker with Surrey County Council before specialising in working with people with learning disabilities in Sussex. She has managed several successful student placements in the learning disability field and has a particular interest in the politics of disabilism and anti-oppressive practice.

Phil Jones is a Child Protection Officer with the NSPCC West Sussex Child Protection Team. Phil has an interest in child protection assessment work, particularly in the field of child neglect and undertaking treatment work with boys and young men who have experienced abuse.

Carol Kedward is a Lecturer in Social Policy and Social Work at the University of Sussex. She is currently Director of the Master in Social Work programme, formerly Practice Placement Organiser and Convenor of Approved Practice Teacher Programme. Her background is in family work, supervision and team-building skills. She is co-author with Dan Norris of *Violence Against Social Workers: The Implications for Practice* (Jessica Kingsley Publishers, 1990).

Hilary Lawson worked for ten years in both specialist and generic social work teams. She worked in training and development in East Sussex Social Services before joining the Social Policy and Social Work Group at Sussex University in 1991. She now lectures on child development and family work on the Masters in Social Work programme, is Director of the Practice Teacher programme and is currently developing other post-qualifying courses for social workers.

Michelle Lefevre is a Senior Practitioner at the Clermont, a multi-disciplinary child protection unit in Brighton which specialises in investigation, assessment and treatment/therapy issues. She recently gained an MA in Social Work Studies and was one of the first practitioners in Surrey and Sussex to gain CCETSW's Post-Qualifying Award in Social Work. Her specialisms include assessment and group therapy with sexual abuse perpetrators, and using music in therapeutic work with children and training.

Fiona Mainstone works as a Senior Practitioner in Children and Families for Brighton and Hove Council. She has been in social work practice since 1977. Having studied with the Institute of Family Therapy in 1992 she became interested in solution-focused ideas and these have gradually come to inform all areas of her practice.

Andy Mantell gained his Post-Graduate Diploma in Social Work from Edinburgh University in 1991. After working in a generic patch team and then in a disability team he became an approved social worker and practice teacher in a general hospital. He is particularly interested in acquired brain trauma, mental health and practice teaching. Recently he has been appointed senior social worker at the Royal Hospital for Neuro-Disability.

Di Metson is a qualified social worker and studied the Practice Teacher programme at Sussex University in 1991. She also teaches the Young Child Observation course for social work students on the Masters in Social Work programme at Sussex University. She started training in Transactional Analysis four years ago and finds it provides useful tools for teaching social work students.

Corinne Pearce is a probation officer with the West Sussex Probation Service. She qualified at Bristol University in 1989 and has since worked with offenders on both an individual and groupwork basis.

Subject Index

Author Index